Department of Economic and Social Affairs

United Nations

E-Government Survey 2012

E-Government for the People

United Nations
New York, 2012

United Nations Department of Economic and Social Affairs

The United Nations Department of Economic and Social Affairs is a vital interface between global policies in the economic, social and environmental spheres and national action. The Department works in three main interlinked areas: (1) it compiles, generates and analyses a wide range of economic, social and environmental data and information on which Member States of the United Nations draw to review common problems and to take stock of policy options; (2) it facilitates the negotiations of Member States in many intergovernmental bodies on joint courses of action to address ongoing or emerging global challenges; and (3) it advises interested governments on the ways and means of translating policy frameworks developed in United Nations conferences and summits into programmes at the country level and, through technical assistance, helps build national capacities. ☙

ST/ESA/PAD/SER.E/150
ISBN: 978-92-1-123190-8
e-ISBN: 978-92-1-055353-7
Sales n° E.12.II.H.2

Printed at the United Nations, New York

Foreword

Today, powerful new technologies can be used to advance sustainable development for all people across the world while including them in the process. In particular, e-government can be an engine of development for the people. In delivering e-government for the people, public services are designed to be responsive, citizen-centric and socially inclusive. Governments also engage citizens through participatory service delivery processes. The evidence base for the latter is strengthened by recent progress in e-government in a growing number of countries where citizens are both users and co-producers of public services.

The increasing role of e-government in promoting inclusive and participatory development has gone hand-in-hand with the growing demands for transparency and accountability in all regions of the world. E-government has strongly shifted expectations of what governments can and should do, using modern information and communication technologies, to strengthen public service and advance equitable, people-centred development.

This report shows that with the right institutional framework, policies and capacity-building efforts, progress in enhancing the contributions of e-government to sustainable development is within reach.

However, the report also explains that adequate funding is needed to enhance e-government. Furthermore, it shows that there are challenges to reducing the digital-divide and increasing access to public services by vulnerable populations and distant communities. More than ever, mobile services, crowd sourcing, cloud computing, e-service kiosks and other innovations of this sort must be nurtured and supported and made available to all segments of society.

The steady diffusion of information and communication technologies and the bridging of the digital divide can help empower all stakeholders to translate commitments into action. I therefore encourage policymakers and public administrators everywhere to apply information and communication technologies and e-government as important tools in advancing sustainable development for all. ☙

Sha Zukang
Under-Secretary-General for Economic and Social Affairs and Secretary-General of the United Nations Conference on Sustainable Development (Rio+20)

Acknowledgements

The 2012 edition of the United Nations e-Government Survey is the result of the efforts, contributions and support of many people from a number of organizations and thanks are extended to all who were involved directly or indirectly. In particular, the following people are acknowledged for their specific roles in its production.

Preparation of the publication was undertaken by a group of senior e-government researchers and advisers at the United Nations Department of Economic and Social Affairs, led directly by Haiyan Qian, Director of the Division for Public Administration and Development Management. She was assisted in this task by Vincenzo Aquaro, Chief of the E-Government Branch, who managed the data collection effort, and John-Mary Kauzya, Chief of the Public Administration Capacity Branch, who helped guide the analytical work.

The core research team comprised DPADM staff members Seema Hafeez who drafted Chapters 1 and 2, Michael Mimicopoulos and John-Mary Kauzya who drafted Chapter 3, Deniz Susar who drafted Chapter 4, Peride Blind who drafted Chapter 5, and Seok-Ran Kim who drafted Chapter 6. Patrick Spearing contributed a background paper on information services in support of sustainable development. Richard Kerby and Jonas Rabinovitch provided case studies and field data. Patrick Spearing and Wai Min Kwok acted as referees in reviews of the various manuscripts.

The survey benefited from advice and guidance on e-government measurement provided by a group of experts who met in New York in December 2010. The group consisted of Abdulla Al Hamid (Bahrain), Kim Andreasson (United States), Roberto Bellotti (Italy), Rowena Bethel (Bahamas), David Eaves (Canada), Tanya Gupta (World Bank), Morten Goodwin Olsen (Norway), Koon Tian Ooh (Singapore), Jeremy Millard (Denmark), Rajkumar Prasad (India), Abir Qasam (United States) Mikael Snaprud (Norway) and Barbara Ubaldi (OECD). Roberto Bellotti and Nicola Amoroso provided advice on the refinement of the statistical methodology.

Under a collaborative agreement between the United Nations and Cornell University in the United States, the collection of data on online services was overseen by Vincenzo Aquaro and Seema Hafeez, supported by Kim Andreasson, Keping Yao, and Thomas O'Toole of the Cornell Institute of Public Affairs (CIPA). The CIPA team included: Samar Alam, Timur Baiserkeev, Hatice Bilici, Santiago Calderon, Viktor Englund, Hadi Fathallah, Nira Gautam, Adalsteinn Hakonarson, Aleks Janjic, Sonia Javed, Rami Jawhar, Resya Kania, Juliana Lima, Haiyue Luo, Margaret Lynch, Andreea Mascan, Grit Mathias, Ammar Naqvi, Michail Panagopoulos, Weng Pong Woo, Vorapat Praneeprachachon, Diego Rios Zertuche, Javad Rostami, Frantz Seide, Sarmad Shaikh, Aditya Shrinivas, Chamnan Sieng, Thitsar Thitsar, Ardak Tukenova, Marc Ufberg, Kim Vallejo, Martina Vanikova, Ana Vanjac and Yucheng Zheng.

Comprehensive second stage data assessment was conducted a group of United Nations interns coordinated by Seema Hafeez. The team included Alisher Djaborov, Aaron Gardner, Kateryna Goychuk, Monica Hernandez, Sonia Javed, Rami Jawhar, Loreta Juskaite, DuyiLi, Sine Soeberg, Desislava Stefanova, AlexanderThomson, Quentin Tourancheau and Yucheng Zheng, in addition to a number of volunteer translators which included Eran Goldshtein, Davaadorj Khulan, Tünde Lázár, Suela Lleku, Michaela Mackuliakova, Inge Meesak, Stephan Nunner, Srinart Poputtachai, Vorapat Praneeprachachon, Alfred Prevoo, Nadja Saveska, Artemis Seaford, Yaroslav Shiryaev, Gracia Sidabutar, Tomohiro Tsuden, Aura Ursu, Vilde Vaeroyvik, Eva van Aalst, Stine Wind and Benjamin Ziga.

Technical data management and support was provided by Aaron Gardner, Rami Jawhar and

Quentin Tourancheau. Kim Andreasson provided the data assessment platform and support to the initial collection of data on online services. Data assessment on access to vulnerable groups was conducted by Christian Rodli Amble, Morten Goodwin and Mikael H. Snaprud and peer review by the University of the United Nations through Tomasz Janoxski.

Telecommunication infrastructure and education data were generously contributed by the International Telecommunication Union and the United Nations Educational, Scientific and Cultural Organization respectively.

Administrative assistance was provided by Rosanne Clarke, Wally Clarkson, Elvira Doyle, Nathan Henninger, Madeleine Losch, and Luis Prugue.

Editorial review and coordination was undertaken by Michelle Alves de Lima-Miller, supported by Silvia Schwarz.

Copyediting services were provided by Mary Lynn Hanley. Creative design was directed and executed by Eliot Sela. CB

Acronyms

C2G	Citizen-to-government		**ITU**	International Telecommunication Union
CIO	Chief information officer		**LDC**	Least developed country
EGDI	E-government development index		**MEA**	Multilateral environmental agreement
EU	European Union		**NGO**	Non-governmental organization
FAQ	Frequently asked questions		**OECD**	Organization for Economic Cooperation and Development
FOI	Freedom of information			
G2C	Government-to-citizen		**OSI**	Online service index
G2G	Government-to-government		**PDA**	Personal digital assistant
GDP	Gross domestic product		**PPP**	Public-private partnership
GII	Government information infrastructure		**RSS**	Real simple syndication
			SMS	Short message service
GNI	Gross national income		**UNDESA**	United Nations Department of Economic and Social Affairs
HCI	Human capital index			
HDI	Human Development Index		**WAI**	Web accessibility initiative
HTML	Hypertext markup language		**WAP**	Wireless application protocol
ICT	Information and communication technology		**WCAG**	Web content accessibility guidelines
IM	Instant messaging		**W3C**	World Wide Web Consortium
ISP	Internet service providers		**WSSD**	World Summit on Sustainable Development

Contents

Boxes

Boxes (cont.)

Figures

Figures (cont.)

Figures (cont.)

Tables (cont.)

Maps

Executive summary

Progress in online service delivery continues in most countries around the world. The United Nations E-Government Survey 2012 finds that many have put in place e-government initiatives and information and communication technologies applications for the people to further enhance public sector efficiencies and streamline governance systems to support sustainable development. Among the e-government leaders, innovative technology solutions have gained special recognition as the means to revitalize lagging economic and social sectors.

The overall conclusion that emerges from the 2012 Survey in today's recessionary world climate is that while it is important to continue with service delivery, governments must increasingly begin to rethink in terms of e-government – and e-governance – placing greater emphasis on institutional linkages between and among the tiered government structures in a bid to create synergy for inclusive sustainable development. An important aspect of this approach is to widen the scope of e-government for a transformative role of the government towards cohesive, coordinated, and integrated processes and institutions through which such sustainable development takes place.

In the current recessionary world climate, in which the lives of people have become ever more interconnected, governments have been harnessing the power of information and communications technologies (ICT) for delivering much needed sustainability in social and economic services to their citizens. As part of this shift towards e-government, there has been an increasing recognition that efforts towards a holistic approach to governance for sustainable development require strategic national planning to ensure efficacy, transparency, responsiveness, participation and inclusion in the delivery of public services. These aims could not be achieved without the underlying notion of sustainable development for the people.

The overall challenge then is to deliver improvements in the standards of living in such a manner that development today does not compromise development tomorrow. Embedded in the concept of sustainability is the viability of (i) national and sub-national governance systems that are citizen-centric, socially inclusive and participatory; and (ii) the associated government operations and services that affect development outcomes. In paying attention to citizen needs, there is a critical need for governments to encompass modalities in working together with citizens in fulfilling service delivery. Therefore the theme of the United Nations E-Government Survey 2012 is E-Government for the People. Areas deserving special emphasis include expanding usage of e-government services, including through multiple channels, and a whole-of-government approach in promoting equity and bridging the digital-divide by extending service delivery to all, particularly vulnerable groups.

The nexus of e-government, institutional linkages and sustainable development

E-government has an important role to play, now and in the future. As the world moves towards 2015, the date set for reaching the Millennium Development Goals, the unmet targets of poverty reduction and other social and economic development goals are being revisited within the ambit of climate change and natural resource conservation. Inherent in this paradigm is a focus on pivotal linkages among public institutions, such that development challenges

can be met with a concerted and coordinated effort that incorporates the environmental dimension into development planning at every stage.

Within this context, national governments need to understand the economic, social and environmental pathways must be adapted to develop or reform their strategic frameworks towards outcomes that promote sustainable development. The basic strategic approach needs to germinate first and foremost in the acceptance of the importance of the inter-linkages among the economic, social and environmental aspects of development.

The role of the government is once again being redefined to reform the governance systems through which services are delivered in a way that maximizes development and minimizes natural resource degradation. A holistic approach to governance includes taking into account the efficiency and distributional aspects of sectoral policies and their outcomes, national development agendas, and international cooperation agreements, so that resulting solutions are sustainable in the future.

The message of the 2012 Survey is that all stakeholders need to recognize the key role that e-government – and e-governance – can play in support of the establishment of effective institutional linkages necessary for sustainable development.

Evidence shows that it is possible to successfully utilize ICT based on governance frameworks that underpin the effectiveness of public sector institutions.

E-government is at the core of building a strategic sustainable development framework. One of its key functions has been to provide an integrated framework of policies, laws and regulations and develop institutions and processes that allow the private sector to provide – and the people to partake of – the benefits of newer technologies.

The underlying principle of e-government, supported by an effective e-governance institutional framework, is to improve the internal workings of the public sector by reducing financial costs and transaction times so as to better integrate work flows and processes and enable effective resource utilization across the various public sector agencies aiming for sustainable solutions. It seeks to establish 'better processes and systems' aimed at more efficiency, effectiveness, inclusion and sustainability. As a key driver of efficiency and coordination, e-governance encompasses institutions, mechanisms and processes for planning, organizing, coordination and implementation of successful socio-economic development programmes.

Utilizing e-government can be the key to the achievement of the integration of economic, social and environment goals for development planning. In this context, national governments need to:

- Recognize the opportunity for synergy among institutions that e-government offers;
- Re-engineer the enabling environment for e-governance to enable institutional inter-linkages within the government; and
- Promote coordination and connectivity between ecosystems and development outcomes.

As the public sector continues to reform structural processes and institutions for greater efficiency and better service delivery; provide a climate conducive for businesses; and offer greater participation for citizens, e-government will increasingly become the key enabler of sustainable development. From putting in place policies and programmes to the design of laws and regulation for ICT access and citizen participation, e-government and e-governance will expand their reach in affecting the living conditions of peoples in all countries of the world in general, and in ameliorating the adverse impact of the digital divide in particular.

One of the key challenges in building the framework of sustainable development is how to employ modern technologies to ensure inter-institutional coordination and the effectiveness of development outcomes while safeguarding natural resource conservation. Lessons of experience in a few of the vanguard countries indicate that by deploying innovative ITC solutions e-governance endeavours can optimize solutions to hither-to-fore intransigent development challenges.

There is a growing recognition that e-governance can support development by improving inter-organizational linkages and consolidation of government systems. This emerging e-government paradigm, allied to the twin objectives of efficacy in government functioning and achieving improvements in service delivery, is bringing about new perceptions of the inter-linkages between e-government and the sustainability of systems.

The entry point for economic sustainability is how e-government supports efficiency and effectiveness in government for greater growth and development by employing whole-of-government approaches. Hierarchical and bureaucratic structures need to be transformed into horizontal integrated systems, which facilitate customer orientation and increase levels of transparency and accountability in a move towards public service delivery solutions that are sustainable.

At the same time, social equity and inclusion are possible only if institutional barriers to citizen inclusion are removed and opportunities for their participation through ICTs are equitably distributed. The reach of innovative inclusive solutions to support citizen decision-making processes is just as important as the nature of the participatory process itself. For social sustainability, the role of e-government requires a shift from that of a controller of information and services to that of a facilitator, whereby information and services are geared towards addressing the needs and concerns of the citizenry, especially the vulnerable, and to promoting user uptake.

Finally, e-government can support environmental institutional integration by bringing environment agencies online and linking them with governance structures responsible for development planning so that coordinated solutions can be found that are efficient, effective and sustainable.

The United Nations E-Government Survey 2012: E-Government for the People addresses the conceptual and analytical issues related to how the Member States are utilizing ICTs to support citizen centric service delivery and citizen participation in service delivery to ensure sustainable development.

Global trends in e-government development

The United Nations E-Government Survey 2012 explores the inter-linkages between e-government and sustainable development efforts. While presenting the United Nations e-government development rankings for 2012 it analyses how governments of the world are employing e-government policies and programmes to support efficiency, effectiveness, and inclusiveness as the parameters of sustainable development efforts worldwide.

It addresses conceptual and analytical issues related to an effective e-governance institutional framework as the key enabler for the organizational and regulatory environment that is the necessary ingredient for such development to take place. Building on lessons learnt and best practices identified through previous UNDESA work on e-government, the 2012 Survey highlights the 'silo' or sector-by-sector approach often common to both e-government and environment in development planning. It brings together concepts and best practices such as whole-of-government; effectiveness of multichannel service delivery; increasing access to Internet and mobile use around the world in bridging the digital divide; the importance of e-service to vulnerable groups; and challenges in user uptake. It thereby alerts policy makers to the current need for a holistic vision to sustainable development that emphasizes synergies among various sectors and approaches that will help advance economic sustainability and social equity.

A special focus of this year's Survey is on environment-related services. It assesses the provision of environment and resource conservation information and services to the citizen and presents the first data set on United Nations e-environment indicators.

The message of the 2012 Survey builds upon the findings of the previous United Nations Surveys and sets the importance of e-government firmly within the current global developmental debate. First, underscoring the importance of technological advancements and the role of the government and sustainable development, it highlights the importance of e-government and ICT as integral to sustainable development.

Second, expanding the concept of e-governance it points to the need to place it at the centre of development thinking for a coherent, coordinated and synergistic approach to public sector solutions.

Finally, it draws attention to state-of-the art e-government approaches that are being deployed in vanguard countries as case studies for a whole-of-government framework and inclusion of the disadvantaged in the circle of development.

Thus, it presents the progress made in e-government development around the world since the last Survey (2010) while cautioning against the digital divide that stems from the current worldwide disparity in the use of information technologies. In this way it contributes to a better understanding of the need for e-government to be deployed in order to create the required synergy and integration across institutions and processes that will support Member States' efforts towards sustainable development that includes all.

Key findings from the 2012 Survey

According to the 2012 United Nations E-government Survey rankings, the Republic of Korea is the world leader (0.9283) followed by the Netherlands (0.9125), the United Kingdom (0.8960) and Denmark (0.8889), with the United States, Canada, France, Norway, Singapore and Sweden close behind.

The steady improvement in all the indicators of the e-government development index has led to a world average of 0.4877 as compared to 0.4406 in 2010. This reflects that countries in general have improved their online service delivery to cater to citizens' needs. On a regional level, Europe (0.7188) and Eastern Asia (0.6344) lead, followed by Northern America (0.8559), South Asia (0.3464) and Africa (0.2762).

Despite progress, there remains an imbalance in the digital divide between developed and the developing countries, especially in Africa. The latter region had a mean e-government development index of about 30 per cent of Northern America and about half of the world average. The digital divide is rooted in the lack of e-infrastructure, which has hindered information-use and knowledge-creation. The tremendous difference of broadband width and subscriptions between the developing and the developed world proves that there are yet many milestones to be reached in order to close the gap of the digital divide.

Whole-of-government approaches lead the way in vanguard countries

Employing e-government to improve efficiency and effectiveness of public service delivery in government structures is one facet of economic sustainability. The 2012 Survey finds that many Member States are moving from a decentralized single-purpose organization model, to an integrated unified whole-of-government model contributing to efficiency and effectiveness. The model aims at centralizing the entry point of service delivery to a single portal where citizens can access all government-supplied services, regardless of which government authority provides them. In some countries, the whole-of-government approach helps build a transparent government system with interconnected departments and divisions, feeding into the funnel of greater government efficiency and effectiveness.

Member States are paying closer attention to multichannel service delivery

The increasing power of ICT has also provided governments with the flexibility of providing services and information to citizens through multichannels. Citizens have diverse needs and demands for services; therefore it is no longer sustainable for governments to utilize one preferred way of service provision over the other. It is now ever more essential that governments exploit all possible delivery channels in order to reach out to as many people as possible, no matter how poor, illiterate or isolated. The 2012 Survey shows that 71 Member States partner with third party organizations such as those in the civil society or the private sector to provide e-services.

Progress on the digital divide is far from satisfactory though rapid dispersion of mobile technology gives hope for improvement.

This year's Survey also indicates that global infrastructure access has improved, with the global average ICT index value reflecting an increase in mobile penetration – the global average number of mobile subscriptions per 100 inhabitants is now 88.5. Broadband penetration, however, remains very low, with a global average of only 8.7 fixed broadband connections per 100 inhabitants. Mobile-based technologies have become the most rapidly adapted technologies to provide e-services, playing a pivotal role, especially in developing countries. Rural areas with very little access to telephony can now benefit from mobile and broadband services to access services. According to the 2012 Survey, 25 countries have developed separate m-government websites, and 24 countries provide the option of making payments via mobile phones.

Much more needs to be done to include vulnerable groups in the benefits of technology. With a focus on social sustainability, the underlying approach of the top performers in 2012 is inclusion for all, which has led to the expansion of information and services to vulnerable groups, people who live in isolated rural areas and the disabled. Further, in pursuit of greater efficiency, more and more governments are paying closer attention to citizens' use of online services. The levels still remain low with only around a quarter – or 47 countries – providing information on how citizens use services.

Developing countries make progress in e-participation

Many developing countries have adopted citizen inclusion as key in providing "customer"-oriented services. While the Republic of Korea and the Netherlands are the world leaders, Singapore and Kazakhstan are close behind. Europe has the largest share of the top e-participation countries. Despite progress the gains are not spread evenly, both across and within countries, with the majority still offering low levels of engagement possibilities.

Citizens demand more services

While the primary focus of Member States has been the provision of services from a supplier perspective, recently there has been a shift towards a more consumer demand driven policy and greater emphasis on citizen usage. Nevertheless the level of citizen up-take currently remains at low levels. Usage divides across and within countries is one of the many challenges hindering high levels of citizen up-take. According to the 2012 Survey, only 24 countries openly promote free access to e-government services through free wifi or kiosks. Leveraging social media for the benefit of e-service uptake is another area where a greater effort can make a difference since currently only 40 per cent of Member States are using a social networking site.

A good beginning but e-environment initiatives have a long way to go

With the worldwide focus on sustainable development this year the 2012 United Nations e-Government Survey devoted a special section to examining the effort made by Member States in provision of environment-related online information and services. In keeping with institutional development identified as one of the two main themes for Rio +20, the 2012 Survey assessed Member States' online offerings in three areas cited in the Secretary-General's Report to the Preparatory Committee for the United Nations Conference on Sustainable Development: 1) dissemination of information; 2) institutional integration with respect to environmental matters; and 3) opportunities for citizen engagement on environmental issues. With respect to information dissemination services, Chapter 2 looks particularly at four policy areas related to environmental degradation and natural resources management: clean air, clean water, energy, and resource conservation. Given the importance placed on empowering citizens – particularly marginalized groups – with respect to environmental policy making, it also assesses how e-participation tools are deployed in the environmental domain, at the same time, focusing on the importance of institutional integration at all levels for sustainable development. Chapter 3 assesses how e-government offerings support both sub-national and international integration. Among the top-scoring countries on the environment, four provide considerable environment related information and services to their citizens – Germany, the Republic of Korea, Singapore, and the United States. As in the case of e-government development rankings, developed countries dominate the e-environment service delivery, with 36 per cent of countries providing less than one third of the information and services assessed; another one third providing 34 to 66 per cent; and 56 countries providing 67 to 100 per cent of the e-environment services assessed.

A majority of countries provide online information or education to citizens regarding clean water (111 countries), clean air (105 countries), and resource conservation (104 countries). Nearly half of countries, 86, provide information pertaining to energy. However few countries provide features designed to proactively notify citizens of environmental issues or permit citizens to focus online searches specifically on the environment. Similarly, citizen engagement on environment issues is in its infancy. While Europe takes the lead, other regions are slow to follow.

The way forward

As the way forward the first imperative is to recognize the role of national governments in tapping into the transformative nature of e-government for sustainable development as it relates to whole-of-government approaches and multichannel service delivery. In this regard countries must at a minimum establish a persistent online presence with at least basic services in order to build trust in government.

Second, shifting from a structurally disintegrated government to one that is a more interconnected single-purpose whole-of-government will require collaboration and streamlining not only along the whole spectrum of governance but also with private sector and civil societies. Prerequisites for achieving this shift include long-term vision and leadership commitment, a strategic framework, an IT management programme aligned with the overall strategy, and technical integration of IT systems. Whole-of-government practices will not only boost efficiency of government agencies but also utilization of public services if properly administered in accordance with a clear strategy and motivated leadership.

Third, it needs to be reiterated that the digital divide is still an obstacle we face. With all the cutting-edge technologies and development of social media and networking tools, which have re-shaped parts of our modern world, it is becoming more challenging to diminish the digital divide. Not only is the non-availability of infrastructure such as broadband the main reason behind this divide, but differences in skills and lack of means to access information also play a major role. Therefore it is vital for governments to learn from global best practices and collaborate internationally to develop a harmonized framework with indigenous ICT content. An effective approach must address both access to infrastructure as well as well as barriers to using online services that may persist even when such access is available.

Fourth, there is a need to reach out to all citizens, particularly the disadvantaged and vulnerable groups, in order to bridge the gap and maximize the utilization of online service delivery. However, governance processes for the effectiveness and benefit of all cannot be realized without a well-established coordination framework encompassing the involvement of all national and international stake-holders, including third party organizations, which can play a pivotal role in the process. This is particularly important in the context of multichannel service delivery, where it is important to follow an evolutionary rather than a revolutionary approach to developing new channels. In other words, service delivery via new channels should not come at the expense of service delivery via established channels.

Fifth, low usage and user uptake indicates that e-services up-take has untapped potential for the improvement of service delivery in line with citizen demand.

Finally, the 2012 Survey assessment points to horizontal and vertical e-government linkages among various institutions and nodal points that have created opportunities for greater participation and social inclusiveness. By bringing technology to the people instead of making the people come to technology hubs, and by creating opportunities for online service delivery, e-government has contributed to coordinated efforts for increased e-government among public sector officials, public institutions and citizens.

As the collective global effort, led by the United Nations, gains momentum towards a greater acceptance of the institutional linkages among the economic, social and environmental pillars of sustainable development, there is a need to be cognizant of the importance of e-government that is for the people, in achieving higher standards of living for future generations. ☾

Eliot Sela

Chapter 1

World e-government rankings

Progress in online service delivery continues in most countries around the world. The United Nations E-Government Survey 2012 finds that many have put in place e-government initiatives and information and communication technologies applications for the people to further enhance public sector efficiencies and streamline governance systems to support sustainable development. Among the e-government leaders, innovative technology solutions have gained special recognition as the means to revitalize lagging economic and social sectors.

The overall conclusion that emerges from the 2012 Survey in today's recessionary world climate is that while it is important to continue with service delivery, governments must increasingly begin to rethink in terms of e-government – and e-governance – placing greater emphasis on institutional linkages between and among the tiered government structures in a bid to create synergy for inclusive sustainable development. An important aspect of this approach is to widen the scope of e-government for a transformative role of the government towards cohesive, coordinated, and integrated processes and institutions through which such sustainable development takes place.

E-government innovation and development can position the public sector as a driver of demand for ICT infrastructure and applications in the broader economy.

1.1 Overview of national e-government development

The United Nations Survey 2012 assessment of progress indicates that e-government is increasingly being viewed among countries in the vanguard as going beyond service delivery towards a framework for a smart, inclusive and sustainable growth for future generations. In countries that follow that trend, a focus on institutional integration coupled with online citizen orientation in public service continues to be dominant. Both in terms of information and services, the citizen is increasingly viewed as 'an active customer of public services' with borrowed private sector concepts being applied to improve public sector governance systems.

A key driver for this approach is the need to achieve efficiency in government at the same time that services are being expanded. Advances in technology, which allow data sharing and efficient streamlining of cross-agency governance systems are forming the back end of integrated portals where citizens find a myriad of relevant information arranged by theme, life cycle or other preferred use. The trend towards personalization of services has gained momentum with more countries tailoring substance and presentation in accord with varied preferences. Multichannel service delivery features were found on several portals in 2012 through which the government conducted business with citizens. Citizen inclusion is also expanding both horizontally and vertically with more governments around the world in 2012 accepting and promoting the need to inform – and involve – the citizen in the public decision making process.

E-government innovation and development can position the public sector as a driver of demand for ICT infrastructure and applications in the broader economy. The effect will be more pronounced in cases where government programmes constitute a significant proportion of a country's GDP and where the regulatory environment is conducive to expansion of ICT manufacturing, software and related services.

E-government programmes can be a catalyst in boosting productivity, thereby speeding up the benefits of newer technologies to the people. In the last few years many countries have employed ICT in areas such as entrepreneurship, innovation, research and development, promoting distance learning, e-health, e-agriculture, e-trade and other fields. Accessing these new technologies for development is being recognized as one of the key sources of economic growth. Of particular importance is the effect of cellular technologies. Where national governments have taken a lead, rapid mobile technology proliferation has contributed as much as a one per cent annual increase in economic growth over the last few years.[1]

Notwithstanding these trends, progress remains uneven. In the current recessionary climate some countries have been better able to continue to invest in ICT infrastructure and service improvement. Others are evaluating the marginal utility of such investment, especially taking into account low user uptake of existing services, and reassessing service portfolios where demand for online services is low. Many countries with low levels of infrastructure and human capital remain at lower levels of e-government development with serious issues of digital divide.

In all cases, e-government take a prominent role in shaping development making it more in tune with people's needs and driving the whole process based on their participation.

1.2 Global leaders at a glance

Building upon the transformative nature of ICT and maintaining their focus on e-government development, all of the top 20 countries in 2012 were high-income developed economies.[2] All have values that range from 164 to 190 per cent of the world average. Of the 20, 14 are in Northern America and Europe; 3 in East Asia (Republic of Korea, Singapore and Japan); 2 in Oceania (Australia and New Zealand); and 1 in Western Asia (Israel).

While the Republic of Korea (0.9283) maintains its position as achieving the greatest e-government development, in 2012 it is followed by three European countries, with the Netherlands (0.9125) advancing by three and the United Kingdom of Great Britain and Northern Ireland (0.8960) by one to become the 2nd and 3rd leading e-ready governments in the world. Denmark (0.8889), the United States of America (0.8687), France (0.8635) and Sweden (0.8599) follow close behind among the global leaders.

The top 20 countries have marginal differences among them in the level of e-government development. All have invested, consolidated and aggregated their e-government development offerings in the last two years. Israel, Liechtenstein and Luxembourg, among the high-income countries, joined the group of world leaders in 2012.

In 2012, the United Nations e-government assessment focused on the concept of integrated services that exploit inter-linkages among different public services on a functionally and/or thematically similar one-stop-shop portal, thereby improving and facilitating citizen experience, allowing for back-office integration across governmental departments and strengthening institutional arrangements. Single sign-on integrated services on portals can organizationally transform public service delivery at both the front and the back end. They can increase functional productivity in governments by identifying and improving governance processes and mechanisms across several departments, leading to greater efficiency and effectiveness of services along with needed cost savings. With a focus on governance solutions that enhance service delivery and streamline public sector efficiency, the United Nations e-government rankings in 2012 reflect an assessment of which countries are undertaking their e-government development with a view to integrated, user-centric public service delivery.

The 2012 Survey assesses web portals with a view to the provision of e-information, e-services, which range from interactive to transactional to networked services, e-participation, and features that are the conduit for service flow from government to citizen and consequently a reflection of attention to governance processes. Indicators grouped along the four stages of the model (emerging, enhanced, transactional and connected) range from static information such as links to ministries/departments, archived information, and regional/local government services; to unidirectional government-to-citizen (G2C) information flows such as online policies, laws and regulation, reports, newsletters, and downloadable databases, among other things; to two-way financial and non-financial transactional services and advanced technical features such as mobile apps; and to integrated and participatory services characterized by an integration of

government-to-government (G2G), government-to-citizen, and citizen-to-government (C2G) interactions in the last stage.[3]

The United Nations Survey 2012 finds that models of an integrated portal differ across countries and regions. While a few countries are progressing towards one national integrated portal, others have developed their e-government offerings with a view to more than one portal, with thematic and/or functional services integrated in a manner that finds e-information separate from e-services or e-participation.

Though each of these have integrated services across various departments on the thematic or functional portal, they nevertheless make less convenient the user search for government information, services and participation in one place. The United Nations E-Government Survey 2012 differentiates these as 'integrated services' from a single 'integrated portal.'

In 2012 no country had a true single-sign-on integrated portal. The United States, Republic of Korea, Israel, Australia, Norway, Denmark, Bahrain, Qatar, United Arab Emirates and New Zealand are among the few that come close to a pure one-stop-shop portal with information, services and participation services integrated on one site.

Most countries from the European Union (EU) follow the approach of separate portals for their information, service and participation offerings. In several European countries e-government services focus on the nationally organized one-stop channel for the provision of 20 basic e-services essential to their citizens while the government-provided information forms a separate portal with information services integrated on it from across all sectors.

Lessons of experience from the assessment in 2012 indicate that more services have been integrated across sectors and agencies. While this trend is likely to continue it seems that increasingly complex public sector services in the future will be 'cloud-based' with service providers able to address innovation and productivity upgrades without costly investments by the government. Cloud service equips governments with greater efficiency by helping them scale up their services, including storage capacity, as it evolves. Among the main challenges for large-scale adoption of cloud-based government services are the integrity of service, data security and privacy, and regulatory environment in most countries around the world, which will need

Table 1.1 **World e-government development leaders 2012**

Rank	Country	E-government development index
1	Republic of Korea	0.9283
2	Netherlands	0.9125
3	United Kingdom	0.8960
4	Denmark	0.8889
5	United States	0.8687
6	France	0.8635
7	Sweden	0.8599
8	Norway	0.8593
9	Finland	0.8505
10	Singapore	0.8474
11	Canada	0.8430
12	Australia	0.8390
13	New Zealand	0.8381
14	Liechtenstein	0.8264
15	Switzerland	0.8134
16	Israel	0.8100
17	Germany	0.8079
18	Japan	0.8019
19	Luxembourg	0.8014
20	Estonia	0.7987

The 2012 Survey extends a special recognition to those countries with a population of over 100 million, which have made the tremendous effort to provide e-government services to their people despite the challenges they face.

Figure 1.1 **Emerging leaders in e-government development**

Country	EGDI
Austria	0.7840
Iceland	0.7835
Spain	0.7770
Belgium	0.7718
Slovenia	0.7492
Monaco	0.7468
Russian Federation	0.7345
United Arab Emirates	0.7344
Lithuania	0.7333
Croatia	0.7328
Hungary	0.7201
Italy	0.7190
Portugal	0.7165
Ireland	0.7149
Malta	0.7131
Bahrain	0.6946
Greece	0.6872
Kazakhstan	0.6844
Chile	0.6769
Malaysia	0.6703
Saudi Arabia	0.6658
Latvia	0.6604
Colombia	0.6572
Barbados	0.6566
Cyprus	0.6508

It is somewhat noteworthy that the emerging leaders group includes some developing countries that have begun to catch up with higher-income countries, such as Kazakhstan (0.6844); Chile (0.6769), Malaysia (0.6703), Colombia (0.6572), Barbados (0.6566) and Cyprus (0.6508).

Many of these countries have invested considerable resources in e-government in the last few years. They have expanded infrastructure and human skills on which to build further advances in service delivery and employ the full potential of information technologies for long-term sustainable development. Some of the developing countries have found ways to leapfrog traditional development cycles by deploying mobile technology for bridging the digital divide. They have reoriented their public sector governance systems towards user-centric approaches visible on their websites through multichannel service delivery features.

As in the case of the world leaders, countries in the emerging leaders group have e-government development values close to each other, ranging from 0.6508 to 0.7840. Most of them are providing similar levels of e-services such as in the case of Cyprus, which though ranked lowest for this group, has achieved around 83 per cent of the level of e-government development of Austria, the group leader.

1.2.1 Countries with a large population

continued reform in governance systems and a continued focus on strengthening institutional linkages.

Close behind the top world leaders are the 25 emerging leaders as given in figure 1.1. Among these, 16 are in Europe, 6 in Asia and 3 in the Americas. With close proximity in the e-government development index value, the leaders among this group are Austria (0.7840), Iceland (0.7835), Spain (0.7770) and Belgium (0.7718). Substantial effort was made by some countries, which is reflected in their advancement this year. Notable among these are the Russian Federation (0.7345), the United Arab Emirates (0.7344), and Saudi Arabia (0.6658), all three of which joined the emerging leaders group. Progress was also noted in the case of Italy (0.7190) and Portugal (0.7165).

The raison d'être of the United Nations E-Government Survey is to assess whether countries are deploying e-government for inclusion-for-all.

Since each country faces a different set of factors that can help or hinder its overall progress towards e-government development, this year the United Nations Survey is extending special recognition to those countries which, with a population of over 100 million, have made a tremendous effort to provide e-government services to their people, despite the challenges they face.

Table 1.2 presents e-government development in countries with populations larger than 100 million that have made a special effort to improve service delivery to large swathes of their populations. It should be kept in mind that the E-Government

Table 1.2 E-government development in largest population countries

Country	E-gov. development index 2012	E-gov. development index 2010	World e-gov. development ranking 2012	World e-gov. development ranking 2010	Population (in millions)
China	0.5359	0.4700	78	72	1,341
India	0.3829	0.3567	125	119	1,225
United States	0.8687	0.8510	5	2	310
Indonesia	0.4949	0.4026	97	109	240
Brazil	0.6167	0.5006	59	61	195
Pakistan	0.2823	0.2755	156	146	174
Nigeria	0.2676	0.2687	162	150	158
Bangladesh	0.2991	0.3028	150	134	149
Russian Federation	0.7345	0.5136	27	59	143
Japan	0.8019	0.7152	18	17	127
Mexico	0.6240	0.5150	55	56	113

Development Index (EGDI) is constructed on a comparative basis that rates each country relative to all other Member States.

Lack of access to both ICT and education infrastructure in the developing countries is a major constraint on e-government development. Income per capita imposes another limiting factor, with lower income countries having a higher marginal cost for a dollar spent on ICT. With the economic downturn, online services are at a disadvantage in the competition for resources with safe water, rural health and basic education services. This becomes especially acute if the country has a large population and/or a large land area since e-inclusion demands that online service access and infrastructure be available to all. Large areas require greater investments in providing telecommunication infrastructure. Even with cellular technology on the move, connectivity remains a major challenge for far flung rural areas. Including a population of 200 people living in the Sahara desert denotes a high marginal cost for the government. Large populations also require greater investments in schools and functional literacy. Many developing countries continue to feel the drag of a low level of educational achievement, which pulls down the United Nations E-Government rankings.

Implicit in the concept of inclusion-for-all is that large, low income countries must exert far more effort to achieve a given level of e-government development than small, high income countries. A large country by land area, for example, must lay many

more miles of fibre-optic cable than a small country to provide broadband connectivity to its citizens. Similarly, a country with a very large population must provide many more online access points – via kiosks, mobile phones, or other means – to its citizens than a country with a small population. Conversely, a country with a high income has more resources to apply to e-government development than a country with a low income.

Figure 1.2 India advancing in e-government development

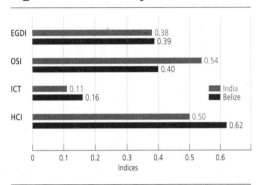

For example, India has about 4000 times the population and about 130 times the area of Belize. Moreover, it has only about one quarter of the Gross National Income of Belize. As such, the effort required by India to provide e-government services is far greater than that of Belize.

Figure 1.3 Impressive gains by China

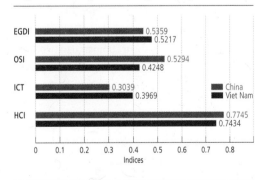

The same is the case of China, which has about 15 times the population of Viet Nam, around 30 times the area, and some 30 per cent the income per capita. This implies that China has a lower availability of resources, skill levels and connectivity, at the margin, to devote to e-government development compared to Viet Nam, and that it must put forth a greater effort to achieve a similar level of e-government development. Despite these challenges the effort made by China has translated into a higher EGDI, at 0.5359.

The converse is true too. Countries endowed with a high income per capita, a small population, and high levels of connectivity face fewer challenges. It is to be expected that with fewer constraints, their e-government development efforts will be more developed so that e-services are available to all, and that high-income developed economies will go the extra mile to deploy ICT for transformation of societies for sustainable development.

This brings into sharp focus two aspects of e-government for development. Countries with a high per capita income, an established ICT infrastructure, and high levels of human capital can easily utilize these advantages to leverage the opportunity afforded by ICT and support sustained socio-economic development. However, in some cases, they may not be doing so fully. Others with lower levels shown by key indicators no doubt need a greater effort, but also have an opportunity to leapfrog long gestation developmental cycles by adroit utilization of ICT for development.

1.3 Regional comparisons

Sustained integration, expansion and consolidation of government online offerings led to more than a 10 per cent increase in the world average of e-government development compared to two years ago. The region of Europe (0.7188) shows the highest e-government development followed by the Americas (0.5403).

Figure 1.4 highlights that despite considerable strides towards bridging the digital divide, infrastructure and human capital limitations in several parts of the world impinge upon the ability of governments to spread – and the citizens to partake of – the benefits of information technology in the delivery of services. With a history of high levels of functional education and widespread telephony infrastructure, Europe and the Americas

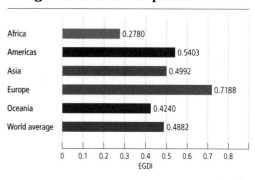

Figure 1.4 **Regional averages in e-government development**

as a whole remain far ahead of the rest of the world regions. Asia, which is home to around three-fifths of the world citizens, has nevertheless only around 70 per cent of the level of e-government in Europe while the level of services in Africa barely squares off at 40 per cent of those in Europe. Within any region, countries at the lower percentile of e-development do not fare well either. This is especially true of the lower income countries in both Asia and Africa. The 10 least e-ready countries in Asia have barely 37 per cent of the level of e-government in Europe while in Africa the figure is little more than 20 per cent.

What is encouraging is the worldwide trend during the last decade. Since 2003 all regions of the world have steadily improved their e-government

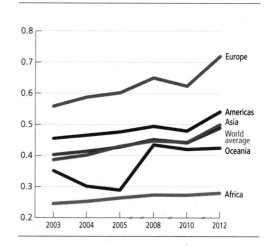

Figure 1.5 **Advances in regional e-government development in the last decade**[4]

development offerings with European countries visibly taking off in the last two years (see figure 1.5). While some countries have advanced considerably over others, Asia as a whole progressed at a leaner rate till 2010 – almost in line with the advances in the world average – and then took off. With an almost flat curve for the period 2003-2012, e-government offerings in Africa advanced minimally, with the region as a whole still remaining least e-ready.

1.3.1 E-government in Africa

The key challenge for the e-government development of Africa remains the widespread lack of infrastructure and functional literacy. Despite recent expansion in mobile telephony, most countries in Africa remain at the tail end of the digital divide. These challenges have translated into a lower than world average e-government development for all sub-regions. Southern Africa (0.3934) consistently outpaces all other sub-regions. Though there has been some improvement in all sub-regions, except for Northern Africa and Middle Africa, it has been minimal, with the least e-ready sub-region being Western Africa (0.2171).

for government ministries and agencies. Table 1.3 shows that Seychelles (0.5192) climbed several points to number one in the region in 2012 followed by Mauritius (0.5066) and South Africa (0.4869). It is notable that all of the African leaders increased their e-government development index value in 2012 but lost in comparative performance around the world, except for Kenya and Morocco, which gained in the world rankings from 124 to 119 and from 126 to 120 respectively. Tunisia (0.4833) and Egypt (0.4611) declined in rank substantially as did Cape Verde (0.4297) because their improvements did not keep pace with those of other countries around the world.

Table 1.3 Top ranked countries in Africa

Rank	Country	E-gov. development index		World e-gov. development ranking	
		2012	2010	2012	2010
1	Seychelles	0.5192	0.4179	84	104
2	Mauritius	0.5066	0.4645	93	77
3	South Africa	0.4869	0.4306	101	97
4	Tunisia	0.4833	0.4826	103	66
5	Egypt	0.4611	0.4518	107	86
6	Cape Verde	0.4297	0.4054	118	108
7	Kenya	0.4212	0.3338	119	124
8	Morocco	0.4209	0.3287	120	126
9	Botswana	0.4186	0.3637	121	117
10	Namibia	0.3937	0.3314	123	125
	Regional Average	**0.2780**	**0.2733**		
	World Average	**0.4882**	**0.4406**		

> The key challenge for the e-government development of Africa remains the lack of widespread infrastructure and functional literacy.

Figure 1.6 Trends in e-government development in Africa 2008-2012

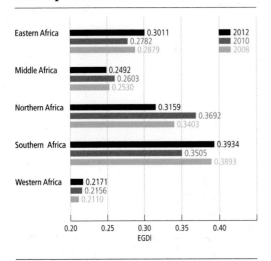

Eastern Africa: 0.3011 (2012), 0.2782 (2010), 0.2879 (2008)
Middle Africa: 0.2492 (2012), 0.2603 (2010), 0.2530 (2008)
Northern Africa: 0.3159 (2012), 0.3692 (2010), 0.3403 (2008)
Southern Africa: 0.3934 (2012), 0.3505 (2010), 0.3893 (2008)
Western Africa: 0.2171 (2012), 0.2156 (2010), 0.2110 (2008)

EGDI

Map 1.1 Sub-regions of Africa

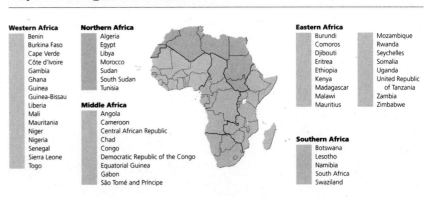

Western Africa
Benin
Burkina Faso
Cape Verde
Côte d'Ivoire
Gambia
Ghana
Guinea
Guinea-Bissau
Liberia
Mali
Mauritania
Niger
Nigeria
Senegal
Sierra Leone
Togo

Northern Africa
Algeria
Egypt
Libya
Morocco
Sudan
South Sudan
Tunisia

Middle Africa
Angola
Cameroon
Central African Republic
Chad
Congo
Democratic Republic of the Congo
Equatorial Guinea
Gabon
São Tomé and Principe

Eastern Africa
Burundi
Comoros
Djibouti
Eritrea
Ethiopia
Kenya
Madagascar
Malawi
Mauritius
Mozambique
Rwanda
Seychelles
Somalia
Uganda
United Republic of Tanzania
Zambia
Zimbabwe

Southern Africa
Botswana
Lesotho
Namibia
South Africa
Swaziland

Africa has seen improvement in e-government with countries in the region looking to increase their online presence through developing websites

Box 1.1 **Seychelles leads in Eastern Africa**

The Government of Seychelles took the initiative to enhance its e-government service offerings in line with an integrated and interdependent strategic approach, which focuses on ICT infrastructure, legal and regulatory framework, human resource development, ICT industry and improvements in the efficiency of the government. It aims at making "Seychelles globally competitive, with a modern ICT enabled economy and a knowledge-based Information Society where strong, efficient and sustainable improvements in social, economic, cultural, good governance and regional integration are achieved through the deployment and effective application of ICT".[5] Seychelles hosts its integrated portal through its *SeyGo Connect* for residents, citizens and businesses which branches out into an e-services gateway, providing a one-stop-shop services ranging from thematic, sectoral, life cycle services to single sign-on tailored for the individual user. ◆

Table 1.4 **E-government development in Eastern Africa**

Country	E-gov. development index		World e-gov. development ranking	
	2012	2010	2012	2010
Seychelles	0.5192	0.4179	84	104
Mauritius	0.5066	0.4645	93	77
Kenya	0.4212	0.3338	119	124
Zimbabwe	0.3583	0.3230	133	129
United Rep. of Tanzania	0.3311	0.2926	139	137
Rwanda	0.3291	0.2749	140	148
Uganda	0.3185	0.2812	143	142
Madagascar	0.3054	0.2890	148	139
Zambia	0.2910	0.2810	154	143
Mozambique	0.2786	0.2288	158	161
Malawi	0.2740	0.2357	159	159
Comoros	0.2358	0.2327	171	160
Ethiopia	0.2306	0.2033	172	172
Burundi	0.2288	0.2014	173	174
Djibouti	0.2228	0.2059	176	170
Eritrea	0.2043	0.1859	180	175
Somalia	0.0640	0.0000	190	N/A
Sub Regional Average	**0.3011**	**0.2782**		
World Average	**0.4882**	**0.4406**		

In 2012, Seychelles undertook further consolidation of infrastructure and its e-government development. Major improvements in mobile telecommunication and integration of thematic services in education, health, and finance with the national portal allowed it to improve its world ranking. Mauritius improved its offerings around 10 per cent with the national portal providing facilities for services such as appointments for vehicle inspections, scholarships and work permits. Although it ranked 2nd in the Eastern Africa region, its efforts could not keep pace in comparison to peers, leading to a decline in its global ranking.

Online services of Mozambique have gained ground in attempting to consolidate all information into one complete site, though this site lacks transactional services. Integrated services across sectors, including important legislation, are available. They include obtaining an identity card, registration of motor vehicles, finding private employment recruitment agencies, and the payment of taxes, to name a few. Progress on back-office integration can be found from the linkages to the various ministries and institutions of the government. Lack of infrastructure, especially broadband, remains a critical factor impeding the e-government efforts in other countries of this

Box 1.2 **Tunisia national portal**

The national government portal provides a 'Most Used Services' section on the home page that provides quick access for citizens to information on services such as obtaining a driver license, and acquiring personal and home loans. Information regarding government services is also laid out by sector, providing quick and efficient access to comprehensive data. ◆

sub-region such as Mozambique and Rwanda as well, despite their progress in expanding services.

The top five countries in the Middle Africa sub-region all improved their service offerings in 2011. However the marginal improvement did not translate into rank improvements on a world level, except in the case of Cameroon (0.3070). The countries of Middle Africa trailed behind other countries of the world.

Gabon (0.3687) was the sub-regional leader followed by Sao Tome and Principe (0.3327) and then Angola (0.3203). Improved features such as Twitter and Facebook on the Gabon national site indicated a move towards greater participation and inclusion of the citizen. The national website

of Sao Tome and Principe, though providing mostly static information, has archived data including sectoral information on health, education and the economy.

For effective e-government to materialize, planning and organization needs to accompany resource availability and an adequate level of human and physical infrastructure on the ground.

Table 1.6 **E-government development in Northern Africa**

Country	E-gov. development index		World e-gov. development ranking	
	2012	2010	2012	2010
Tunisia	0.4833	0.4826	103	66
Egypt	0.4611	0.4518	107	86
Morocco	0.4209	0.3287	120	126
Algeria	0.3608	0.3181	132	131
Sudan	0.2610	0.2542	165	154
South Sudan	0.2239	N/A	175	N/A
Libya	N/A	0.3799	N/A	114
Sub Regional Average	**0.3159**	**0.3692**		
World Average	**0.4882**	**0.4406**		

Though most countries of Northern Africa increased their e-government offerings since the last Survey, they slipped in overall world rankings this year primarily because other countries overtook them in infrastructural development, especially in mobile telephone access. Tunisia (0.4833) maintained its position as the leader of e-government in the sub-region. Morocco improved its e-government

Table 1.5 **E-government development in Middle Africa**

Country	E-gov. development index		World e-gov. development ranking	
	2012	2010	2012	2010
Gabon	0.3687	0.3420	129	123
Sao Tome and Principe	0.3327	0.3258	138	128
Angola	0.3203	0.3110	142	132
Cameroon	0.3070	0.2722	147	149
Equatorial Guinea	0.2955	0.2902	151	138
Congo	0.2809	0.3019	157	135
Democratic Republic of the Congo	0.2280	0.2357	174	158
Chad	0.1092	0.1235	189	182
Central African Republic	N/A	0.1399	N/A	181
Sub Regional Average	**0.2492**	**0.2603**		
World Average	**0.4882**	**0.4406**		

value (0.4209) reaching 120th. Algeria increased its e-government development value by 13 per cent and maintained its global rank. Egypt did not improve

Table 1.7 **E-government development in Southern Africa**

Country	E-gov. development index		World e-gov. development ranking	
	2012	2010	2012	2010
South Africa	0.4869	0.4306	101	97
Botswana	0.4186	0.3637	121	117
Namibia	0.3937	0.3314	123	125
Lesotho	0.3501	0.3512	136	121
Swaziland	0.3179	0.2757	144	145
Sub Regional Average	0.3934	0.3505		
World Average	0.4882	0.4406		

much and declined to 107th. South Sudan became the 193rd United Nations Member State and at the same time came online with a world ranking of 175th. At the same time, domestic political turmoil impacted

Figure 1.7 **Limitations of infrastructure impeding e-government in Africa**

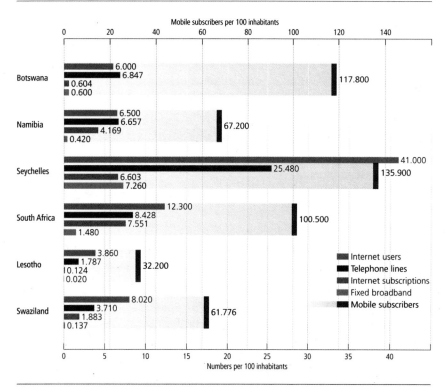

upon the virtual presence of the Government in Libya (formerly the Libyan Arab Jamahiriya), which went offline at the time of the survey assessment.

South Africa (0.4869) was the sub-regional leader, followed by Botswana (0.4186) and Namibia (0.3937). South Africa developed a solid presence covering many of the basic services and features while simultaneously developing transactional facilities and venturing into the networked presence stage. Though providing slightly higher online services than in 2010 and advances in mobile telephony, all countries in Southern Africa, except for Lesotho, fell behind due to continued low availability of infrastructure, especially for the use of broadband.

Table 1.8 **E-government development in Western Africa**

Country	E-gov. development index		World e-gov. development ranking	
	2012	2010	2012	2010
Cape Verde	0.4297	0.4054	118	108
Ghana	0.3159	0.2754	145	147
Gambia	0.2688	0.2117	161	167
Nigeria	0.2676	0.2687	162	150
Senegal	0.2673	0.2241	163	163
Côte d'Ivoire	0.2580	0.2805	166	144
Liberia	0.2407	0.2133	169	166
Togo	0.2143	0.2150	178	165
Benin	0.2064	0.2017	179	173
Mauritania	0.1996	0.2359	181	157
Guinea-Bissau	0.1945	0.1561	182	179
Mali	0.1857	0.1815	183	176
Burkina Faso	0.1578	0.1587	185	178
Sierra Leone	0.1557	0.1697	186	177
Niger	0.1119	0.1098	188	183
Guinea	N/A	0.1426	N/A	180
Sub Regional Average	0.2171	0.2156		
World Average	0.4882	0.4406		

Cape Verde (0.4297) was the sub-regional leader. Although half of all countries, including Ghana (0.3159), Gambia (0.2688), Senegal (0.2673), and Liberia (0.2407) increased their offerings in 2012 all countries of the sub-region remained below the world average. Despite the upsurge in mobile telephony online in recent years, services in Africa remain circumscribed by lack of infrastructure.

1.3.2 E-government in the Americas

As part of their effort to advance citizen services, developed countries are paying greater attention to the concepts of an integrated government portal and the re-engineering of back-office processes in designing their e-government capabilities. E-government strategies are geared towards user-centric solutions, which serve to synergize governance processes and systems across multiple public administration domains.

As noted in figure 1.8, the sub-region of Northern America (0.8559), encompassing only the United States and Canada, is the world leader with values far higher than the world average and all other sub-regions. In 2012, all sub-regions collectively improved performance in the Americas, including the Caribbean (0.5133) and South America (0.5507).

Figure 1.8 Regional e-government in the Americas

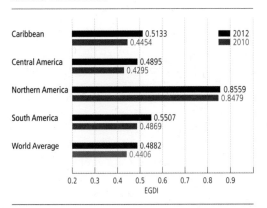

The top ranked countries in the Americas remained the United States followed by Canada, both of which were also among the world leaders. All countries of the region improved their e-government in the past two years, which contributed to around 12 per cent improvement in the sub-regional average. The majority of the countries were also among the top 60 in world rankings.

Table 1.9 Top ranked countries in the Americas

Rank	Country	E-gov. development index		World e-gov. development ranking	
		2012	2010	2012	2010
1	United States	0.8687	0.8510	5	2
2	Canada	0.8430	0.8448	11	3
3	Chile	0.6769	0.6014	39	34
4	Colombia	0.6572	0.6125	43	31
5	Barbados	0.6566	0.5714	44	40
6	Antigua and Barbuda	0.6345	0.5154	49	55
7	Uruguay	0.6315	0.5848	50	36
8	Mexico	0.6240	0.5150	55	56
9	Argentina	0.6228	0.5467	56	48
10	Brazil	0.6167	0.5006	59	61
	Regional Average	**0.5403**	**0.4790**		
	World Average	**0.4882**	**0.4406**		

The United States was found, as before, a best practice example of an integrated portal that provides easy to navigate design and collects and consolidates all information and services for citizens in one place, including agency services at the state and local level, which vastly increases the effectiveness of user search and uptake.

Barbados (0.6566) has been and remains the sub-regional leader among the Caribbean countries in 2012 followed by Antigua and Barbuda (0.6345) and the Bahamas (0.5793). The national site of Barbados offered a user friendly approach of "channels" such as the Government Channel, Citizens &

E-government strategies in the Americas are geared towards user-centric solutions, which serve to synergize governance processes and systems across multiple public administration domains.

Map 1.2 Sub-regions of the Americas

Table 1.10 **E-government development in the Caribbean**

Country	E-gov. development index		World e-gov. development ranking	
	2012	2010	2012	2010
Barbados	0.6566	0.5714	44	40
Antigua and Barbuda	0.6345	0.5154	49	55
Bahamas	0.5793	0.4871	65	65
Trinidad and Tobago	0.5731	0.4806	67	67
Dominica	0.5561	0.4149	73	105
Grenada	0.5479	0.4277	75	99
Saint Kitts and Nevis	0.5272	0.4691	81	75
Saint Vincent and the Grenadines	0.5177	0.4355	85	94
Dominican Republic	0.5130	0.4557	89	84
Saint Lucia	0.5122	0.4471	90	88
Jamaica	0.4552	0.4467	108	89
Cuba	0.4488	0.4321	110	96
Haiti	0.1512	0.2074	187	169
Sub Regional Average	**0.5133**	**0.4454**		
World Average	**0.4882**	**0.4406**		

Table 1.11 **E-government development in Central America**

Country	E-gov. development index		World e-gov. development ranking	
	2012	2010	2012	2010
Mexico	0.6240	0.5150	55	56
Panama	0.5733	0.4619	66	79
El Salvador	0.5513	0.4700	74	73
Costa Rica	0.5397	0.4749	77	71
Guatemala	0.4390	0.3937	112	112
Honduras	0.4341	0.4065	117	107
Belize	0.3923	0.3513	124	120
Nicaragua	0.3621	0.3630	130	118
Sub Regional Average	**0.4895**	**0.4295**		
World Average	**0.4882**	**0.4406**		

Residents Channel, Businesses Channel, etc., making it easier for the user to find relevant information. Moving towards transactional offerings, it allowed for calculation of land taxes.

Improvements in online offerings along with investments in telecommunications and human capital allowed Antigua and Barbuda to advance to a world ranking of 49th in 2012. Similarly, in Dominica and in Grenada, substantial investments in access infrastructure, especially broadband, contributed to an advance in world rankings.

All countries of the Central America sub-region increased their offerings in 2012. Mexico (0.6240) was the leader with e-government offerings around 27 per cent higher than other countries of the sub-region. Closely following Mexico as number two in the sub-region, Panama (0.5733) improved its world ranking from 79 in 2010 to 66 in 2012. It is followed by El Salvador (0.5513) and Costa Rica (0.5397). On the other hand, even as mobile telephony increased in El Salvador, broadband and other access infrastructure remained low, impeding its online service delivery uptake. Other countries of the sub-region that improved e-services are also demonstrating that the expansion of mobile infrastructure has allowed them to complement, and indeed supplement, traditional access to narrow the digital divide.

Mexico upgraded its offerings in 2011 to include a comprehensive search service, which indexes federal, state and municipal web portals daily. With more than 400 million registries in its index, the national portal greatly expanded online services to citizens, including an open government initiative, special offerings for vulnerable groups, and a facility for the anonymous reporting of issues of concern to authorities. It allows for greater inclusion of the citizen through social media such as Twitter and Facebook and is among the select 19 per cent of world countries providing a single sign-on service.

Though Panama improved its online services, the main contributor to its advancement in this year's rankings is the expansion of mobile infrastructure, which is becoming an affordable technology among other countries as well. Panama has one of the highest penetrations of mobile subscribers in the region. As part of its Modernization Plan, to be completed in 2014, Panama is aiming to provide free access to the Internet for all citizens.

The United States (0.8687) leads this sub-region followed closely by Canada (0.8430). Since the United Nations Survey started tracking e-government development in 2003 both countries have been among the top world leaders with integrated

Box 1.3 Mexico's alternative approach

Mexico takes an alternative approach to e-services. Its portal, simply speaking, is a search engine with integrating services that respond to users' specific search criteria. It contains information filtering features that allow users to filter content in order to narrow down searches for specific information. The portal has the ability to filter information by image, videos or news, following the style of Google's main filtering features, as well as being able to filter through other themes such as laws at state and federal levels. Users are also able to filter information that narrows down search results to those that are near the user. A translation feature allows users to translate their searches into the various languages that Google offers. Another feature is 'The Government Recommends' side-bar that suggests useful pages to users so they can quickly gain access to information. ◆

Table 1.12 E-government development in Northern America

Country	E-gov. development index		World e-gov. development ranking	
	2012	2010	2012	2010
United States	0.8687	0.8510	5	2
Canada	0.8430	0.8448	11	3
Sub Regional Average	0.8559	0.8479		
World Average	0.4882	0.4406		

closest to a pure integrated portal with access to interlinked searchable information from the United States Government, state governments, and local governments all in one place. Substantial back-office integration has gone into the user interface, which offers a simple convenient and easy-to-use facility for everything from government departments and agencies to verifying a social security number, getting an employer identification number, multiple online participation efforts and much more.[6] Early recognition of the use of ICT for rolling out citizen portals and increasingly inclusive citizen services spread across theme, functionally and now by life cycle and events. For example, the United States e-government portal (http://www.usa.gov) comes

Figure 1.9 E-government in Northern America

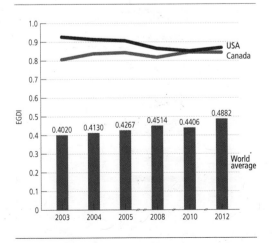

Table 1.13 E-government development in South America

Country	E-gov. development index		World e-gov. development ranking	
	2012	2010	2012	2010
Chile	0.6769	0.6014	39	34
Colombia	0.6572	0.6125	43	31
Uruguay	0.6315	0.5848	50	36
Argentina	0.6228	0.5467	56	48
Brazil	0.6167	0.5006	59	61
Venezuela	0.5585	0.4774	71	70
Peru	0.5230	0.4923	82	63
Ecuador	0.4869	0.4322	102	95
Paraguay	0.4802	0.4243	104	101
Bolivia (Plurinational State of)	0.4658	0.4280	106	98
Guyana	0.4549	0.4140	109	106
Suriname	0.4344	0.3283	116	127
Sub Regional Average	0.5507	0.4869		
World Average	0.4882	0.4406		

Box 1.4 **Brazil: Expanding services**

Brazil's national portal (http://www.brasil.gov.br) has looked to further build upon its strengths by offering greater access and improvement of services to citizens and increasing transparency of government actions. The layout of the national portal is thematic with a 'For' section, which targets the student, worker and business person with a supplemental 'About' section differentiated by topics such as health, education, environment and citizenship. Government services, such as payment of income taxes, fines, utilities and application for social welfare benefits, are easily accessible in an A to Z search from the national portal, which connects users to the various ministries and government departments.

An innovative feature of the national portal is 'MeuBrasil' (My Brazil), where users can personalize queries by choosing their favourite themes that allow updated and user-tailored content. An innovative approach is noticeable on the linked Ministry of Health portal, (http://portal.saude.gov.br/portal/saude/default.cfm). Here, through a live webcast, radio users can receive the latest news and information on health issues while a micro site offers health crisis information. At the time of assessment, available material related to dengue fever, informing on symptoms and methods of prevention and providing a map showing the risk of the disease in each state of the country. ◆

centric services has contributed to the United States' top rankings in the last decade. As the figures indicate, both the United States and Canada have consistently had e-government development levels far above the world average from 2003 to 2012.

Chile (0.6769) is the sub-regional leader in South America, followed by Colombia (0.6572). Whereas collectively the sub-region improved its e-government development by 13 per cent, of the 12 countries that make up this sub-region all declined in the world rankings except Brazil (0.6167) and Suriname (0.4344), indicating that countries within the region as well as around the world are investing in – and expanding – services faster than the countries of this sub-region.

1.3.3 **E-government in Asia**

Asia is home to 60 per cent of humanity. With some Asian countries, including China and India, averaging around 8 to 9 per cent of the continent's GDP, Asia as a whole continued to expand e-government services further. Investments were made horizontally to expand infrastructure, including support for broadband and mobile access, while at the same time governments reached out to provide greater online services and improve e-governance. In 2012, three of the world's top 20 e-leaders are from Asia,

and the region as a whole has a higher level of e-government development than the world average. While there has been improvement in providing e-services across the continent, some of the largest gains are found in Western Asia.

The Republic of Korea (0.9283), the world leader in e-government, is also the top performer in Asia with around double the average world e-government offerings. The 2nd slot is taken this year by Singapore (0.8474) followed by Israel (0.8100) and then Japan (0.8019). The performance of the

> In 2012, three of the world's top 20 e-leaders are from Asia, and the region as a whole has a higher level of e-government development than the world average.

Figure 1.10 **Regional e-government in Asia**

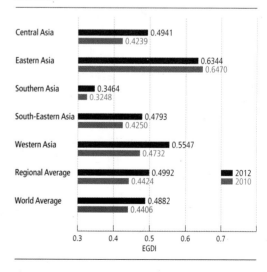

Table 1.14 E-government leaders in Asia

Rank	Country	E-gov. development index 2012	2010	World e-gov. development ranking 2012	2010
1	Republic of Korea	0.9283	0.8785	1	1
2	Singapore	0.8474	0.7476	10	11
3	Israel	0.8100	0.6552	16	26
4	Japan	0.8019	0.7152	18	17
5	United Arab Emirates	0.7344	0.5349	28	49
6	Bahrain	0.6946	0.7363	36	13
7	Kazakhstan	0.6844	0.5578	38	46
8	Malaysia	0.6703	0.6101	40	32
9	Saudi Arabia	0.6658	0.5142	41	58
10	Cyprus	0.6508	0.5705	45	42
	Regional Average	**0.4992**	**0.4424**		
	World Average	**0.4882**	**0.4406**		

United Arab Emirates (0.7344) is especially notable as it advanced 21 positions to the ranking this year of 28th globally and 5th in Asia. The rapid progress of the United Arab Emirates is a best practice case highlighting how effective e-government can help support development. With double the population and three quarters of the GDP per capita, the United Arab Emirates has achieved around the same level of online services as those offered in Norway, a global leader at the 8th position.

Figure 1.11 E-government in Norway and the United Arab Emirates

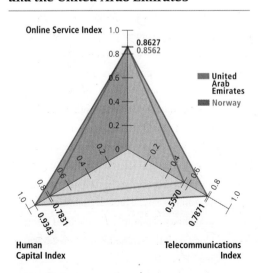

Commensurate with global progress, all countries of Central Asia improved their service offerings, pulling up the sub-regional average by around 17 per cent. Kazakhstan was the sub-regional leader, improving its global ranking by around eight positions in 2012.

Kazakhstan in recent years has made efforts to modernize the public sector, including technology-based reform of administrative governance systems. A parallel effort has been a focus on the use of ICT

Table 1.15 E-government development in Central Asia

Country	E-gov. development index 2012	2010	World e-gov. development ranking 2012	2010
Kazakhstan	0.6844	0.5578	38	46
Uzbekistan	0.5099	0.4498	91	87
Kyrgyzstan	0.4879	0.4417	99	91
Tajikistan	0.4069	0.3477	122	122
Turkmenistan	0.3813	0.3226	126	130
Sub Regional Average	**0.4941**	**0.4239**		
World Average	**0.4882**	**0.4406**		

for provision of services and inclusion. As in other developing countries the acceleration of informatization is aimed at increasing the efficiency of the government and exploiting synergies towards a sustainable model of development.

Ranked 2nd in the e-government development index in Central Asia, Uzbekistan has taken slow but significant steps toward increasing its online presence with the Government Portal of the Republic of Uzbekistan

Map 1.3 Sub-regions of Asia

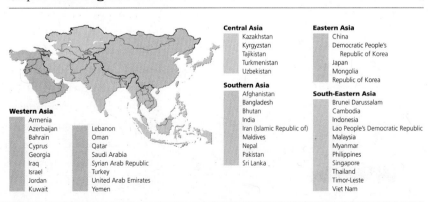

Box 1.5 **Integrated services in Kazakhstan**

The official homepage provides more than 1300 codes, laws, decrees, and orders with all legislation integrated into the main site. Each e-service has several icons stating whether this service can be paid online or obtained through electronic signature. There are other convenient sites such as ePay (http://www.epay.gov.kz) and eLicense (http://www.elicense.kz) where you can get specific services and payments. Another site, (http://www.goszakup.gov.kz), offers participation online in almost all procurement procedures. The main driver behind the improvement in services is the electronic public procurement portal featuring digitization of 59 e-services of state bodies, the e-license database, frequent open public web conferences, often with the with active participation of high-level government officials, and blog platforms in many ministries and agencies. ◆

(http://www.gov.uz). Though the country slipped in overall rank, it improved its services by around 13 per cent. If several years ago the website was merely informative and not at all interactive, government initiative and consequent legislative changes in 2007 and 2009 made possible a more comprehensive e-government portal. Compared to its earlier versions, the national site has added the following notable characteristics and features: effective organization of information; integrated archived information (laws, policies, etc.); an increased number of ministries linked to the portal; technical and web design features (RSS, audio, video, language, etc.) and static online downloadable forms.

The Republic of Korea offers around 87 per cent of all services assessed in the United Nations E-Government Survey 2012. The country's emergence as the world leader in information and communication technologies in fields such as broadband, semiconductors and third generation mobile devices – has guaranteed its fast growth and development in the area of e-government. Japan follows as number two in the sub-region, at 18th in world e-government development rankings. It is notable that all countries of Eastern Asia improved their service offerings and that the Democratic People's Republic of Korea came online.

Box 1.6 **World leader in e-government development 2012: Republic of Korea**

The Government's main website has developed into an integrated portal where citizens can find almost every service they want, on both national and local level. The main government portal is a gateway to services through multiple channels, by theme and subjects; citizens can also have a customized channel by inputting their own age, gender and services of interest. Back-office integration across many departments brings together a powerful search engine offering advanced categorizing function, which can list results by websites, services, and news, including at the local level.

A key reason for continued leadership in world e-government progress is significant development and provision of downloadable mobile applications that are available from its national portal. The cross sector mobile apps for citizens are both iPhone and Android compatible including for e-Learning, which allows students to learn on their mobile phone in areas such as social studies, math and English. For employment opportunities, *Jobcast* provides information on availability of jobs in the Republic of Korea along with the relevant legislation governing labour. ◆

Box 1.7 China: Enhancing transparency and openness

China has been making efforts to improve the level of its Government portal by providing comprehensive information, more integrated services of different sectors, and interactions between government officials and citizens.

One thing worth mentioning is China's endeavour to promote the open government initiative. In order to improve transparency, there is a separate section on the government's main portal that enables citizens to search for and refer to archived policy documents and notifications of different sectors. ◆

Among others, China has made steady progress in overall e-government development. This is no small feat since it is a country of 1.2 billion people and a large land mass – both of which require more effort from the government, especially if the population is widely dispersed, than would a country with a small population living within a limited area. China has enhanced the quality of its government portal by providing comprehensive information, more integrated services across different sectors, and greater interactions between government officials and citizens.

All countries of Southern Asia fall in the lower half of the e-ready countries with approximately an equal number of them above and below the regional average. A low GDP per capita, a still evolving infrastructure and lower levels of functional literacy translate

Table 1.16 E-government development in Eastern Asia

Country	E-gov. development index		World e-gov. development ranking	
	2012	2010	2012	2010
Republic of Korea	0.9283	0.8785	1	1
Japan	0.8019	0.7152	18	17
Mongolia	0.5443	0.5243	76	53
China	0.5359	0.4700	78	72
Dem. People's Rep. of Korea	0.3616	N/A	130	N/A
Sub Regional Average	**0.6344**	**0.6470**		
World Average	**0.4882**	**0.4406**		

Box 1.8 India looks to sustainable development by including all

In addition to the national portal, the Government has also developed an India Development Gateway. This is "the National portal of India developed as a single-window access to information and services, with the specific objective of reaching the 'un-reached' rural communities of India, especially women and the poor. It catalyzes the use of ICT tools for knowledge sharing, leading to development." (http://www.indg.in/india/about-c-dac/ view?set_language=en). A variant of the National Portal, but targeted towards a specific group of people, this site contains specific topics aimed at the rural poor: agriculture, rural energy, etc., and features forum discussions and an "ask an expert" section. Making it available in English and in eight local dialects, the government's main objective is to stimulate women, the poor, and people in the remote rural areas to use technology to their own advantage. ◆

Box 1.9 **Pakistan in the forefront of e-passport**

In Pakistan, the Ministry of Interior and the National Database and Registration Authority (NADRA) have introduced a chip-based e-passport that would help further secure the identity of the citizens, making Pakistan one of the first countries in the world to issue the Multi-biometric e-Passport compliant with ICAO standards. The e-Passport solution uses security features on the data page supported by sophisticated technology and business logic, which makes it one of the most modern passports of this era. NADRA has already issued the passports to millions of Pakistani citizens. ◆

into low service provision and user uptake for the majority of the populations of India, Bangladesh, Bhutan, Pakistan and Nepal, with e-government development levels ranging from 0.2664 to 0.3829.

Maldives (0.4994) leads in the sub-region followed by the Islamic Republic of Iran (0.4876) and then Sri Lanka (0.4357). Service provision in Maldives builds on providing easy access to information to citizens and businesses. Through an 'I Want To' section organized by theme and life cycle, users can find information on service procedures, including how to obtain driver licenses, obtain ID cards and register vehicles. The national site of the Islamic Republic of Iran is available in two languages: Persian and English. Transactional service offerings in the Islamic Republic of Iran are joint public-private partnerships with some available online but also though banks and other local and national institutions.

Table 1.17 **E-government development in Southern Asia**

Country	E-gov. development index		World e-gov. development ranking	
	2012	2010	2012	2010
Maldives	0.4994	0.4392	95	92
Iran (Islamic Republic of)	0.4876	0.4234	100	102
Sri Lanka	0.4357	0.3995	115	111
India	0.3829	0.3567	125	119
Bangladesh	0.2991	0.3028	150	134
Bhutan	0.2942	0.2598	152	152
Pakistan	0.2823	0.2755	156	146
Nepal	0.2664	0.2568	164	153
Afghanistan	0.1701	0.2098	184	168
Sub Regional Average	0.3464	0.3248		
World Average	0.4882	0.4406		

Box 1.10 **Singapore in the vanguard of countries**

Singapore is among the leaders in the use of private cloud computing for leveraging ICT infrastructure and services. In September 2009, it became the first government in Asia to equip all its teachers with Web 2.0 communication and collaboration tools under an open standard cloud platform. Singapore's citizen's portal provides an extensive range of online payment services that lists by agency as well as bill type. Payments range from taxes, fees, fines and licenses that can be made through multichannels such as credit card, direct debit as well as internet banking and even by phone. ◆

Box 1.11 **Israel consolidates e-services**

Israel has improved its e-government development and has now become the leading country in the Western Asia region. The Government portal is well organized. Citizens can access information on government services in three different ways: by target audience, topics and life events. Citizens can also use the portal's electronic identity management feature 'My Gov' to filter content that interests them and to access the full range of online government services and make online payments. ◆

With 1.2 billion people and challenges associated with a large population, e-services in India are in the formative stage. The Government of India has made substantial efforts in the last few years to overcome the challenges, including that of connectivity to its 70 per cent rural population. Looking towards sustainable growth the government has announced that Rural Broadband Connectivity to all 250,000 Panchayats (local governments) in the country will be provided in three years to bridge the digital divide.[7]

Other countries in the sub-region such as Pakistan are also providing more e-services. In line with the Government of Pakistan's policy to digitize e-services, the Multi-biometric e-Passport project aims at improving transparency in the public sphere.

Tenth in the world ranking, Singapore (0.8474) is the leader in the South Eastern Asia region and a best practice example. It is among

Table 1.18 **E-government development in South-Eastern Asia**

Country	E-gov. development index		World e-gov. development ranking	
	2012	2010	2012	2010
Singapore	0.8474	0.7476	10	11
Malaysia	0.6703	0.6101	40	32
Brunei Darussalam	0.6250	0.4796	54	68
Viet Nam	0.5217	0.4454	83	90
Philippines	0.5130	0.4637	88	78
Thailand	0.5093	0.4653	92	76
Indonesia	0.4949	0.4026	97	109
Lao People's Dem. Rep.	0.2935	0.2637	153	151
Cambodia	0.2902	0.2878	155	140
Myanmar	0.2703	0.2818	160	141
Timor-Leste	0.2365	0.2273	170	162
Sub Regional Average	**0.4793**	**0.4250**		
World Average	**0.4882**	**0.4406**		

Box 1.12 **Saudi Arabia offers innovative e-services**

A big development in the Saudi e-services is the eDashboard portal, which verifies the identity of the citizen (Digital Verification) and serves as a single sign-on portal where citizens can access all services provided. The Saudi Government also offers an Open Data Initiative, which provides citizens with documents and reports from ministries and government agencies, all publicly available. It encourages e-participation to gather public opinion through surveys, public consultations and blogs. ◆

Box 1.13 Qatar's Hukoomi: Working towards integration

http://portal.www.gov.qa/wps/portal/frontpage

Hukoomi, Qatar's official government gateway that integrates government services, programmes and initiatives. Among its goals are to improve efficiency, responsiveness to users and accessible to all. Accessible through the Internet as well as a mobile device, *Hukoomi* integrates back-office processes to allow easy access to over 100 topics and articles with detailed information about Qatari law and society. The portal provides direct links to sub-portals, such as on the employment and recruitment service and e-tendering; and links to application forms from a wide range of government ministries, agencies and public services.[8] ◆

the vanguard countries employing advanced technology for innovative future solutions, organizing information in a seamless structured and user-targeted manner. Malaysia (0.6703) continues to be the 2nd leading country in the South-Eastern Asia region in 2012, not least because of its impressive service provision through an A-Z topics section as well as a life cycle feature targeting the user as a child, teenager, adult or elderly person. An impressive national health portal, *MyHealth*, uses ICT to inform citizens on health issues in Malaysia.

Like other leading countries, the key to the advancement of Israel, the leader in Western Asia, is its integrated approach to e-government development. Israel has added 10 points to its ranking, advancing from 26th position in 2010 to 16th in 2012.

Close behind are Saudi Arabia (0.6658) and Qatar (0.6405), both of which have undertaken to expand citizen centric services as reflected in their notable performance, which raised their global rankings to 41st and 48th respectively. The principle goals of the Saudi Arabian e-government offerings are to raise the productivity and efficiency of the public sector, increase the return on investment in ICT and provide easy-to-use, timely accurate services. A separate e-payment portal has been developed through which citizens are able to handle all online transactions.

In accordance with the strategy of the Supreme Council of Information and Communication Technology (ictQATAR), Qatar developed a strategic plan for the implementation of an integrated government programme. The plan aims to provide an enabling ICT environment through legislation, policies, guidelines and standards, such as the e-commerce policy, security policy, and data protection policy. It addresses ICT 'readiness' by offering e-services through a unified system of government networks; provides a centralized, secure, government data centre and a payment platform; and seeks

Table 1.19 E-government development in Western Asia

Country	E-gov. development index		World e-gov. development ranking	
	2012	2010	2012	2010
Israel	0.8100	0.6552	16	26
United Arab Emirates	0.7344	0.5349	28	49
Bahrain	0.6946	0.7363	36	13
Saudi Arabia	0.6658	0.5142	41	58
Cyprus	0.6508	0.5705	45	42
Qatar	0.6405	0.4928	48	62
Kuwait	0.5960	0.5290	63	50
Oman	0.5944	0.4576	64	82
Georgia	0.5563	0.4248	72	100
Turkey	0.5281	0.4780	80	69
Lebanon	0.5139	0.4388	87	93
Armenia	0.4997	0.4025	94	110
Azerbaijan	0.4984	0.4571	96	83
Jordan	0.4884	0.5278	98	51
Syrian Arab Republic	0.3705	0.3103	128	133
Iraq	0.3409	0.2996	137	136
Yemen	0.2472	0.2154	167	164
Sub Regional Average	**0.5547**	**0.4732**		
World Average	**0.4882**	**0.4406**		

to improve 'usage' by increasing the number of e-services such as businesses' registration, visa services and resident permits. Hukoomi, the national portal of Qatar, integrates back-office processes to allow easy access to over 100 topics and articles with detailed information about Qatari law and society. Online services available include, among others, payment for utilities, renewal of health cards, settlement of traffic violations, visa applications, and licenses.

1.3.4 E-government in Europe

Europe as a region has been in the vanguard of information technology and setting the pace for others to follow. Building on the existing strength of high levels of human capital and infrastructure, the transformative role of ICT has been recognized and adopted to further streamline e-government services. Moving beyond improving public sector efficiency, Europe is now looking to adapt innovative technologies to human development and economic sustainability in the future.

Table 1.20 **Top 10 in Europe**

Rank	Country	E-gov. development index		World e-gov. development ranking	
		2012	2010	2012	2010
1	Netherlands	0.9125	0.8097	2	5
2	United Kingdom	0.8960	0.8147	3	4
3	Denmark	0.8889	0.7872	4	7
4	France	0.8635	0.7510	6	10
5	Sweden	0.8599	0.7474	7	12
6	Norway	0.8593	0.8020	8	6
7	Finland	0.8505	0.6967	9	19
8	Liechtenstein	0.8264	0.6694	14	23
9	Switzerland	0.8134	0.7136	15	18
10	Germany	0.8079	0.7309	17	15
	Regional Average	**0.7188**	**0.6227**		
	World Average	**0.4882**	**0.4406**		

With a common e-government framework, EU countries are encouraged to deploy advanced technologies, institute better governance and provide expanded services with concomitant pursuit of greater transparency, efficiency and inclusion. Notwithstanding, differences remain between regions and within them. Key European countries spend more than double the EU average amount per capita on ICT; others, around half of it.

The Netherlands (0.9125) made substantial gains, advancing to the top position in Europe and 2nd in world rankings, followed by the United Kingdom (0.8960) in 3rd place and Denmark (0.8889), which also advanced and occupies the

Moving from improving public sector efficiency, Europe looks to take this role further in adapting innovative technologies to human development and economic sustainability in the future.

Figure 1.12 **Regional e-government in Europe**

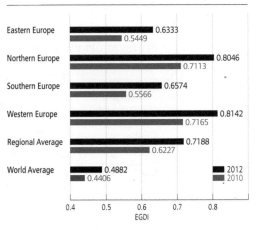

The European region has the highest level of e-government development, which is around 50 per cent higher than that of the world as a whole. Western and Northern Europe offer the most online services but considerable gains were made by Southern and Eastern Europe as well in 2012.

Map 1.4 **Sub-regions of Europe**

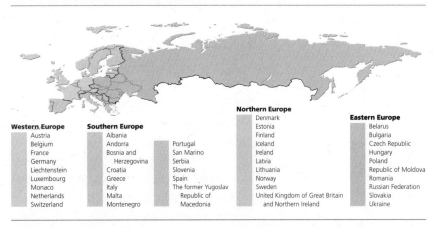

Box 1.14 EU leads the way to innovative application of ICT to sustainable development

http://www.europe2020.org

Europe 2020, EU's growth strategy for the coming decade, involves an innovative use of technology to challenges of economic growth, employment, education, social inclusion and climate/energy. Expanding the reach, EU countries are looking towards ICT as the key enabling technology to underpin future development in the region.

The EU Member States have earmarked a total of € 9.1 billion for funding ICT over the duration of the Seventh Framework Programme.[9] One of the three Flagship Initiatives to achieve *Smart Growth* in Europe 2020 is the *Digital agenda for Europe*, a blueprint for creating a single digital market based on fast or ultra-fast internet and interoperable applications. Targets include:

- By 2013: broadband access for all by 2020: access for all to much higher Internet speeds (30 Mbps or above)
- By 2020: 50 per cent more European households with Internet connections above 100 Mbps.

The strategy for the near future aims at development of common platforms and reference architectures, interoperability and data exchange standards in order to build a competitive advantage in technology solutions, which will yield high value added. ◆

4th position this year. Within the aforementioned common e-government framework, all of the top countries of Europe offered more or less the same level of user centric services to their citizens resulting in marginal assessment difference among them. For example, Germany (0.8079), the 10th leading country in Europe as a whole, achieved about 89 per cent of the e-government development level of the regional leader, the Netherlands.

Advancing 32 positions in the world rankings, the Russian Federation (0.7345) became the leader in Eastern Europe followed by Hungary (0.7201) and the Czech Republic (0.6491).

As in other parts of Europe, all countries of the sub-region improved their e-government development in 2012, advancing the sub-regional average by 16 per cent even though they could not maintain their rankings, except for Belarus and the Russian Federation. Being the largest country in the world and consisting of eight federal districts influences the development of e-government in the Russian Federation. The Government recently announced investments of around 80 billion rubles for the informatization of federal government bodies and other initiatives related to the development of e-government. In Hungary, the focus of programmes to develop the information society encompassed support for improving ICT skills in the labour

market, targeting small and medium enterprises and increasing the number of ICT experts.

E-services were increasingly the norm in other countries as well. In 2010, Moldova, another country that improved its ranking, in collaboration with the World Bank, started implementation of a *Strategic Programme for Technological Modernization of the Government*, aimed at ICT-led

Table 1.21 E-government development in Eastern Europe

Country	E-gov. development index		World e-gov. development ranking	
	2012	2010	2012	2010
Russian Federation	0.7345	0.5136	27	59
Hungary	0.7201	0.6315	31	27
Czech Republic	0.6491	0.6060	46	33
Poland	0.6441	0.5582	47	45
Slovakia	0.6292	0.5639	53	43
Bulgaria	0.6132	0.5590	60	44
Belarus	0.6090	0.4900	61	64
Romania	0.6060	0.5479	62	47
Ukraine	0.5653	0.5181	68	54
Republic of Moldova	0.5626	0.4611	69	80
Sub Regional Average	0.6333	0.5449		
World Average	0.4882	0.4406		

Box 1.15 **Denmark: Providing multiple choices**

Denmark's services portal is the gateway to the entire public sector in Denmark and provides access to an enormous amount of information and services. It paves the way for an efficient user interface with effective streamlining of public sector departments. The slogan of the page is *"your access to the public"*. It is, for example, possible to report an address change on this website, apply for student loans and student grants scholarships, see and modify tax issues, apply for a state pension, and report changes in income or marital status. Feedback is offered through a mailbox called *E-Box*, which collects all the mail that the citizen receives from both public authorities and private companies. ◆

institutional reform to increase access to information and promote digital services (e-services), and to improve public administration. By improving the governance frameworks the programme is expected

Table 1.22 **E-government development in Northern Europe**

Country	E-gov. development index		World e-gov. development ranking	
	2012	2010	2012	2010
United Kingdom	0.8960	0.8147	3	4
Denmark	0.8889	0.7872	4	7
Sweden	0.8599	0.7474	7	12
Norway	0.8593	0.8020	8	6
Finland	0.8505	0.6967	9	19
Estonia	0.7987	0.6965	20	20
Iceland	0.7835	0.6697	22	22
Lithuania	0.7333	0.6295	29	28
Ireland	0.7149	0.6866	34	21
Latvia	0.6604	0.5826	42	37
Sub Regional Average	**0.8046**	**0.7113**		
World Average	**0.4882**	**0.4406**		

to result in simplification and consolidation of administrative procedures leading to transparency and effectiveness.

Six out of ten countries of Northern Europe were among the world leaders. Number three in the world, United Kingdom (0.8960) was the leader in Northern Europe followed by Denmark (0.8889 – 4th) and Sweden (0.8599 – 7th). The focus on integration of back-office departments for improvement of user interface is evident in the integrated services on the United Kingdom's *DirectGov* (http://www.direct.gov.uk), which provides a one-stop-shop for all government information and services. Its comprehensive 'Do It Online' page lists all public services, forms, tools and transactions that the government provides in a user-friendly manner. The *Jobcentre Plus* page located on the portal allows citizens to search one of the United Kingdom's largest online databases of job vacancies.

With a focus on service delivery, government national portals are organized according to domains in most of the EU countries. Denmark's overall strategy appears to go well beyond simply providing a single portal. Rather, it seems to be focusing on multiple entry points to government based on various interest groups and constituencies. Early adoption of online transactional services has resulted in substantial cost efficiencies. In Denmark, for example, electronic invoicing saves taxpayers €150 million and businesses €50 million a year. According to one estimate, similar efforts all across the EU would result in annual savings of around €50 billion.[10]

In Northern Europe, the progress of Finland was especially noteworthy as it gained 10 positions to rank 9th in the world. The National Knowledge Society Strategy 2007-2015 in Finland focuses on the provision of multichannel, interactive e-services together with interoperability of information systems in the public administration. The *suomi.fi* (http://www.suomi.fi/suomifi/suomi) portal provides a single access point to online public services offered from both state and local authorities, organized around daily life events.

Some other Northern European countries also fortified their e-services, providing greater access and inclusion to citizens. Though they did not maintain their global ranking, other countries such as Lithuania (0.7333 – 29th), Ireland (0.7149 – 34th), and Latvia (0.6604 – 42nd) also improved e-government applications, networking, and other web services. The e-government gateway of Lithuania (http://www.ep-aslaugos.lt) has been developed under the auspices of the Information Society Development Committee for the purpose of providing seamless public administration services and information to residents and business. Covering content in both the Lithuanian and English languages, the gateway provides 211 first-level public services, 167 second-level services, 33 third-level services and 12 fourth-level services.[11] The one-stop-shop portal of Ireland approaches the delivery of e-services in such a way that enables users to tailor those services to their needs at a place and time that suits them, together with an overview of the extent of public services online. Latvia's one-stop-shop portal (https://www.latvija.lv) offers 29 e-services and online banking (e-payments). Points of Single Contact allow service providers to obtain information through a single entry point and complete required administrative procedures electronically in order to commence provision of services in a chosen business sector in Latvia. An advanced users authorization system through bank or ID cards ensures users privacy and security. The online banking system allows users to employ the system more efficiently and securely (e.g., for income tax declaration).

Even though its global ranking dropped, Spain (0.7770) remained the leader in Southern Europe, followed by Slovenia at 25th and Croatia at 30th in world rankings. The national site of Spain is available for the user in five languages with information services and easy-to-navigate features. In Slovenia the public sector reforms have included digitization of governance processes and services for improved functioning. The State portal of the Government of Slovenia (http://e-uprava.gov.si) organizes information to citizens by links to 18 life event categories such as work and employment, health and social affairs, personal finance and taxes, environment, education and youth, and social welfare so that information on government services can be easily and quickly accessible.

Table 1.23 E-government development in Southern Europe

Country	E-gov. development index		World e-gov. development ranking	
	2012	2010	2012	2010
Spain	0.7770	0.7516	23	9
Slovenia	0.7492	0.6243	25	29
Croatia	0.7328	0.5858	30	35
Italy	0.7190	0.5800	32	38
Portugal	0.7165	0.5787	33	39
Malta	0.7131	0.6129	35	30
Greece	0.6872	0.5708	37	41
Serbia	0.6312	0.4585	51	81
San Marino	0.6305	N/A	52	N/A
Montenegro	0.6218	0.5101	57	60
Andorra	0.6172	0.5148	58	57
The former Yugoslav Rep. of Macedonia	0.5587	0.5261	70	52
Bosnia and Herzegovina	0.5328	0.4698	79	74
Albania	0.5161	0.4519	86	85
Sub Regional Average	**0.6574**	**0.5566**		
World Average	**0.4882**	**0.4406**		

Among other countries that increased their world rankings are Italy, Portugal, Greece and Serbia. Particularly notable is Serbia's performance, which advanced 30 positions to arrive at 51st in the world rankings. In Serbia, the Digital Agenda Authority is

Table 1.24 E-government development in Western Europe

Country	E-gov. development index		World e-gov. development ranking	
	2012	2010	2012	2010
Netherlands	0.9125	0.8097	2	5
France	0.8635	0.7510	6	10
Liechtenstein	0.8264	0.6694	14	23
Switzerland	0.8134	0.7136	15	18
Germany	0.8079	0.7309	17	15
Luxembourg	0.8014	0.6672	19	25
Austria	0.7840	0.6679	21	24
Belgium	0.7718	0.7225	24	16
Monaco	0.7468	N/A	26	N/A
Sub Regional Average	**0.8142**	**0.7165**		
World Average	**0.4882**	**0.4406**		

responsible for introducing online services to improve economic efficiency and citizens' quality of life, and for implementing e-government in accordance with a "one-stop-shop" principle. Among other initiatives, the Authority created Serbia's e-services portal, eUprava (http://www.euprava.gov.rs), which aggregates services and information from more than 27 governmental authorities, including municipal authorities.

Of the countries of the region which are global leaders, several offered examples of best practice. In the Netherlands, efficiency and citizen inclusion are the objectives of the e-government strategy. Integration of a back-office management system has been undertaken with a belief that citizens should provide information once. The government is building an e-government infrastructure encompassing citizen access to government processes including electronic authentication, uniform identification numbers for both citizens and businesses and electronic personal identification. As part of its broader ICT strategy the focus of e-government in the Netherlands was on improving efficiency of services concomitant with reduction of administrative cost and burden.

Based on extensive technological infrastructure, the recently concluded National Implementation Programme (NUP) for Better Services and e-Government laid out agreements among the national government, provinces, and municipalities to improve service delivery. Its high levels of broadband connectivity ensured further enhancements in e-services undertaken during the last few years.

Luxembourg's services portal (http://www.guichet.public.lu/fr/citoyens/index.html) is helping to simplify the citizens' interaction with government by providing a quick and easy access to all information and services by public bodies to citizens and businesses and it allows users to use the electronic signature LuxTrust.

Table 1.25 **E-government development in Oceania**

Country	E-gov. development index		World e-gov. development ranking	
	2012	2010	2012	2010
Australia	0.8390	0.7863	12	8
New Zealand	0.8381	0.7311	13	14
Fiji	0.4672	0.3925	105	113
Tonga	0.4405	0.3697	111	116
Palau	0.4359	0.4189	113	103
Samoa	0.4358	0.3742	114	115
Micronesia (Federated States of)	0.3812	N/A	127	N/A
Tuvalu	0.3539	N/A	134	N/A
Vanuatu	0.3512	0.2521	135	155
Nauru	0.3242	N/A	141	N/A
Marshall Islands	0.3129	N/A	146	N/A
Kiribati	0.2998	N/A	149	N/A
Solomon Islands	0.2416	0.2445	168	156
Papua New Guinea	0.2147	0.2043	177	171
Sub Regional Average	**0.4240**	**0.4193**		
World Average	**0.4882**	**0.4406**		

1.3.5 **E-government in Oceania**

Two of the world leaders – Australia and New Zealand – outpace others in the region. With many countries in the range of 113–177 in global rankings, the region as a whole scored around 13 per cent less than the world average.

Figure 1.13 **Regional e-government development: Oceania and the world**

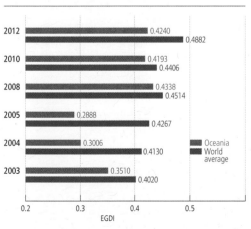

	Oceania	World average
2012	0.4240	0.4882
2010	0.4193	0.4406
2008	0.4338	0.4514
2005	0.2888	0.4267
2004	0.3006	0.4130
2003	0.3510	0.4020

EGDI

Map 1.5 **Region of Oceania**

Australia and New Zealand
Australia
New Zealand

Melanesia
Fiji
Papua New Guinea
Solomon Islands
Vanuatu

Micronesia
Kiribati
Marshall Islands
Micronesia (Federated States of)
Nauru
Palau

Polynesia
Samoa
Tonga
Tuvalu

Australia continues to be the leader in the Oceania region. The national portal (http://australia.gov.au) acts as a one-stop-shop that connects citizens to the information and services of around 900 government websites and state and territory resources. Information can be quickly and easily accessed through the 'People' and 'Topics' sections, which categorically filter specific content while the 'Services' section allows citizens to perform many functions such as making payments for taxes, driver license renewals, vehicle and business registrations, lodging online forms and making online inquiries. The integrated portal of the Government of New Zealand provides a one-stop-shop portal for information, images and resources from all New Zealand government agencies and government funded sites.

1.4 Least developed countries

The least developed countries (LDCs) group was led by Samoa (0.4358) at 114th place, followed by Tuvalu (0.3539) which, at 134th, made considerable progress since 2010.[12] Notable advances were also made by Vanuatu (0.3512) and Rwanda (0.3291), which moved up to 135th and 140th, respectively. Overall, the LDCs remain hampered by a lack of infrastructure, both physical and human. Despite advances in mobile communication lack of functional skills limit user uptake.

Though there is considerable progress in the expansion of online services, one of the primary challenges that remains is integration of back-end processes with efficient, user friendly, and target-oriented services delivery. Countries around the world are increasingly adopting integrated, multichannel and user-centric services online. Though efforts towards deploying ICT for sustainable development are evident, the extent, design and approach to user interface vary depending on several factors, including leadership and vision, planning and organization, level of income and absorptive capacity in the country.

> Though there is considerable progress in the expansion of online services, one of the primary challenges that remains in LDC's is integration of back-end processes with efficient, user friendly, and target-oriented services delivery.

Table 1.26 E-government development in least developed countries

Country	E-gov. development index 2012	E-gov. development index 2010	World e-gov. development ranking 2012	World e-gov. development ranking 2010
Samoa	0.4358	0.3742	114	115
Tuvalu	0.3539	N/A	134	N/A
Vanuatu	0.3512	0.2521	135	155
Lesotho	0.3501	0.3512	136	121
Sao Tome and Principe	0.3327	0.3258	138	128
United Rep. of Tanzania	0.3311	0.2926	139	137
Rwanda	0.3291	0.2749	140	148
Angola	0.3203	0.3110	142	132
Uganda	0.3185	0.2812	143	142
Madagascar	0.3054	0.2890	148	139
Kiribati	0.2998	N/A	149	N/A
Bangladesh	0.2991	0.3028	150	134
Equatorial Guinea	0.2955	0.2902	151	138
Bhutan	0.2942	0.2598	152	152
Lao People's Dem. Rep.	0.2935	0.2637	153	151
Zambia	0.2910	0.2810	154	143
Cambodia	0.2902	0.2878	155	140
Mozambique	0.2786	0.2288	158	161
Malawi	0.2740	0.2357	159	159
Myanmar	0.2703	0.2818	160	141
Gambia	0.2688	0.2117	161	167
Senegal	0.2673	0.2241	163	163
Nepal	0.2664	0.2568	164	153
Sudan	0.2610	0.2542	165	154
Yemen	0.2472	0.2154	167	164
Solomon Islands	0.2416	0.2445	168	156
Liberia	0.2407	0.2133	169	166
Timor-Leste	0.2365	0.2273	170	162
Comoros	0.2358	0.2327	171	160
Ethiopia	0.2306	0.2033	172	172
Burundi	0.2288	0.2014	173	174
Democratic Republic of the Congo	0.2280	0.2357	174	158
Djibouti	0.2228	0.2059	176	170
Togo	0.2143	0.2150	178	165
Benin	0.2064	0.2017	179	173
Eritrea	0.2043	0.1859	180	175
Mauritania	0.1996	0.2359	181	157
Guinea Bissau	0.1945	0.1561	182	179
Mali	0.1857	0.1815	183	176
Afghanistan	0.1701	0.2098	184	168
Burkina Faso	0.1578	0.1587	185	178
Sierra Leone	0.1557	0.1697	186	177
Haiti	0.1512	0.2074	187	169
Niger	0.1119	0.1098	188	183
Chad	0.1092	0.1235	189	182
Somalia	0.0640	N/A	190	N/A

1.5 Post-conflict countries

Post-conflict situations are associated with weak and fragile states where legitimacy and governance are ineffective and services non-existent. As a special case, in table 1.27 the 2012 Survey presents e-government development in a few select countries that have witnessed conflict in the past decades. For the definition of post-conflict countries, please refer to the United Nations Development Programme's *Crisis Prevention and Recovery Report 2008*, available online.[13]

1.6 Conclusion

In conclusion, the 2012 Survey finds that Member States have begun to move from a decentralized single-purpose organization model of e-government to an integrated unified whole-of-government model for the people. This approach supports the strengthening of institutional linkages with interconnected departments and divisions; greater efficiency and effectiveness of governance systems; and better public service delivery. However, the efforts of countries at all levels of development are still affected by a lack of integration of administrative simplification with e-government development plans, lack of infrastructure and human resource capacity and a gap between e-services supply and demand. Low-income countries, in particular, continue to contend with traditional barriers to ICT investment such as lack of technical skills, high costs of technology, and ineffective government regulation. ⌀

Table 1.27 **E-government development in post-conflict countries**

Country	E-gov. development index		World e-gov. development ranking	
	2012	2010	2012	2010
Croatia	0.7328	0.5858	30	35
Georgia	0.5563	0.4248	72	100
El Salvador	0.5513	0.4700	74	73
Bosnia and Herzegovina	0.5328	0.4698	79	74
Lebanon	0.5139	0.4388	87	93
Azerbaijan	0.4984	0.4571	96	83
Indonesia	0.4949	0.4026	97	109
Guatemala	0.4390	0.3937	112	112
Sri Lanka	0.4357	0.3995	115	111
Tajikistan	0.4069	0.3477	122	122
Namibia	0.3937	0.3314	123	125
Nicaragua	0.3621	0.3630	130	118
Rwanda	0.3291	0.2749	140	148
Angola	0.3203	0.3110	142	132
Uganda	0.3185	0.2812	143	142
Cambodia	0.2902	0.2878	155	140
Congo	0.2809	0.3019	157	135
Mozambique	0.2786	0.2288	158	161
Nepal	0.2664	0.2568	164	153
Côte d'Ivoire	0.2580	0.2805	166	144
Solomon Islands	0.2416	0.2445	168	156
Liberia	0.2407	0.2133	169	166
Timor-Leste	0.2365	0.2273	170	162
Ethiopia	0.2306	0.2033	172	172
Burundi	0.2288	0.2014	173	174
Democratic Republic of the Congo	0.2280	0.2357	174	158
Papua New Guinea	0.2147	0.2043	177	171
Eritrea	0.2043	0.1859	180	175
Guinea-Bissau	0.1945	0.1561	182	179
Afghanistan	0.1701	0.2098	184	168
Sierra Leone	0.1557	0.1697	186	177
Haiti	0.1512	0.2074	187	169
Chad	0.1092	0.1235	189	182

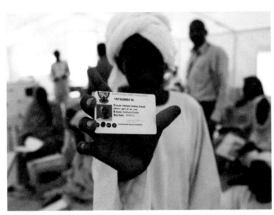

UN Photo/Albert Gonzales Farran

Chapter 2

Progress in online service delivery

Information and communication technologies support development. When that development is effective, efficient and enduring it is called sustainable. E-government impacts directly on sustainable development through the use of ICT in public sector social and economic development programmes. In this context, the emerging imperative today is to rethink e-government development in order to understand how the opportunities offered by new technologies promote development for the people and with their integral participation. There is a need to assess how and to what extent governments of the world are employing e-government, which furthers greater efficacy and effectiveness for sustainability in this specific and people-focused sense.

The 2012 Survey assesses four different types of indicators encompassing: information such as documents on laws, policies etc., across sectors of education, health, finance, social welfare and labour; public services such as taxes, fines, licenses; e-participation information and services; and technical features (audio, video, RSS, etc.), which provide a conduit for these kinds of information and services to flow from the government to the citizen.

Box 2.1 **Bahrain, a leader in Western Asia**

Bahrain's e-government strategy is based upon "delivering customer value through collaborative government." The government sees citizens as customers who have different needs and demand different services and at the same time demand value for money. Thus the aim of e-government is to provide all services, integrated, to all citizens and upon their choice of channel. The Kingdom provides delivery of services through the following channels: e-government portal,

mobile portal, national contact centre (a 24-7 call centre) and e-services centres and kiosks. Bahrain has introduced the "Listen" feature, which enables people with visual disabilities to hear any text available on the website with the click of a button. Another very innovative feature is the e-government toolbar, which can be downloaded permanently to your browser. This allows direct access to e-services and RSS feeds without having to go to the main portal. ◆

Within the framework of sustainable development, the 2012 Survey has attempted to take into account Member States' efforts with regard to the rising importance of a whole-of-government approach and integrated online service delivery, as well as the effectiveness of multichannel services and how these approaches will help advance economic efficiency and effectiveness in government service delivery with people's participation. At the same time, the 2012 Survey has paid attention to an assessment of the increasing emphasis on service usage and citizen satisfaction, including online services that are effectively responding to the demands of the people, and particularly those of vulnerable groups, to ascertain whether e-infrastructure is playing the prescribed role in bridging the digital divide.

at the same level as some high-income economies, such as Bahrain and the United Arab Emirates, which are at the level of Australia and Japan, and Colombia, which is at the level of Sweden.

This is highlighted by the example of Saudi Arabia and Bahrain – two countries that devoted especial attention to expanding and consolidating online services in the last few years and now offer online services close to those of global leaders such as Norway and Denmark.

Table 2.1 **Top 20 countries in online service delivery**

Country	Online service index
Republic of Korea	1.0000
Singapore	1.0000
United States	1.0000
United Kingdom	0.9739
Netherlands	0.9608
Canada	0.8889
Finland	0.8824
France	0.8758
Australia	0.8627
Bahrain	0.8627
Japan	0.8627
United Arab Emirates	0.8627
Denmark	0.8562
Norway	0.8562
Israel	0.8497
Colombia	0.8431
Sweden	0.8431
Estonia	0.8235
Saudi Arabia	0.7974
Malaysia	0.7908

2.1 **Online service rankings**

Three countries – the Republic of Korea, Singapore and the United States – are tied as world leaders in online services this year. Devoid of the level of infrastructure and human capital in the country, the online service index is a measure of 'how much' the governments are putting online. Of all the online services assessed of the United Nations Member States, the Republic of Korea, Singapore and the United States provide the most. Among the top 20 in 2012 are several developing countries, which are

Figure 2.1 **Progress in online service provision 2003-2012 in selected countries**

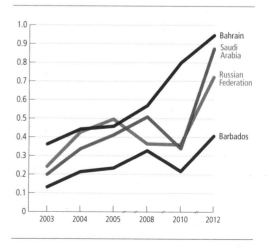

Recognizing the potential of e-government for development is key to the provision of online services. Notwithstanding issues of the marginal utility of ICT

Box 2.2 **Russian Federation: Investments for service delivery improvements**

In 2006 the Government of the Russian Federation adopted a new version of the Federal Target Programme eRussia (2002-2010) to improve efficiency of government operations and enhance citizen services. Standards were crafted and put in place, departments were interlinked and information management systems were integrated.

The national government portal of the Russian Federation (http://government.ru) has been modified and redesigned and now looks very solid and representative, with links to all ministries/agencies and rich technical features. The portal of public services is one of the key elements of the project to create "electronic government" in the country. The portal provides a single point of access to all references on state and municipal services through the Internet and provides citizens and organizations the opportunity to receive these services electronically. Monthly visits by users of the public services portal range between 200,000 and 700,000. For example, citizens are now able to get or exchange a driver license through this portal. ◆

investment, cognizance of the fact that new technologies along with access to services can support efficiency and efficacy of development solutions is necessary for a meaningful expansion of citizen services.

Take the case of Latvia and Belarus: at around the same levels of GDP per capita, telecommunication infrastructure and human capital, Latvia provides around 51 per cent of online services assessed, compared to 36 per cent in the case of Belarus, pulling up its EGDI ranking to 42 compared to 61 for Belarus.

Figure 2.2 **E-services in Latvia and Belarus**

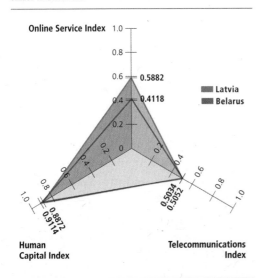

2.2 **Trends in e-service provision**

An increasing focus on improving efficiency and efficacy has led to an increasing trend towards innovative and transformational use of ICT in online service delivery. The section below provides an assessment of the type – and extent – of service offerings.

2.2.1 **Review of online services**

The review of online government service provision during the last decade indicates two notable trends. First, United Nations Member States have steadily made progress in establishing an online presence. In 2003, when the United Nations started tracking, 18 countries were not online. Since then many have begun online offerings, including Chad, Dominica and Eritrea. In 2012, only three countries (Central African Republic, Guinea and Libya) did not have a web presence. These countries are excluded from the 2012 Survey. Second, it was noticeable that whereas the collective world progress improved over the years, a few countries were sporadic in their offerings by being online in one year and offline the next. Zambia, which had a presence in 2003, went offline in 2004-05 and again had no web presence in 2008. Similarly, Turkmenistan, which was online until

Member States have steadily made progress in establishing an online presence. In 2003, when the United Nations started tracking, 18 countries were not online. In 2012, only three countries did not have a web presence.

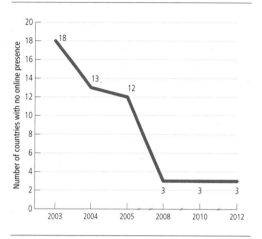

Figure 2.3 **United Nations Member States' online presence, 2003 – 2012**

current and updated within the last three months. Two thirds offered a site map or index to guide the user through the services. However, advanced features had an inverse relation to the number of countries represented.

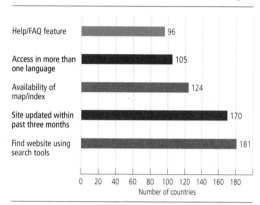

Figure 2.4 **Online features availability**

2004, discontinued its offerings in 2005 but came back online again in 2008. Guinea, which had been online since 2003, was not available to its citizens at the time of the 2012 Survey.

Consistency of online service can be a key factor in building trust in the institutions of the government. It is important to recognize that an important precursor for an effective utilization of ICT for sustainable development is the maintenance of services even at a basic level.

Notwithstanding domestic conflict and/or natural disasters, which may affect the ability of a country to provide online services to its citizens, intermittent provision of service does not build trust in government. It may be that during times of natural disaster and/or conflict the citizen could be more in need of vital information, especially in far flung cut off areas, and such information can be provided to the outermost reaches via the use of ICT. In this context, the role of e-government in treating information as a key service to the citizen becomes increasingly important and lends credence and significance to the need for maintenance and sustainability of online service delivery.

A cursory glance at the characteristics of online presence of countries in 2012 indicates a greater number of features than in previous years and a growing recognition of the importance of providing relevant and up-to-date information. The majority of countries (88 per cent) were involved in ensuring that their online e-government offerings were

The fact that only 96 countries provided an advanced search feature on the website, fewer (79) had a privacy statement and only 39 countries offered a secure website is indicative of the large number of countries that still have a long way to go in terms of exploiting the full potential of e-government.

Table 2.2 **Advanced features available on websites**

	Advanced search options	Privacy statement	Tag cloud or 'hot topics'	Secure website
Number of countries	96	79	56	39
Percentage of countries	50%	41%	29%	20%

Services and features targeted to a thematic area were also on the rise. One hundred and seventy-nine countries provide some form of documentation related to finance. The most common among them were tax forms. Laws, policies and other documentation of interest to the citizen on education, health, social welfare and other sectors were increasingly being integrated within the overall national portal and/or on the agency portals. More than two thirds of the countries provided options for directly sending updates via email, RSS or a mobile device to the citizen. Whereas the more advanced countries may have provided multiple choices, the fact that countries in early stages of e-government development such as Afghanistan, Burundi, Iraq, Mali, and Senegal also provided some form of citizen alert mechanism testifies to a wider recognition of the importance of citizen inclusion.

Figure 2.5 **Sectoral user services online**

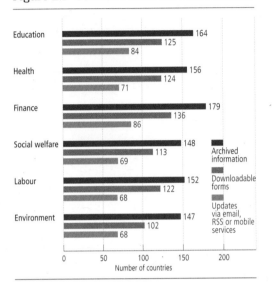

Online transactional[i] capability, such as making payments online, is substantially more complicated than simply providing information. Increasing online provision of transactional services such as payments indicates maturity as well as greater integration because payments made through a single site may need to be routed to any number of accounts held by various branches of the government. Conversely, in some countries, even payments collected from various points of sale must make their way to a single governmental entity, such as a treasury department. Countries must have a well-developed electronic banking infrastructure, including electronic clearing systems and adequate security safeguards. Society must also trust that the electronic banking system is reliable.

However once these pre-requisites exist it is a relatively easier task to add transactional capabilities to multiple sectors. In 2012, a greater number of countries were providing transactional services online than before. With governments keenly aware of the role technology can play in revenue generation online, tax payments became available in 40 per cent of the countries in 2012. With greater back-office integration, other forms of transactions such as payment for utilities and birth and car registrations were

Table 2.3 **Transactional services online**

	Income taxes	Utilities	Fines	Birth certificates	Car registration	ID cards	Driver licenses
Number of countries	77	55	46	43	41	34	34
Percentage of countries	40	28	24	22	21	18	18

increasingly placed online. In 34 to 55 countries, citizens could obtain driver licenses, ID cards and birth certificates online.

Despite considerable progress in online service, only 22 countries offer 66 per cent or more of the online services assessed. E-services in around 171 countries are below 66 per cent with around half – or 95 countries – providing less than 33 per cent, including three that are not online at all.

Trends in e-government development around the world in 2012 indicate that e-services in a country are a function of the level of development, resource availability, and human and technological infrastructure. The complex pattern of developments across a myriad of these factors has a bearing on how many e-government services are available – and how much they are utilized.

Figure 2.6 **Extent of e-service delivery**

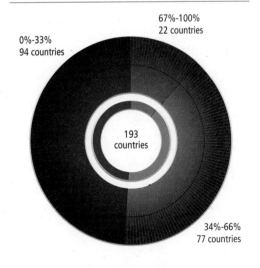

Despite progress, service availability levels are generally low around the world. Except for the top performers most countries have a long way to go in providing online services, which remain between low and non-existent. A selected few are shown in

Table 2.4 **Extent of service delivery in top performers, selected countries**

	Stage I: Emerging presence	Stage II: Interactive presence	Stage III: Transactional presence	Stage IV: Networked presence	Total
67%-100% utilization					
Republic of Korea	100	79	92	87	87
Singapore	100	79	94	86	87
United States	100	90	88	83	87
United Kingdom	100	95	79	81	85
Canada	100	83	81	68	78
Finland	100	90	75	67	77
France	100	79	85	65	77
Bahrain	100	76	81	67	75
United Arab Emirates	100	74	83	67	75
Colombia	100	76	65	74	74
Sweden	92	90	71	62	74
Estonia	100	69	65	74	72
Saudi Arabia	92	60	77	67	70
Malaysia	100	64	79	59	69
New Zealand	100	79	69	57	69
Kazakhstan	92	64	52	80	69
34%-66% utilization					
Chile	100	62	67	61	66
Qatar	83	64	62	64	65
Mexico	100	69	62	57	64
Lithuania	83	67	54	59	61
El Salvador	100	71	38	59	59
Portugal	100	74	42	51	57
Serbia	100	64	38	42	50
Cyprus	100	62	46	35	49
Uruguay	100	60	38	39	48
India	100	64	33	38	47
China	92	55	40	38	46
Peru	83	45	31	49	45
Costa Rica	92	45	31	43	43
Trinidad and Tobago	92	64	23	35	42
South Africa	100	60	17	35	40
Bangladesh	100	60	21	29	39
Cape Verde	92	48	23	35	38
Viet Nam	100	52	17	32	37
Belarus	100	55	25	22	36
Jordan	83	48	31	20	34

Table 2.5 **E-services in selected developing countries**

	Stage I: Emerging presence	Stage II: Interactive presence	Stage III: Transactional presence	Stage IV: Networked presence	Total
0%-33% utilization					
Honduras	92	52	15	25	33
Grenada	83	50	8	28	31
United Rep. of Tanzania	92	55	2	28	31
Saint Lucia	83	50	8	26	30
Senegal	75	31	12	36	30
Cameroon	83	48	4	20	26
Ghana	83	38	2	28	26
Lesotho	92	38	4	25	26
Zimbabwe	67	45	4	25	26
Tonga	100	33	2	14	21
Turkmenistan	67	19	4	16	17
Burundi	42	5	8	17	13
South Sudan	58	19	2	9	13
Swaziland	50	24	2	7	13
Marshall Islands	25	26	2	9	12
Togo	42	14	6	10	12
Solomon Islands	42	24	4	4	11
Dem. People's Rep. of Korea	58	12	4	6	10
Sao Tome and Principe	58	7	4	9	10
Guinea-Bissau	33	12	2	9	9
Myanmar	50	17	0	4	9
Chad	25	14	2	7	9
Equatorial Guinea	25	10	4	9	9
Nauru	33	14	2	6	9
Haiti	33	19	0	3	8
Comoros	42	7	2	4	7
Congo	33	14	2	1	7
Mauritania	33	7	2	6	7
Kiribati	33	5	2	4	6
Tuvalu	17	2	2	6	5

stage II and a third in stage IV but only 17 per cent in the transactional stage. As expected, transactional stage utilization depends, among other factors, on the level of development of the financial system in the country. Putting up stage III services would also require a regulatory framework and governing rules of security and privacy, which are still to be fully developed in many of the developing countries.

Some of the least developed countries had the lowest availability of e-services, which were barely a third of those in the forefront of e-government.

table 2.4, which also indicates that there is no apparent linear correlation between the level of development and stages of e-services. A country such as Viet Nam may offer all services in stage I, around half in

---

Box 2.3 **Kazakhstan: A leader in e-participation**

Kazakhstan has improved from 2010 in terms of providing online features that allows citizens to engage with government. An interesting online participation feature is the government's Blogs site, where citizens can communicate with the government agencies' executives by posting comments and questions. The executives may then respond and post their answers on the blog. The site also contains statistical information on the questions and comments an agency executive has received as well as how many times he/she has responded. ◆

Many of these countries are in Africa which, as already noted, also is the least e-ready region in the world. Senegal, Cameroon, Ghana, Lesotho and Zimbabwe all had utilization levels ranging from 26-30 per cent. Others included Democratic People's Republic of Korea, which came online in 2012, at 10 per cent; Myanmar, Chad, and Equatorial Guinea at 9 per cent; while Tuvalu had a bare minimum offering at 5 per cent.

Though there is considerable progress in the expansion of online services, the digital divide has remained more or less the same for the majority of countries in the world. As previous surveys have maintained, there are wide disparities between and among regions and countries in their online service offerings. Governments in the high income countries are far advanced in their provision of public information, online services, communications and outreach to citizens, as well as overall electronic access to government. Their distance from the bottom 40 countries remains substantial.

2.2.2 **Citizen inclusion and e-participation**

For e-participation to contribute to sustainable development and the socio-economic uplift of the people, the role of government requires a shift from that of a controller of information and services to that of a proactive facilitator. In this context, it is imperative that information and services are geared toward promoting user uptake, addressing the needs and concerns of the citizenry, especially the vulnerable. It also requires viewing the citizens not only as passive receivers of information through web-based services, but also as active partners who are engaged and supported to interact with the government through ICT-based dissemination of relevant government information.

The best performing countries in e-participation appear in table 2.6. Once again the Republic of Korea tops the list, but this year it is joined by the Netherlands. Kazakhstan (0.9474), a developing country, which was noted in the 2010 Survey for its commitment to e-participation, moved up 16 places to be ranked second and tied with Singapore. Among this group several other countries were tied for the same spot, such as Australia, Estonia, and Germany, which were all at the 5th position. With the use of consultation tools, including social media, other developing countries have also caught up to the developed countries as e-leaders. Notable among these are Bahrain, Egypt, the United Arab Emirates, Colombia, and Chile.

The pie in figure 2.7 shows the geographic distribution of the top 20 countries. Europe's share of the top ten fell from 51 per cent in 2010 to 38 per cent this year. This change was primarily the result of the Americas increasing from 14 per cent to 19 per cent with Chile and Colombia joining the leaders, along with the appearance of Egypt from Africa, and Bahrain and the United Arab Emirates from Western Asia.

Table 2.6 **Top e-participation leaders**

Rank	Country	Index
1	Netherlands	1.0000
	Republic of Korea	1.0000
2	Kazakhstan	0.9474
	Singapore	0.9474
3	United Kingdom	0.9211
	United States	0.9211
4	Israel	0.8947
5	Australia	0.7632
	Estonia	0.7632
	Germany	0.7632
6	Colombia	0.7368
	Finland	0.7368
	Japan	0.7368
	United Arab Emirates	0.7368
7	Egypt	0.6842
	Canada	0.6842
	Norway	0.6842
	Sweden	0.6842
8	Chile	0.6579
	Russian Federation	0.6579
	Bahrain	0.6579

Figure 2.7 **Geographic distribution of top performers in e-participation**

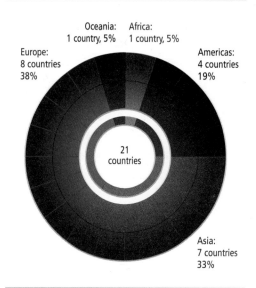

Oceania: 1 country, 5%
Africa: 1 country, 5%
Europe: 8 countries 38%
Americas: 4 countries 19%
21 countries
Asia: 7 countries 33%

Table 2.7 **Extent of e-participation**

	Country	E-infor-mation	E-consul-tation	E-decision making	Total
Over 67%	Netherlands	75	84	67	81
	Republic of Korea	75	78	100	81
	Kazakhstan	100	76	67	77
	Singapore	75	76	83	77
	United Kingdom	100	70	83	74
	United States	75	78	50	74
	Israel	75	73	67	72
34%-66%	Estonia	75	65	33	62
	Colombia	75	59	50	60
	United Arab Emirates	50	54	100	60
	Egypt	25	54	83	55
	Bahrain	50	49	83	53
	Chile	25	59	33	53
	Russian Federation	50	59	17	53
	Qatar	75	51	33	51
	Saudi Arabia	50	49	67	51
	Mongolia	75	43	67	49
	France	50	43	67	47
	Mexico	25	51	33	47
	Denmark	25	51	17	45
	El Salvador	0	54	17	45
	Lithuania	100	38	33	43
	Brazil	0	43	50	40
	Brunei Darussalam	50	38	33	38
	Hungary	50	30	67	36
	Oman	50	32	50	36
1%-33%	Peru	50	35	0	32
	Rep. of Moldova	25	32	33	32
	Austria	50	27	33	30
	Portugal	50	32	0	30
	Ethiopia	0	32	17	28
	Greece	0	30	33	28
	Thailand	0	30	17	26
	Argentina	50	22	17	23
	Croatia	25	19	50	23
	Kyrgyzstan	0	30	0	23
	Czech Republic	0	27	0	21
	Italy	0	27	0	21
	Guatemala	50	19	0	19
	Liechtenstein	25	22	0	19
	Uzbekistan	0	24	0	19
	Bolivia (Plurinational State of)	0	19	17	17
	China	25	14	33	17
	India	25	14	17	15
	South Africa	0	16	0	13
	Ukraine	0	14	17	13
	Pakistan	50	8	0	11
	Saint Lucia	0	11	0	9
	St. Vincent and the Grenadines	0	11	0	9
	Viet Nam	0	8	17	9
	Bahamas	0	5	17	6
	United Rep. of Tanzania	25	5	0	6
	Algeria	0	5	0	4
	Vanuatu	0	5	0	4

> One of the main goals of European e-government development is to empower citizens and businesses by providing greater access to public service information and greater transparency of governments.

There are several countries among the top from the European region, including the Netherlands, the United Kingdom, Finland, Sweden, and the Russian Federation. There is strong political emphasis on e-participation in Europe. One of the main aims of European e-government development, laid out through the European Commission's Action Plan 2011-2015, is to empower citizens and businesses by providing greater access to public service information and greater transparency of governments as well as effective measures to enable public participation in policy-making processes. The national portal of the United Kingdom (http://www.direct.gov.uk) provides a fine example through its e-petition page, where citizens have the ability to lodge online petitions on issues for governments to propose to parliament if enough signatures are acquired. The government also provides great transparency by providing the outcomes of previous petitions, showing how many signatures were obtained.

Despite broad regional representation, e-participation for social equity remains largely unexplored for many other countries as a norm. The concept, which derives from an acceptance of online inclusion of citizens for effective sustainable development, envisions provision of information followed by consultation, feedback and inclusion of citizen views in active decision-making. The pre-requisites for this life cycle of e-participation are technology access and also a conducive political regime with leadership and vision in support of collective societal approaches to public policy challenges.

Figure 2.8 shows how deep the e-participation services are. The majority of countries offer less than two thirds of all e-participation services assessed. Advanced features of e-participation and citizen incluson assessed in the 2012 Survey are not yet adopted by most Member States. More than one third of all countries do not offer any e-participation services.

Figure 2.8 **Depth of e-participation**

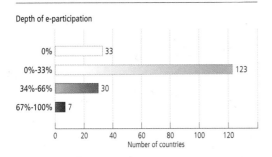

Table 2.7 shows the extent and type of e-participation for selected countries. Of all the services assessed in the survey, the Netherlands and the Republic of Korea tied for the number one spot, providing 75 per cent in e-information, 84 and 78 per cent respectively in e-consultation, and 67 and 100 per cent respectively in e-decision making. It is noteworthy that Kazakhstan, the United Kingdom and Lithuania offer all e-information assessed. A cursory glance at the results indicates that though e-participation has found adoption among many countries, only the top seven countries provide more than 70 per cent of the services assessed.

Governments have started consulting more with citizens in a bid to boost transparency and allow for a partnership approach to public policy making. They provide policies and information on when participatory events are available on which citizen can give feedback. More recently, information has begun to be provided if the government commits itself publicly to considering the results of e-participation in its decision making process as well. Even though e-consultation is more widespread across countries, it is not so deep. It is noteworthy that the Republic of Korea and the United Arab Emirates are the only two

countries that score 100 per cent on whether the government takes citizen's views into decision-making.

As in the case of overall online services, e-participation also does not follow any linear model: the level of each category is a function of political regimes, leadership, commitment and openness. For example, Guatemala, Liechtenstein and Pakistan provide 25-50 per cent of e-information but zero in considering citizens' views. Overall, fewer countries provide evidence of active citizen views in decision-making.

Promotion of opportunities

Despite the gap among countries, e-participation has been on the rise as countries become more open to the idea of collective solutions to societal issues. The 2012 Survey found that 61 countries – nearly one third–provide an e-participation policy online. Whereas most of these are developed economies where e-participation is well rooted, others such as Senegal, Pakistan, India, Nicaragua and China are also in the group. A smaller number (26 per cent), follows up on this with a public statement that citizen feedback will be taken into account but only about 14 per cent actually have calendar listings of participatory events, though this is a useful feature. In January 2011 the Government of Ukraine accepted a resolution to promote e-participation in the country and allow its citizens to take part in shaping the country's policies. This resulted in the creation of the new e-participation portal "Civil Society and Government" (http://e-gov.net.ua), with features such as a calendar showing upcoming events to promote dialog between the citizens and the government.

Table 2.8 **Extent of government's commitment to e-participation**

	Number of countries	Percentage
E-participation policy available online	61	32
E-decision making commitment publicized online	50	26
E-participation calendar available online	27	14

Consultation tools

A majority of countries, 123, have some means – even if only a simple feedback form – of collecting citizen opinions online. Less than half that number, 57, administer surveys specifically with the aim

Box 2.4 **Colombia: E-participation**

Colombia's government portal contains numerous participation features for citizens to use to engage with government. Citizens can employ tools such as online forums, blogs and online polls. The portal also allows users to participate through social networking features such as Facebook, Twitter, Wordpress, YouTube and Flickr, where they can post comments and express their views. ◆

of improving their online service offerings. From the developing countries these include, among others, Angola, Cameroon and Burkina Faso in Africa; Albania and Croatia in Europe; Sri Lanka, Kyrgyzstan, and Uzbekistan in Asia; and Uruguay and Venezuela in the Americas.

Thanks to the provision of government information through social networks such as Facebook and Twitter, citizens are able to make comments and suggestions to governments while these sites also offer governments a useful tool for reading into public opinion.

Table 2.9 **Collecting citizen feedback**

	Number of countries	Percentage
Facility for citizen feedback	123	64
Surveys regarding improving online services	57	30

More countries now provide online surveys or feedback forms – 87 compared to 55 in 2010. Notable among these are Afghanistan, Albania, Bangladesh, Benin, Cuba, El Salvador, and India. Online polls are also available in many more countries (54 compared to 30 in 2010) including Ghana, Montenegro, Mozambique, Nigeria and Uganda. A much smaller number of countries provide chat room features, which edged up only slightly from 11 to 14 countries, while listservs and newsgroups edged down slightly from 16 to 14.

The use of other interactive tools jumped 73 per cent, from 33 to 58 countries in 2012. The fact that assessment in this category included social networking tools such as Facebook helps to account for this increase. For example, a key pillar of the strategy the Latin American region has followed is to take advantage of social networking media features to promote online participation of citizens, especially among the younger demographic whose members are the main users of these networks.

Figure 2.9 **E-consultation tools used by governments**

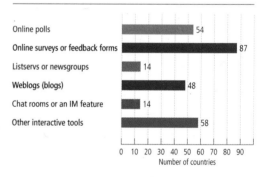

Some countries in the vanguard have gone even further to implement multichannel methods of online consultation. A common method of online public consultation in Australia and New Zealand is through the government providing draft regulations in a downloadable format for users to read. Citizens can then submit their comments and suggestions via email to the respective ministry that is responsible for the consultation. In Latin America, Panama's citizen participation (http://www.participa.gob.pa) portal contains a blog section where users can comment on government programmes while Brazil's Electronic Government site (http://www.governoeletronico.gov.br) contains a forum section that allows users to send comments and

Box 2.5 **Australia: E-participation**

Australia's national portal provides numerous features enabling citizens to engage with government in the policy-making process. The government provides a 'Have Your Say' section that is located on the homepage of the portal. This section links to a public consultations section where citizens can send their comments and suggestions on draft regulations to the respective ministry, mainly by email. The government also provides the outcomes of previous consultations online. Also located in this section is a 'blogs' page that provides links to various government blogs as well as a Twitter page that shows a table of all government Twitter pages that users can access and respond to with their comments and suggestions. ◆

suggestions regarding e-government, such as accessibility and integration of services, while also containing a public consultation section on draft regulations. In Mexico, online public consultation features allow users to participate in the policy-making process with government. Citizen input is then moderated by a government official and subsequently published, promoting greater government transparency.

The 2012 Survey found that Twitter and Facebook are increasingly being deployed by governments as vehicles for consultation. The 24-7 reach of these tools provides a cost effective mechanism for citizen alerts as well as for views on how the government is doing. In Hungary for example, on the e-democracy site (https://edemokracia.magyarorszag.hu) government officials and agencies respond to citizens' comments and suggestions as well as moderating the forums.

The number of countries encouraging government officials to respond to citizen input more than doubled, from 16 to 38.

The number of countries where officials moderated e-consultations also more than doubled, from 8 in 2010 to 17 in 2012. Similar or greater increases occurred in the use of online discussion forums (32 to 78) and online petitions (17 to 42). For example, in the Russian Federation officials provide feedback to citizens' views. Lithuania's national portal (http://www.lrv.lt) contains a public consultation page that displays current consultations as well as previous consultations that the government has undertaken with the public. It contains a number of ways that citizens may participate with government such as being able to send in their opinions via e-mail to the named government authority or by submitting an online form containing their comments and suggestions. In Africa, a case in point in improvement in this area is in Mozambique, where both the Ministry of Education's (http://www.mec.gov.mz)and the Ministry of Health's (http://www.misau.gov.mz) websites, provide online discussion forums where users can comment and make suggestions on education and health policy issues.

ICT-enabled participation in decision-making

One quarter of all countries publicly commit to considering the results of e-participation in the policy-making process, including, among others, Plurinational State of Bolivia, Brazil, India, Hungary and Panama. Governments are increasingly mindful of how 'well' they are doing. In an effort towards greater inclusion, 25 countries are providing feedback from citizens on their services, including Mongolia, Morocco, the Islamic Republic of Iran, Saudi Arabia, and Malta, among others.

As a final note, online service delivery remains skewed in favour of developed countries with the digital

Table 2.10 **Web 2.0 tools used in e-decision making**

	Number of countries	Percentage
Government officials respond to citizen input	38	20
Government officials moderate e-consultations	17	9
Online bulletin boards	76	39
Online discussion forums	78	40
Online petitions	42	22
Online voting	18	9

Box 2.6 Providing outcome on feedback received from citizens concerning the improvement of their service

Bahrain, Brazil, Canada, Croatia, Egypt, Finland, France, Germany, Islamic Republic of Iran, Israel, Japan, Kazakhstan, Malaysia, Malta, Mongolia, Morocco, Oman, Republic of Korea, Republic of Moldova, Singapore, Slovenia, Switzerland, Thailand, United Arab Emirates and United Kingdom. ◆

Table 2.11 E-decision making features

	Number of countries	Percentage
Government commitment to considering the results of e-participation in decision making	50	26
Government provides confirmation receipt on citizen sent communication	45	23
Government provide outcome on feedback received from citizens concerning the improvement of their services	25	13

Table 2.12 Top countries on environment survey

Country	Index
Germany	1.0000
Republic of Korea	1.0000
Singapore	1.0000
United States	1.0000
Austria	0.9412
Israel	0.9412
Japan	0.9412
Malta	0.9412
Mexico	0.9412
New Zealand	0.9412
Russian Federation	0.9412
United Kingdom	0.9412
Australia	0.8824
Canada	0.8824
Finland	0.8824
France	0.8824
Mongolia	0.8824
Norway	0.8824
Portugal	0.8824

divide a continued challenge. Assessment in 2012 reinforces the need to continue to focus on expansion and consolidation of relevant services for the user, supported by increasing efficiency and integration of the different government departmental processes and institutional arrangements relevant for sustainable development.

2.2.3 Online environmental information services

With the worldwide focus on sustainable development, the 2012 Survey devoted a special section to examining the effort made by Member States in provision of environment-related online information and services. The data collection effort was global in scope and covered 193 countries. Though not comprehensive, the prototype survey is indicative of the general trends in national 'e-environment' performance and the amount of effort invested by Member States in addressing environment as a national development priority.

Effective information dissemination regarding how resources are managed represents a fundamental requirement if economic development is to benefit all rather than selected groups only. While some environmental degradation is apparent to all, many forms of pollution or resource depletion

may not be. Global warming, for example, is only indirectly perceptible. The greenhouse gases themselves can only be measured with scientific instruments, while personal observations of the effects are not conclusive evidence for their existence. Similarly, groundwater pollution may take years or even decades before its effects are apparent via birth defects or other health outcomes.

There is widespread acceptance that current institutions are inadequate to address the challenges of sustainable development and that new arrangements are needed to achieve economic, environmental and social objectives in a balanced and integrated manner at national and local levels.[2] Much of the success in this field depends on broad public awareness and on access to reliable information for decision-making. Yet information gaps occur in a range of disciplines with the net result that public appreciation of the challenges of sustainable development and scope for action are highly circumscribed in many countries.

The purpose of the survey depicted here was to determine the extent to which national governments have been using online media to promote public awareness, promulgate environmental information and encourage stakeholders, chief among them the average citizen, to express their views on the issues of the day.

The top-scoring countries on use of online media vis-à-vis the environment are listed in table 2.12. Four countries – Germany, the Republic of Korea, Singapore, and the United States –earned a perfect score. As in the case of e-government development rankings, developed countries dominate in e-environment service delivery.

In terms of overall provision of information and services, the countries are evenly distributed, with 69 countries (36 per cent) providing less than one

Figure 2.10 Overall environmental e-service provision

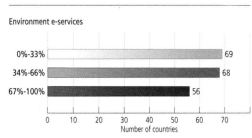

Environment e-services

	Number of countries
0%-33%	69
34%-66%	68
67%-100%	56

third of the information and services assessed, another one third providing 34-66 per cent, and 56 countries providing 67-100 per cent.

Figure 2.11 **Africa sub-regional average scores as percentage of regional average score**

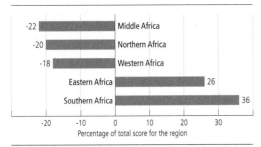

Performance within regions varied widely, with Middle, Northern, and Western Africa scoring about 20 per cent less than the regional average, while Eastern and Southern Africa scored 26 and 36 per cent more than the regional average, respectively.

Figure 2.12 **Americas sub-regional average scores as percentage of regional average score**

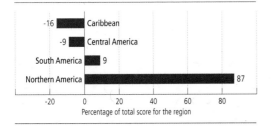

In the Americas, North America greatly exceeded the regional average, while South America scored slightly above nine per cent.

Similarly in Asia, Eastern Asia was 46 per cent above the regional average score, followed by Central Asia, which was 12 per cent above the regional average.

Although in Europe Southern and Eastern Europe trailed the rest of the region, the overall sub-regional variation in Europe was considerably smaller than in the other regions, ranging from 11 per cent less than the regional average score to greater than 11 per cent.

E-environment performance is closely correlated with wealth as figure 2.15 suggests. In fact, some 90

Figure 2.13 **Asia sub-regional average scores as percentage of regional average score**

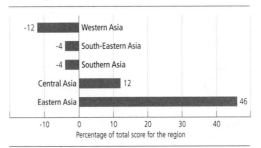

per cent of the difference in cumulative scoring on the selected indicators could be explained by differences in gross national income (GNI) per capita. Every time GNI per capita is doubled, the predicted e-environment score increases by approximately 5 per cent under this informal assessment. The result tracks closely with e-government development scores in general, suggesting that wealth is a powerful determinant of e-government success across sectors as evidenced by Germany, the Republic of Korea and Singapore, high income economies that fared best in this assessment.

Though the connection between affluence and online environmental information services is strong, having to contend with a low income economy does not of necessity mean that progress cannot be made as the case of Bangladesh suggests. Nor is size automatically a strictly limiting factor as the case of Kyrgyzstan shows. The bubbles in figure 2.15 represent the number of Internet users in a country. Countries with large numbers of Internet users, such as the United States and China, score comparatively well in this area. National e-environment initiatives may thus be reaching a considerable proportion of

Figure 2.14 **Europe sub-regional average scores as percentage of regional average score**

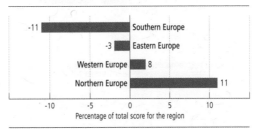

Figure 2.15 **Relationship between e-environment performance and gross national income per capita**

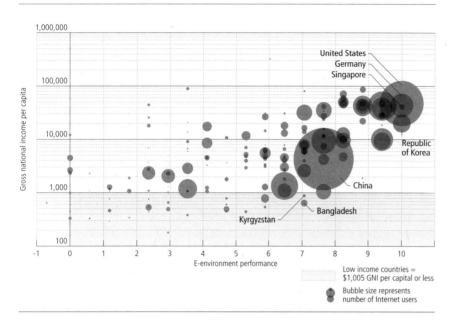

Low income countries = $1,005 GNI per capital or less

Bubble size represents number of Internet users

The higher the income group, the more likely a country is to promote awareness of environmental issues online.

the world population although there are no global statistics available to substantiate this hypothesis.

The Russian Federation, Canada, the United States, China, Brazil and Australia together account for almost half of the world's total land area, in addition to having substantial industries devoted to

Figure 2.16 **Use of e-government to raise awareness of sustainable development**

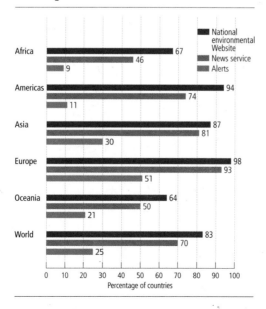

the extraction of marine resources from oceans and seas. All appeared in the top quintile of countries in this basic assessment of national websites.

A majority of countries have a section within the officially designated national government website dedicated to environmental issues (49 per cent), a separate national website dedicated to environmental issues (78 per cent) or some combination of the two (83 per cent). However, results vary by income group. Whereas 96 per cent of high-income countries maintain an environment website, only 60 per cent of low-income countries do the same. The higher the income group, the more likely a country is to promote awareness of environmental issues online, as noted earlier. Differences in performance based on income also translate into geographic variations as shown in figure 2.16. The concentration of low income countries in sub-Saharan Africa and among small island developing states of the Pacific results in less extensive use of online tools to promote public awareness in those regions.

Just over half of national governments publish an easily accessible policy document or similar statement setting out environmental management strategies (57 per cent). National environmental policies support sustainable development by articulating objectives, identifying relevant actors and guiding management of information for decision-making. While not all countries have comprehensive strategies so clearly spelled out, all have laws and regulations that, together, embody national environmental policy and are most likely to be implemented when openly supported.

Shortcomings in communication may be due, in part, to questions of leadership and accountability as in other areas of public affairs. More often than not, national sustainable development focal points are located within these ministries. As figure 2.17 illustrates,

Table 2.13 **Selected environmental online features and content**

	Number of countries	Percentage
'What you can do' section	38	20
News section focused on environment	136	70
Alerts pertaining to environment	48	25
Searches can be filtered for environment	62	32
Environment strategy available online	110	57

Box 2.7 **Trinidad and Tobago: Wealth of information on environment**

Trinidad and Tobago's Environmental Management Authority's website offers a wealth of information on environmental policy, laws and regulations, as well as technical reports detailing how the government manages natural resources. In addition, the site includes links to the Authority's Facebook page and YouTube channel. The latter features nearly 30 videos on a variety of environmental topics. ◆

three out of every four national websites identify the person responsible for leading the development of environmental policy at national level, for example, as head of an environment ministry or similar national regulatory agency (74 per cent). The number rises slightly, to 85 per cent, among those countries with dedicated environmental portals, as might be expected. These omissions notwithstanding, contact information for environment ministries is readily available for all countries from other sources.[3]

Figure 2.18 **Countries offering education or information on public policy concerns**

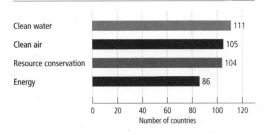

Current news plays a pivotal role not only in raising awareness and support for sustainable development, but also in giving a stronger voice to citizens and in monitoring commitments made by political leaders.[4] Recognizing the potential of news media to influence attitudes and behaviours, a majority of countries (70 per cent) maintain an online environmental news service. However, countries that do not produce an online environmental news service also tend to be among those without a national website

dedicated to environmental issues, with sub-Saharan Africa and Pacific Island countries, as usual, lagging behind other regions.

News alerts and messages such as those used in disaster management require somewhat greater e-government capacity. Only one quarter (25 per cent) of countries have been able to overcome the hurdles presented by the technology. Among these, the European States (51 per cent) have had somewhat more success than others, while Africa and the Americas trail far behind (9 per cent and 11 per cent, respectively). Given the near universality of mobile cellular access in developing regions, the inherent value of public messaging services to vulnerable areas appears to be considerably underexploited.

Figure 2.17 **Online leadership promotion and accountability in environmental sustainability**

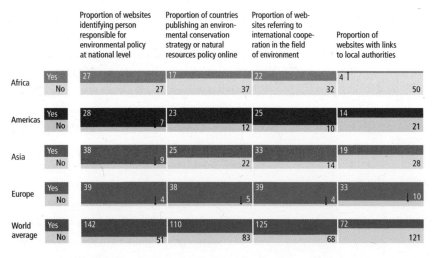

Box 2.8 **Brazil: Special section on Rio +20**

The website of Brazil's Environment Ministry includes a tag cloud of most frequent searches and a calendar of public consultations on the environment. There is also a special section of the site dedicated to Rio +20, including an electronic questionnaire soliciting citizen feedback in formulating Brazil's position. ◆

With respect to selected other questions pertaining to information dissemination, relatively few countries provide features designed to proactively notify citizens of environmental issues or permit citizens to focus online searches specifically on the environment. However, more than half of Member States do provide information focused on the environment and how citizens can help to preserve and manage natural resources, and a substantial majority of countries (57 per cent) make their strategy on resource use and conservation available online.

Clean air and water represent basic requirements for life. As such, they can reasonably be expected to be the first subjects of information to be disseminated online. Energy, a clear necessity for economic development, represents another key area about which citizens need information. Finally, resource conservation in general, including biodiversity maintenance, is critical, given that many people in poor communities rely on agriculture for their sustenance.

A majority of countries provide online information or education to citizens regarding clean water (111 countries), clean air (105 countries), and resource conservation (104 countries). Nearly half of countries (86) provide information pertaining to energy.

On specific public policy concerns, 58 per cent of environmental websites provide information on water quality while 54 per cent supply air quality information. The connection between public concerns and public information is more tenuous when it comes to resource efficiency. Whereas natural resource depletion is generally considered a serious problem, only about half of the national websites promote awareness of energy efficiency (45

per cent) and resource conservation (54 per cent), as depicted in figure 2.19. Not all countries make it easy for users to discover content for themselves, however, with only one-third of sites (32 per cent) offering advanced search options for locating environmental information. Most rely on the logic of the site to guide interested individuals to the information they seek.

Figure 2.19 **Reflection of public concerns on national environmental websites**

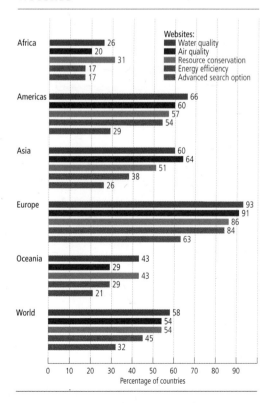

Likewise, some two-thirds of countries (65 per cent) use online tools to publicize their commitments to international environmental cooperation. There are more than 200 multilateral environmental agreements in effect[5] and all countries without exception are party to at least 7 key global and regional treaties.[6] Online disclosure of international commitments is a sign of leadership and reinforces accountability. However, ratification of a treaty is not the same as compliance and there may be reasons why this information is not readily apparent, such as government incapacity that can make the obligations of multilateral environmental agreements (MEAs) seem less relevant in the day-to-day lives of ordinary people.

Table 2.14 **Environment-related online citizen feedback**

	Number of countries	Percentage
Polls, surveys, discussion forums or chats	45	23
Social networking tools	56	29
E-consultations	34	18

One key aspect of engaging the public on environmental issues is putting a face on environmental policy. Three out of every four countries identify the person responsible for leading the development of environmental policy at the national level, for example as head of an environment ministry or similar national regulatory agency (74 per cent). As many as 88 per cent of the countries with a national website identify the person responsible for environmental policy; the number is 85 per cent for the countries with a dedicated environmental portal.

The environment survey also assessed government online tools for feedback from the citizen. As might be expected, the use of e-participation tools specifically for environment is slightly less common than that found across portfolios in the main E-Government Survey. The use of polls, surveys, discussion forums or chat rooms in the general survey ranges from only 14 countries for chats to up to 87 countries for online surveys or feedback forms. On an environment-specific basis only 45 countries use any one of these features.

The use of Facebook, Twitter, YouTube or other third party tools with social networking aspects was found in 78 countries in the main survey, but only in

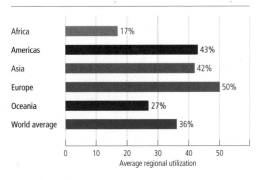

Figure 2.20 **Citizen participation in environmental affairs by region**

56 countries in the environmental survey. Only e-consultations in the environmental domain exceeded the general one – 9 per cent versus 8 per cent of countries. A possible reason for this inconsistency is that the question pertaining to e-consultation in the main survey focused on whether government officials moderate e-consultations. This restriction was not applied to the environmental survey, where unmoderated e-consultations could be counted as well.

On a regional basis, citizen engagement utilization on environmental issues is strongest in Europe, followed by the Americas and Oceania. However, given that average utilization for Europe is only 50 per cent, it appears that more can be done worldwide to employ e-government in support of citizen engagement on sustainable development.

> Online disclosure of international commitments is a sign of leadership and reinforces accountability.

2.3 **Conclusion**

In conclusion, the 2012 assessment indicates that websites aim at centralizing the entry point of service delivery to a single portal where citizens can access all government-supplied services, regardless of which government authority provides that service. But despite attention to e-government, there are substantial gaps in most countries and regions that continue to inhibit development and delivery of online services. To ensure benefits, Member States need to have a clear strategic vision of development planning and establish a regulatory environment for promotion of access and use of newer technologies by the government, the private sector and the citizen. ∞

Bioraven/Shutterstock.com

Chapter 3

Taking a whole-of-government approach

In recent years, there has been a change in emphasis away from structural devolution, disaggregation, and single-purpose organizations towards a more integrated approach to public service delivery.[1] Variously termed "one-stop government," "joined-up government" and "whole-of-government," the movement from isolated silos in public administration to formal and informal networks is a global trend driven by various societal forces such as the growing complexity of problems that call for collaborative responses, the increased demand on the part of citizens for more personalized and accessible public services, which are to be planned, implemented and evaluated with their participation, and the opportunities presented by the Internet to transform the way the government works for the people.

The ability of agencies to work together and citizens to engage in wide-ranging dialogue with government become especially important in the context of putting e-government to the service of inclusive and people-centred sustainable development. Integrated policy approaches, enabled by cohesive institutional mechanisms and modern technology, contribute to the overall objectives of long-term development while lending greater legitimacy to government activities. The absence of a whole-of-government approach, by contrast, can inhibit progress in many areas, notably in low-income countries where limited coordination can undermine delivery of social services, provision of physical security, sound economic management and inclusive political processes.[2]

What needs to be clear, however, is that whole-of-government is not the same as e-government even if the use of ICT can be useful to the practice of whole-of-government. Three questions need to be answered separately. One concerns how the application of ICT can help the practice of whole-of-government. The second is about the institutional reorganization governments need to carry out in order to make whole-of-government effective. A third question concerns what whole-of-government has to do with sustainable development and how whole-of-government can help in implementing it.

Taking the United Nations E-Government Survey 2012 data, this chapter attempts to shed light on these questions. It assesses trends in whole-of-government for all 193 United Nations Member States and analyzes whether governments around the world are employing online tools to enhance institutional coordination and strengthen public services that respond effectively to people's needs and does so with their effective participation.

3.1 E-government harmonization in practice

The entry point for an integrated approach to whole-of-government is to determine the baseline conditions which allow for collaboration, across and between departments, through institutional arrangements so that the ensuing system is holistic, synergistic and coordinated in the delivery of public services.

3.1.1 National coordinating authorities

To realize a national strategy, strong leadership is required. Among other things, top e-government officials can bring together key stakeholders across ministries and agencies, define shared needs, identify potential gaps and redundancies in implementing strategic goals, and guide e-government innovation in service delivery. They can also steer process redesign efforts, facilitating communication among departments, highlight best practices, and leverage shared solutions. Given the mandate to do so, they can identify and remove common barriers to one-stop service provision as well. It is therefore vital to e-government transformation that governments appoint an official with real authority across departmental and ministerial boundaries to facilitate strategy and decision-making regarding the country's ICT architecture, and assist agencies in their efforts to run more effective and efficient programmes.

One measure to be taken is the establishment of a coordinating authority in the form of a chief information officer (CIO) or equivalent at the national level. Since 2008, United Nations E-Government Surveys have assessed governments' organizational commitment to a whole-of-government approach by asking whether they have identified a government-wide CIO or similar official responsible for overseeing e-government strategy. As seen in figure 3.1, the number of countries publicizing such a post has steadily increased. In the current Survey, 60 countries – 31 per cent of Member States – were found to have an e-government CIO or equivalent. This is up from 32 countries in 2010 and 29 countries in 2008.

Figure 3.1 **Countries with CIO or equivalent overseeing e-government**

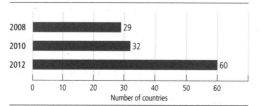

Number of countries

Table 3.1 **Chief information officer or equivalent by region**

	Countries with CIO or equivalent	Number of countries in region	% of countries with a CIO or equivalent
Africa	9	54	17%
Americas	12	35	34%
Asia	19	47	40%
Europe	18	43	42%
Oceania	2	14	14%

As shown in table 3.1, Africa and Oceania lag behind the other regions with only 17 per cent and 14 per cent, respectively, of countries identifying a CIO or equivalent. The percentages of countries installing a CIO or equivalent in the Americas (34 per cent), Asia (40 per cent), and Europe (42 per cent), however, are roughly comparable.

In developed countries, the CIO or equivalent is typically responsible for providing policy leadership, supporting and monitoring open government initiatives, coordinating ICT projects across government to ensure they are aligned with overall strategy, and monitoring and reporting on spending. In developing countries, the role is often described in similar terms, but with the addition of building technology competence among government officials and improving and expanding ICT infrastructure and international cooperation with donors and NGOs on e-government initiatives.

The CIO function may be situated at any level within a national administration, from a technical support group to a ministerial office. Given the emphasis on ICT inherent in CIO functions, responsibility for e-government coordination at the national level is assigned to a technology unit more often than not, frequently within a communications department. Only some 10 per cent of countries have a CIO or equivalent official placed in a senior position in the cabinet office, finance ministry or public administration department, among them many top-performing high-income countries such as the United States, the Republic of Korea, the Netherlands, Canada and France.

Association of the national coordinating authority with the executive or reform elements of public administration serves a dual purpose. First, business ownership of e-government at a high-level assigns responsibility for government modernization to those responsible for the design and management of public services. Second, it imparts to the CIO function a significant convening power that facilitates national strategy development and ongoing collaboration. The authority to bring different constituencies together to address common problems may be especially important in large countries having a substantial number of administrative divisions. The institutional realignment needed for effective e-government echoes responses to questions of coordination and participation that arise in other areas. In particular, the e-government experience can be taken as an important lesson learned in the design of institutional frameworks for sustainable development.

However, despite its evident value, the CIO or official with an equivalent function is not always easy to identify. Fewer than 10 per cent of leading e-government officials use "Chief Information Officer" as their functional title, preferring instead appellations such as "Director-General" or "Head" of the organizational unit mandated to undertake e-government coordination activities. The variety of arrangements and difficulty establishing exactly who is responsible for overseeing administrative reform processes at the national level is indicative of the evolving nature of the institutional frameworks for e-government development and the absence of global norms in this area.

3.1.2 Public sector interoperability

A whole-of-government strategy necessarily implies that the systems deployed throughout government are able to communicate with one another. However, different government entities have different technology needs. A treasury department has little need for a database of geo-spatial and seismic data; while conversely, a mining ministry likely has little use for a system that detects suspicious financial transactions.

Many governments may bear sunk costs from significant historical technology investments that, along with new purchase and implementation costs, prohibit migration to entirely new systems. The challenges above are only exacerbated when multiple levels, such as regional and/or local governments, are involved. Thus, interoperability and integration are at a premium with respect to both new technology purchases and upgrading existing systems.

Interoperability in the public sector is defined as the ability of government organizations to share and integrate information by using common standards.

The 2012 Survey includes several indicators focused on the degree to which countries have implemented systems that can seamlessly exchange information. One such indicator looks for identity management features. To be counted, the feature must enable the government to positively identify an individual citizen in the course of an online transaction. At a minimum, the availability of such a feature implies that the government has dynamically connected its repositories of uniquely identifying information – such as birth certificates, passports, and/or citizen ID numbers – with the system or systems offering a particular service.

Specific countries with an identifying management feature include Albania, the Bahamas, Bulgaria, Canada, Colombia, Finland, Georgia, Japan, Kazakhstan, Maldives, New Zealand, Qatar, Serbia, Singapore, and Ukraine. In some cases, particularly among European countries, the system is also integrated with an electronic ID card database and/or tied to the citizen's mobile phone. One such example is Austria, where citizens can get personalized information and services by signing on to the services portal (https://www.help.gv.at) using their ID card or mobile phone, and can even electronically sign documents using their mobile phones.

Another interoperability indicator is an online tracking system that permits citizens to check on the status of online transactions. As with an identity management feature, such a system implies that the citizen-facing system – the national website or portal – is able to communicate with the system that government officials are using to process the transaction.

Given the expense and difficulty of achieving interoperability that is required for these features, it is unsurprising that a relatively low proportion of countries offer them. Only about a quarter of countries offer

electronic identity management, while slightly more than a third have an online tracking system. Examples of countries with an online tracking system include Argentina, Bangladesh, Cape Verde, China, Colombia, Croatia, Denmark, Greece, India, Japan, New Zealand, the Russian Federation, and South Africa.

3.1.3 Online service integration

Some countries have set up portals that aggregate large amounts of information and services into a single website. A key objective of such portals is to facilitate citizen navigation and use of the content. Although during the Survey assessment period no country's portal completely integrated all information, services, and features assessed, several came close. Some of these vanguard countries include: the Republic of Korea, the United Arab Emirates, and the United Kingdom.

A common approach in this model includes organizing content around life themes and/or specific audiences, such as the young, elderly, women, job seekers, students, etc. These portals also typically include an advanced search feature that may index content from dozens of government websites; usa.gov includes all of these features.

The 2012 Survey includes a specific indicator that assesses whether a country has integrated portals under the rubric "one-stop-shops." The Australian Government has been one of the early

Table 3.2 **Interoperability and back-office integration**

	Countries	Percentage
Electronic identity management	52	27%
Online tracking system	66	34%

Figure 3.2 **Countries offering a one-stop-shop**

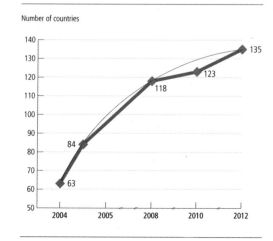

Number of countries

adopters of a one-stop portal. Its portal offers citizens numerous interactive services ranging from birth certificates to registering on the electoral roll. It offers three ways to access services: by service type (paying a bill, applying for a grant); by life event (giving birth); or by location (of government agency or department). Now, one-stop-shops are the norm in most developed countries such as Austria, Belgium, Japan, and Singapore. Further, the trend has been increasing. As seen in figure 3.2, the number of countries deploying one-stop-shops increased in the past eight years from 63 in 2004 to 135 in 2012. Among developing countries, Angola, Costa Rica and Egypt all have developed one-stop-shop portals.

While not all countries may yet be able to achieve substantial interoperability, the Survey includes a proxy for intent to move in that direction: the number of government websites linking to the national page or portal. By providing such links governments not only aid citizens in finding the information and services they seek, but demonstrate that their different branches are in fact collaborating in the online sphere. By this measurement, the majority of coun-

The Survey also measures how many countries provide a gateway to regional and/or local governments by linking to them from their national page or portal. Roughly half of all countries – 96 – provide such links. Some specific countries providing this feature include Armenia, Australia, Belgium, Plurinational State of Bolivia, Bosnia and Herzegovina, Canada, Chile, China, Egypt, France, Germany, India, Kenya, Latvia, Nigeria, Norway, Peru, the Philippines, the Russian Federation, Uganda, the United Kingdom, the United States, and Venezuela.

Figure 3.4 **Percentage of national sites or portals linking to government ministries**

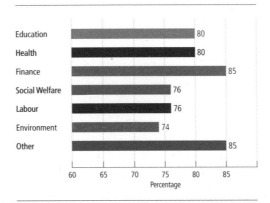

Another way in which the 2012 Survey measures whole-of-government strategy execution is by assessing how many government websites provide information and services in key government portfolios covering citizens' basic needs. As can be seen from figure 3.4, the vast majority of countries provide links from their national portal to their

Figure 3.3 **Countries with government websites linking to a national website or portal**

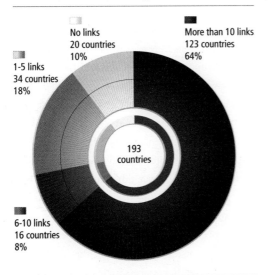

Figure 3.5 **Policy information online**

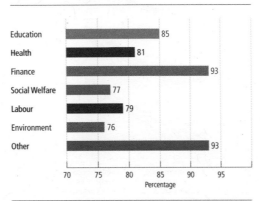

tries are making a strong effort in this area, with 123 countries having at least 10 government sites linking to their national site or portal and only 20 countries having no government sites with such a link.

Box 3.1 **Usa.gov leads in integrated portals**

Usa.gov is perhaps the best example of a highly integrated portal. It is carefully organized, starting from a sufficient level of abstraction for the citizen who does not need to know, say, exactly for which form he/she is looking. Yet by drilling down through increasing levels of specificity, the citizen ultimately – and with remarkably little effort – arrives at a very specific item or service. This process is aided on virtually every page by "Popular Topics," "In Focus," and other helpful boxes that bubble up content that is likely to be relevant. In the event that the citizen cannot find what he/she needs by browsing, a comprehensive, detailed and searchable FAQ is available. Failing that, the citizen can use the general advanced search feature, which indexes dozens of federal and even state and municipal websites. Finally, the site provides myriad ways for the citizen to communicate with the government on any topic, ranging from technical support for the site to substantive policy issues. ◆

ministries having education, health, finance, social welfare, labour, and environmental portfolios. The differences in percentages are largely reflective of the fact that some countries do not have websites for all of their ministries: where the national site provides any links to ministry websites it usually links to all of them. Among the basic needs sectors, the highest proportion of countries link to a finance ministry (85 per cent), while the lowest proportion link to a social welfare (76 per cent) or labour (76 per cent) ministry.

Similarly, a large majority of countries provide information on policies and laws for each of the key portfolios on their websites. Among the basic needs sectors, the highest proportion provide information on finance (93 per cent), while one of the lowest proportions provide information on social welfare (77 per cent).

Overall, 78 per cent of countries have a separate website for the environment, and in all regions a majority of countries scored this question. Far fewer countries – only 49 – have taken the additional step of integrating environmental information into their national and sub-national governance structures. Only in Europe have a clear majority of countries progressed to this point. Roughly half of the countries in the Americas and Asia include environmental information in their portals, while Africa trails substantially.

E-government can support environmental institutional integration not only by including environment ministries/departments but also by linking vertically and horizontally institutional structures responsible for environmental governance so that information and service flows are consistent, efficient and effective. While the e-government Survey does not focus on G2G interaction per se, certain aspects of governments' online G2C offerings may be taken as proxies for this type of information flow. While G2C offerings necessarily will overlook dedicated, login-protected websites containing sensitive information for government officials only, it seems likely that government officials from various institutions will make at least as much use as citizens of the publicly available information.

Figure 3.6 **Institutional integration efforts in environment**

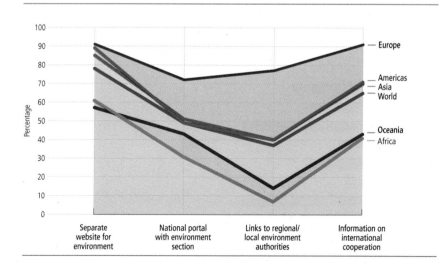

The Survey asked specifically whether Member States help support vertical institutional integration by providing a gateway to regional and/or local environmental authorities as well as providing information on international cooperation on environmental issues. Once again Europe is a leader in this area, with 77 per cent of countries providing the former and 91 per cent the latter. Very few countries in Oceania and Africa provide a gateway to local authorities. This may be explained in part by a lack of multilevel governance in general in these areas, particularly among the small island nations of Oceania. After the question on a separate website for the environment, information on international cooperation is the most commonly scored question, with 65 per cent of countries providing this information overall.

3.1.4 Overall commitment

As measured by factors that focus on commitment to a whole-of-government approach, several countries stand out. The top performers can be seen in table 3.3. Specific factors in the 2012 Survey encompassing the whole of government approach include: 1) identification of an e-government CIO or equivalent; 2) the number of links to and from the cabinet level and other government and regional/local websites; and 3) whether a one-stop-shop is offered. The commitment to a whole of government approach among these countries is evident by their higher scores even though some of them remain at a lower level of overall online service delivery.

Table 3.3 Whole-of-government top performers

Country	Country	Country
Republic of Korea	Malaysia	Serbia
Singapore	New Zealand	Cyprus
United States	Spain	Uruguay
Netherlands	Germany	Argentina
Canada	Austria	Peru
France	Mexico	Slovakia
Bahrain	Lithuania	Indonesia
United Arab Emirates	Luxembourg	Philippines
Japan	Oman	Costa Rica
Norway	Slovenia	Iran (Islamic Republic of)
Israel	Russian Federation	Mauritius
Colombia	Malta	Viet Nam
Sweden	Egypt	Sri Lanka
Saudi Arabia	Latvia	

As seen in figure 3.6, the majority of countries provide links from their government websites to the cabinet level as well as sub-national websites. A majority of countries also link other government websites to the portal. In addition, there is a trend toward installing more e-government CIOs and deploying more one-stop-shops. Finally, the specific countries that display the greatest commitment to the whole-of-government approach include many with relatively low levels of e-government development.

Taken together, these indicators suggest that countries are generally motivated to pursue a whole-of-government approach by integrating services and information as much as possible. The particular form of integration is affected by

Box 3.2 Mauritius, an A to Z thematic approach

The "Citizen" portion of Mauritius' integrated portal is organized primarily around key services, but also groups information by audience and includes an A – Z thematic index. Additional features that aid the citizen in quickly finding content include a "Quick Links" box, a "Related Subject Areas" box, and a government directory. The directory can be displayed according to hierarchy or in alphabetical order by ministry or department name. ◆

Box 3.3 **Germany chooses integrated services on multiple portlets**

One portlet, Die Bundesregierung, focuses primarily on information. It includes news from across the government, links to laws, policy documents, thematic websites in particular policy areas, and links to all government ministries. A second portlet, Bund De, focuses primarily on services. It includes a searchable directory of government offices, services and links, as well as links that direct citizens to the specific services or offices they are seeking. ◆

considerations of: the technical challenges involved in linking dramatically different systems of varying provenance and vintage; the technical complexity of setting up authentication and security systems that can be scaled up to adequately protect an increasingly integrated infrastructure; the costs involved; and political and organizational tensions that may inhibit different organs within governments from cooperating effectively.

A common variation on portal organization is to segregate information into categories for citizens, businesses, government, and sometimes foreigners. Bahrain's portal and Mauritius' portal (box 3.2) are both organized according to this principle.

Following closely behind such portals are those of countries that may not have a single integrated portal but integrated 'portlets' each with multi-sector, multifunctional integrated services or information from across multiple departments and agencies. Many European countries appear to follow this model, with separate information and services portlets, each integrated across thematic and functionally relevant sectors. One example is Germany, described in box 3.3. Other countries pursuing variations of the portlets model include the Netherlands, France, Spain, and Portugal.

Box 3.4 **Malaysia "no wrong door" policy**

A whole-of-government strategy, introduced in the 10th Malaysia Plan for development covering 2011-2015, urges public sector agencies to work across portfolio boundaries to provide high quality public services to citizens across all areas of economic activity, and ultimately to improve the capacity of public sector agencies to work together to address the economic, social and environmental challenges of globalization. A "one service, one delivery, no wrong door" policy is intended to enable easy access to public services by ensuring that government agencies are well-coordinated, well-informed and customer-friendly. Using various service delivery channels, it is expected that citizens and businesses will be able to deal with government agencies in a fast, simple and transparent manner, resulting in increased customer satisfaction. One of the most visible manifestations of the policy is the country's myGovernment website providing one-stop access to a variety of services from a multiplicity of agencies. ◆

Source: The Malaysian Public Sector ICT Strategic Plan: Powering Public Sector Digital Transformation 2011-2015, 7 July 2011

3.2 Challenges and opportunities of integrated e-service delivery

In the section below, we examine how e-government harmonization requires strong leadership and commitment in order to achieve interoperability and integration of the various public sector organizations, which is a crucial pillar of whole-of-government practice.

3.2.1 Revisiting institutional arrangements

As the 2012 Survey findings show, the vertical and horizontal fragmentation, which is typical of public administration, constitutes one of the key challenges of one-stop government implementation. Public sector initiatives where services cross departmental boundaries present a formidable challenge. The fragmented and 'siloed' government structure complicates easy communication among persons in each silo, which might result in customer dissatisfaction. Service delivery channels might not be developed based on a shared vision and could have different objectives.[3]

For example, whereas one channel might focus on personal interaction, another channel of the same organization could emphasize efficiency. Furthermore, there might be a gap between strategy and operational processes. Strategies are high level and can be interpreted and implemented in many, sometimes even conflicting, ways. Also, strategies are often formulated by politicians. They may reflect their political ambitions but fail to consider limiting factors like scarce resources, path dependencies, legacy systems and public agencies' time constraints.

The issue here is to overcome existing power structures and build a culture of cooperation. Department/agency heads may fear losing power over human and financial resources and thus fail to make them available for advancing one-stop government. Building trust among departments and agencies is therefore key to successful one-stop e-government implementation, as is incorporating change management mechanisms in the whole-of-government programme.

One important step towards this end is the development of a national strategic framework that articulates the government's vision, objectives and milestones, as well as basic roles, technical standards and constraints for realizing a one-stop e-government system. Such a framework also addresses issues of privacy and security, maintenance, and interface standards. The strategy should help departments and agencies in both central and sub-national government to cooperate in new partnerships that will enable them to offer their services in ways that make sense to the customer. Such a strategy can usefully point to partnerships with innovators in the private sector who can find new ways of meeting changing patterns of demand.

To realize the national strategy, a high level of initial investment may be needed, which must be embodied in long-term vision and strategic planning in order for an integrated and sustainable e-government solution to be successfully implemented. Service delivery platforms often require the integration of telecom and IT capabilities and the creation of services that cross technology and network boundaries. In this process, established, hierarchical and bureaucratic structures must be supplanted with horizontal one-stop government network structures that facilitate customer orientation and increase levels of transparency and accountability. The end result must be seamless, knowledge-enhanced e-government solutions that are sustainable.

At the same time, governments need to guard against creating parallel structures or institutions because these further complicate the difficult job of coordination and go contrary to the requirements of the whole-of-government approach. Creating parallel institutions would also be more of a throw-back to traditional hierarchical governmental organization. The practice of whole-of-government mainly requires the establishment of networks and partnerships within government agencies, as well as with other key players, such as those in the non-government sector. Beyond the engagement of leading e-government officials and institutions, one-stop government may require the acquisition of new skills by public employees and customers alike.

Vertical and horizontal fragmentation, which is typical of public administration, constitutes one of the key challenges of one-stop government implementation.

Alongside analysis and interpretation skills, which are necessary at every stage of an e-government project, skills in information management can ensure that information is treated as a valuable organizational resource with due regard for content, quality, format, storage, transmission, accessibility, usability, security and preservation. Depending on the type of e-government challenge an organization is facing, higher order technical skills may be required to implement the chosen solution. Communication skills are important because of the need throughout the project to convey goals, progress, issues and results. Finally, project management skills are essential to plan, organize, allocate resources, negotiate, track progress and measure results.[4]

An analysis of 40 case studies on interoperable government collected in Europe points to three further conclusions regarding human resources. First, strengthening of existing collaborations in order to create new ones; interoperability (vertical or horizontal cooperation) is easier to implement when the actors are used to collaborating. Even then, it takes time. Second, collaboration yields better results than imposition: "things change naturally and it is not necessary to inflict them. Changes impact the heart of organizations, practices and culture. This can only be done gradually."

Third, project implementation, in almost all the cases analyzed, is based on extensive training sessions. Training in the implementation process is essential. Training contributes to cultural change, to knowledge transfer, and to enabling civil servants to use the technology.[5]

Notwithstanding common issues that arise in the design of effective institutional frameworks for e-government development, there is no one institutional arrangement that can be recommended for all governments. Much depends on the national context and the interplay of organizational changes that may be advised in the pursuit of a whole-of-government approach as table 3.4 suggests.

3.2.2 Promoting citizen-centric design

The distinguishing characteristic of the whole-of-government approach is that government agencies and organizations share objectives across organizational boundaries, as opposed to working solely within an organization. It encompasses the design and delivery of a wide variety of policies, programmes and services that cross organizational boundaries.[6] From the citizens' perspective, a whole-of-government approach to e-government permits them to access information and services without needing to know anything about the structure of government. It 'flattens' government structure so that even if a particular administrative process involves two or three government departments, the citizen need have only a single point of contact with the government. One way to implement a whole-of-government approach is to aggregate government services and information into a limited number of websites. Another is to deploy advanced search technology that indexes websites throughout government.

One-stop government refers to the integration of public online services from a customer's viewpoint via a single entry point, irrespective of whether these services are actually provided by different departments or authorities. The customer may be a citizen or a business. One-stop online service provision requires the interconnectedness of all public authorities, with the effect that customers are able to

Table 3.4 Selected organizational changes needed in the pursuit of a whole-of-government approach

Objective	Strategy
Adopt a new and different culture and philosophy	Incorporate whole-of-government values into all departments and agencies
	Promote information sharing and cooperative knowledge management
	Effectively align top-down policies with bottom-up issues
Adopt new and different ways of developing policies, designing programmes and delivering services	Pursue a collegiate approach
	Focus on whole-of-government outcomes
	Consult and engage with clients and users
Adopt different working methods	Exercise shared leadership
	Emphasize expertise
	Apply flexibility and promote teamwork
	Focus on outcomes
Employ new incentives and accountability mechanisms	Recognize and reward shared outcomes
	Promote horizontal management
	Be flexible around service outcomes

access all available public services through a single entry point. Since from a customer's perspective knowledge of the functional fragmentation of the public sector is irrelevant in terms of accessing information, customers should be able to access one-stop online services in terms of life events and business situations directly from the responsible unit.

The one-stop-shop should offer a point of entry for citizens and businesses to all relevant services from the central and sub-national governments. It should be capable of personalization, matching citizens' and businesses' circumstances and needs. It should also facilitate push technology, so that at citizens' and businesses' choices, it can send reminders about services or information by email. Government online resources should also be well indexed and easy to find.

Some additional characteristics include a well thought out structure, a comprehensive navigation system, and a consistent look for the web pages – all cornerstones of an effective government website. It is also necessary to present the content in a way that is understandable for a normal user according to life/business events. Personalization is likewise very important to improve the acceptance of a national website. Since authentication of a citizen is necessary for transactions anyway, the same mechanism can also be used for personalization purposes. The demand of businesses for personalization is even higher than that of citizens, since a business is likely to use the portal more often. The user needs to be informed as to what happens with his/her data, for whom it is accessible and how it is protected. This creates confidence in the site.[7]

Another requirement for a one-stop-shop is that it be intuitive. For example, if a user wants to use a specific public service, she/he should be automatically connected to the right agency (e.g., marriage – registry office) in the right jurisdiction. Use of more advanced e-services can be described as a set of phased transactions corresponding to the citizen's view of the exchange. In the information and intention building phase, users search for information regarding possible intended public services. In the contracting phase, the user already knows what she/he needs to do and either fills in the online application form or downloads the corresponding form from the server and completes it. In the service

delivery and payment phase, the processes to complete the service are performed, the results are conveyed to the customer and the customer pays for the service. The last phase addresses aftercare, where aspects of citizen (or customer of public administration) relationship management and complaints management are addressed.[8]

While general principles such as the foregoing together constitute a helpful guide to e-government development, the quest for citizen-centric design implies an understanding of the specific needs of different segments of society and their capacity to benefit from online and mobile services. How these needs are matched with available channels, taking into account characteristics of the various phases of service delivery, is explored in Chapter 4. Differentiation in e-service design can, moreover, reinforce efforts to bridge the digital divide by reaching out to vulnerable populations, as discussed in Chapter 5. More generally, citizen-centric design with a strong user focus has a direct bearing on increasing usage of e-services to realize their full potential benefits, a subject explored in detail in Chapter 6.

3.2.3 Standards setting and systems integration

Citizen-centric design is dependent on a fully-integrated operational model usually requiring significant systems integration and accompanying transformation of business processes. Two types of integration can be discerned: vertical integration involving cooperation among different tiers of government, for example between national and local authorities engaged in environmental management; and horizontal integration within a single jurisdiction, such as connecting the finance ministry with government departments involved in provision of social services. In both cases, citizens and businesses are best served when responsibility for the requisite communication among different agencies is assumed by government, subject to applicable legal and regulatory constraints, rather than transferred to individual actors.

Building a common architecture for a one-stop government portal requires secure and trusted interoperable systems that adopt existing Internet standards for government agencies at all levels. Establishing an interoperable system within one government means that agencies can easily "talk to one another" whether by sending email or exchanging information, without any technical problems that hinder the smooth operation of government. In practice, various approaches to interoperability are possible with tighter and looser forms of integration. Three principle types of interoperability can be identified:[9]

- *Organizational interoperability* is the ability of systems and interfaces to overcome different business processes in different regions, in order to process a certain transaction or request. All three types of interoperability are of great importance if one wants to achieve the goal of a one-stop e-government portal.

- *Semantic interoperability* is about the ability of systems to exchange information, to combine it with other information resources and to subsequently process it in a meaningful manner. When semantic interoperability is achieved, information is made understandable for different applications and consequently it can be reused in different settings.

- *Technical interoperability* of e-government solutions for sustainable development demands the establishment of an IT infrastructure that allows for the efficient exchange of information among different levels of administration, both horizontal and vertical. It also presupposes that there is homogeneous equipment among all the actors involved and a significant number of end-users.

Many governments have started creating interoperability frameworks spanning agency boundaries that, among other things, facilitate the deployment of multichannel delivery of government services. Achieving interoperability in government organizations is difficult. In many cases, agencies are reluctant to change existing processes, open data and services to external parties, and renegotiate their way of operating with external parties. Open standards are particularly recommended as they are platform independent and cannot be controlled by any single agency. Legal offices, academia, and other organizations involved in interoperability can be invited to discuss key issues. An inter-ministerial board can also be set up as a working group to agree

on interoperability standards. Other measures can include getting political support from top management and developing policy and regulation in support of interoperability within the government.

As far as online services are concerned, there is what is known as the 'portal' approach, which is designed for information provision and sharing. It aggregates content coming from various sources and allows the easy localization of information delivery by use of co-branding solutions. This solution, however, needs significant investment supported by a single main actor and an efficient networking of all other actors involved, which influences the quality and updating of information. A basic requirement for a one-stop government portal is that there should be a government information infrastructure (GII).[10] This is a network that connects all government agencies. Building a GII however is a costly undertaking that requires cross-agency, cross-government planning. In order to assess the cost implications of such an undertaking, a financial feasibility study should be conducted.

There is also a so-called 'platform' approach. The platform approach does not aim at centralizing and dispatching the data but provides common tools and common functionalities (security, data exchange mechanisms, electronic signature) that allow service delivery. In this configuration, local actors are directly responsible for service provision and have to coordinate their actions (technical and organizational interoperability).[11] Both have been successfully employed separately and in combination by different countries.

The experience of the United Arab Emirates in managing its e-government initiative is instructive in this respect. While the Emirate of Dubai centrally controlled and monitored the e-services development overall, government departments were given the freedom to creatively build their own e-services in an early phase of the project. This not only accelerated development, but also helped the government departments to meet the initial target of 70 per cent of government services to be online by 2005.[12]

Similarly, Dubai adopted a hybrid approach to implementing its e-government initiative whereby government departments focused on e-service enablement while the central authority focused on building common parts (e.g., payment, customer support, etc.) needed by all offices. This balance between centralization of common aspects of e-services implementation and decentralization of e-services enablement was one of the key pillars of success in the Dubai e-government initiative, which resulted in standardization, best practices sharing, cost savings, and reduced time to market.

Implementation can be augmented by adding identity management and single-sign-on functionality. The former allows the government to verify the citizen's identity, which in turn permits a broader range of online service offerings. However, it also permits government to more easily tie together information about individual citizens from multiple data repositories. This enables the government to increase efficiency by reducing data duplication and administrative overhead while providing more personalized services to citizens. Single-sign-on functionality adds the ability for citizens to only log on once regardless of with how many disparate government ICT systems they interact. The whole-of-government model of information and service delivery benefits citizens by simplifying their interaction with government. As a result, it can be expected to drive user take-up of government information and services.

3.2.4 **Privacy and security matters**

There must also be a strong emphasis on a legal framework that embodies elements of trustworthiness, traceability, security and privacy of citizens' data. One-stop government often requires the adaptation of laws to make e-government solutions legally binding. Among the legal issues to be investigated for a successful one-stop government are: data protection, access to sensitive data, networking of authorities and databases, equal opportunities, electronic signature, etc.[13]

A central challenge of one-stop government is how the new technology can be used not only to increase efficiency for public administration, but also to strengthen confidence in privacy measures by creating mutual transparency between public administration and citizens.[14] For example, while secure systems are needed to impede unauthorized access to data, such personal data must be made accessible to a citizen who wishes to verify the use, authenticity and accuracy of his or her own personal data.

Protection of personal data calls for a number of organizational and technical measures to prevent unauthorized access and processing, for example by:[15]

- Protecting premises, equipment and systems software, including input-output units;
- Protecting software applications used to process personal data;
- Preventing unauthorized access to personal data during transmission thereof, including transmission via telecommunication means and networks;
- Ensuring effective methods of blocking, destruction, erasure, or anonymization of personal data;
- Enabling subsequent determination of when individual personal data were entered into a filing system, used or otherwise processed, and the person responsible, for the period covered by statutory protection of the rights of an individual with regard to unauthorized supply or processing of personal data.

Creating a trusted framework for digital authentication is also a crucial factor in assuring the integrity of online and mobile financial transactions. Digital signature is only a beginning. Concrete applications have to be developed, and they require a lot more legal changes. Individual laws, governing both the operation of public administrations and policy-specific issues, have to institute digital signatures as an accepted way of identification and authentication.[16] A key concept with security issues is scalability. At the same time, the security framework should take into consideration the fact that a majority of administrative transactions do not need high levels of protection and that secure procedures are expensive, difficult to implement and not always well accepted by the end user.[17]

Given the complexities, implementation of trusted security and privacy measures constitutes a major challenge to one-stop-shops, which many governments have yet to tackle. Only about one fifth of national portals clearly indicate the presence of security features with significant regional variation. According to the 2012 Survey, almost half of the countries in Europe display secure links on their national websites, while only one in Africa appears to do so, underscoring the continuing difficulty that African governments face in moving to the transactional and connected stages of e-government development.

> A central challenge of one-stop government is the need to strengthen confidence in data privacy and security measures, for example by allowing citizens to verify the accuracy of personal records.

Box 3.5 **Cloud computing**

Cloud computing has been a big beneficiary of virtualization, enabling organizations to share computing resources and, depending on service level agreements, pay only for what they use. In the United States, as part of the new Cloud First Initiative, government agencies are required to consider cloud options before making new IT investments. With virtualization, data can reside across a shared pool of storage devices, but the devices themselves do not have to be equal. Critical information that needs to be accessed frequently can be sent to high performance storage – the

equipment with the fastest response times – while less important data can go to lower cost devices with slower response times. Data that is rarely accessed or needed only in emergencies can be sent in devices that are less advanced and less costly. Virtualization enables organizations to use their most expensive storage devices for their most important data and to buy fewer of them.[18]

Another possible advantage of virtualization is that it can contribute to green IT when data centres are established in areas with access to renewable energy sources. One of the

major vendors of cloud computing equipment reports that virtualization has enabled the Municipality of Copenhagen, Denmark to cut the number of servers it uses from 638 to just 32. That meant not only less infrastructure to maintain but also lower power consumption, reducing carbon emissions by 77 per cent.[19]

A major caveat, however, is that data about citizen-government transactions and the content of those transactions is better off kept under governmental control to protect privacy and ensure that use of data complies with applicable regulations. ◆

3.2.5 **Issues in infrastructure development**

Relevant infrastructure issues to be considered here include the country's existing infrastructure, current level of Internet penetration, telephone density, existing speed of technology change, allowances for convergence, and investment in broadband.

Table 3.5 **National portals clearly indicating a security feature**

	Portals with a security feature indicated	Number of countries in region	Percentage
Africa	1	54	2%
Americas	4	35	11%
Asia	12	47	26%
Europe	19	43	44%
Oceania	3	14	21%
World	**38**	**193**	**20%**

The advantage of having one's own backbone is that government communications are open and secure and operating 24-7. However, this may imply regular funding for upgrades and maintenance of the network, and for hiring a team to support the network full-time.

Given the cost and time implications of building a backbone, governments may opt for an existing private telecommunications backbone, usually one

run by a large telecommunications carrier. With this alternative, the government entrusts the security of the network to the operator, who will also be assuming the costs of regular network maintenance and technical support and the risks of possible network sabotage.

In order to minimize the threat of security risks, governments that choose to ride on a private backbone will have to set up specific security measures, including: firewalls, intrusion detection software, encryption, and secure networks (such as Virtual Private Networks, Wide Area Networks or Local Area Networks) for government agencies that require high levels of security.

One-stop e-government requires IT support. It is therefore necessary to develop the appropriate technical infrastructures, such as a full-fledged electronic network among agencies, including applications for communication and electronic filing.

Standardization and intelligent functionality has to be provided for the portal, front-office (intake and communication) as well as the back office.[20] Specific attention has to be paid to small units of government in rural regions, which otherwise would never get a chance to use the required government infrastructure. In this respect, the need for cooperative, shared architectures and infrastructures to avoid lack of skilled resources and to lower investment and maintenance costs becomes important too.

With the silos being phased out, IT resources become much more tightly linked and collaboration becomes crucial. Increasing flexibility and efficiency in e-government operations can now be achieved via virtualization, which enables organizations to pool computing resources and use the same servers and storage devices for many different users and applications. On-demand computing is the new model for organizations looking to get the best returns from their technology investments.

3.3 Conclusions

Employing e-government to improve efficiency and effectiveness of public service delivery, and to promote development for the people helps governments use available resources to their best advantage, thus contributing to economic sustainability. In the past, e-government development efforts tended to focus on the short term, in particular on getting isolated services online, publishing information without providing for regular updates and adding new features to websites in response to changes in technology. This approach has helped meet the immediate needs of specific agencies while bypassing reform of institutional frameworks, enabled by technology, in response to the long-term financial and operational challenges of the public sector.

The 2012 Survey finds that many Member States are moving from a decentralized single-purpose organization model, to an integrated unified whole-of-government model, contributing to efficiency and effectiveness. The model aims at centralizing the entry point of service delivery to a single portal where citizens can access all government-supplied services, regardless of which government authority provides that service. In some countries, the whole-of-government approach helps build a transparent government system with interconnected departments and divisions.

Although there is widespread support for the principles of whole-of-government, there remain major problems in implementing the concept related to issues of ensuring accountability for publicly funded activities and overcoming the 'silos' created by departmentalism or vertical styles of management while avoiding fragmentation and lack of coordination. Knowledge and attitudes of public servants to the whole-of-government vision are also seen as critical elements to its success.

Why is integrated service delivery so hard, and what are the key lessons that can be extracted from reviewing the literature? The problem lies not with the technology but in the political challenge of re-wiring a range of public sector programmes delivered by different levels of government – often with different qualification requirements – for the people. Adding to the complexity is the fact that an increasing number of these services are delivered on behalf of a government by a network of private and non-profit organizations with a common mission such as reducing poverty, improving education or helping teens find jobs.

The network model for service delivery has evolved because traditional hierarchical government has failed to figure out how individual agencies can interconnect and deliver services that successfully deal with the complex and tough social and economic challenges facing societies. For some, networked service delivery avoids the inefficiencies inherent in earlier efforts to reorganize government agencies into single large units. Instead, it focuses on engaging existing agencies in joint problem solving without realignment of formal authorities.[21]

The key lessons that can be drawn from the preceding analysis are:

- *On strategy:* It is essential to begin with a strategic framework. That involves defining the framework for the whole-of-government, basic roles of the public as well as the private sector, and strategic decisions to be taken, as well as identifying constraints to be considered for realizing and implementing a one-stop government.

- *On leadership, commitment and vision:* If effective one-stop government is to materialize in any shape or form, public officials must have a long-term coherent vision that identifies, articulates and advocates the benefits of a one-stop government programme. They must also be aware of potential resistance to change, which is always inherent in projects like one-stop government. Since tradition is deeply rooted in public administration, leaders must address

Despite widespread support for whole-of-government, there remain major problems in overcoming departmental silos, reducing fragmentation and enhancing coordination.

and explain what the one-stop government portal is, inviting the opinion of personnel in the process and emphasizing the importance of continuous communication while developing and implementing the project. Leaders must also provide all necessary resources to personnel to carry out their work effectively, while training them in an adequate and continuous way during the whole process.

There are many examples illustrating that in the search for appropriate institutional arrangements for implementing whole-of-government for sustainable development, whether supported by ICT or not, there is a need to emphasize collaboration, partnerships, mainstreaming, and inter-agency or interdepartmental coordination across the whole spectrum of governance. This includes collaboration and partnership with private sector and civil society organizations.

- *On funding:* Governments fund their e-government programmes in a variety of ways: financing through a general fund, user fees, and public-private partnerships. When good economic conditions prevail, tax revenues can be an effective way to pay for a one-stop government portal. When economic hardship prevails however, spending on e-government and one-stop portals becomes more difficult as it must compete with spending for education, health care, and other social welfare concerns. Therefore, it may make sense to embark on ambitious one-stop portals during economic boom times.

- *On systems transformation:* The objective of one-stop government should be to focus on the depth of services, integrating them as deeply as possible, especially those frequently in high demand. The breadth of services should be the next focus. Such an undertaking implies developing seamless links from the front to the back office.

An e-government system may have both centralized and decentralized processes for implementing and executing e-government goals for the people. Neither system guarantees the success of these goals while each has its advantages and disadvantages. Centralized administrative systems allow IT requests to

be filtered through one agency, reducing the variation and duplication of e-government systems. Decentralized e-government systems allow individual agencies more control over e-government administration and content. Agencies can choose which firms to use when they outsource e-services.

The argument can also be made that decentralized information provision is more accurate because it is as close to the source as possible. Decentralized systems can provide agencies with a sense of ownership that can encourage better site management and design.[22] The decision to develop a centralized or decentralized e-government system depends on the economic and political circumstances within a government and the objectives stated in its e-government strategy. In either case, there needs to be smooth cooperation among government authorities (central government, local government and other administration bodies).

- *On sustainability and efficiency:* A study on the strategies of the European Union plus 21 other countries showed that the most prominent strategic objectives that appear among e-government strategies are: enhancement of public sector capacity for better services; networked government; efficiency; simpler procedures to boost business participation; business facilitation; simplification of life; increasing public value; and human capacity building, respectively.[23] One of the study's most striking findings is that the most frequent guiding principle is to always consider efficiency while devising solutions. The second most prevalent guiding principle is to design e-government in such a way as to allow greater participation from the constituents. Clearly, this is a social requirement that also calls for government to become more responsive and considerate vis-à-vis users of its services. A responsive government aims at offering better services. To achieve this, internal efficiency also needs to be attained. The third most important guiding principle for e-government is to achieve universal access, while the fourth was found to be user-centricity. All of these four goals, in turn, feed directly into making sustainable development citizen-centric and participatory.

It is important to note that creating a one-stop portal is a great step forward towards establishment of a one-stop-shop. However, the portal per se does not guarantee such an outcome. That requires connecting all the e-government systems so that no matter where the user starts his/her quest, he/she will always be pointed to the desired service.[24] This clearly needs collaboration among all government units. Internal efficiencies and government networking are therefore needed to make systems sustainable.

Herein lies perhaps the biggest conundrum facing whole-of-government approaches. While whole-of-government approaches and the technological benefits to be derived thereof require cooperation across the boundaries that separate one agency from another, and the government from the private sector, sustaining cooperation among diverse entities is almost always difficult if not a Herculean task. However, given the substantial benefits for both governments and citizens that can result, many governments are finding it well worth the effort. ☙

IQoncept/Shutterstock.com

Chapter 4

Supporting multichannel service delivery

Increasingly powerful and user-friendly technologies are creating opportunities for governments to offer new ways to interact with citizens in order to respond to their needs more effectively and with their integral participation. Taking advantage of the introduction of devices such as smartphones, interactive voice response systems, digital television, and self-service terminals, the private sector has been making use of multiple channels for a long time.[1] Such initiatives encourage citizens to envision new forms of interaction with the desire that service providers – public and private – be as accessible and responsive as modern technology allows. Although many governments are aware of this trend, few developing countries are exploiting the full potential of multichannel service delivery to serve their constituents.

Multichannel service delivery is the provision of public services by various means in an integrated and coordinated way. Citizens can make selections according to their needs and circumstances and receive consistent information and services across channels resulting in an increase in their satisfaction and trust in government.[2]

Table 4.1 **List of countries utilizing all channels**

Australia	Malaysia
Austria	Netherlands
Bahrain	Oman
Canada	Qatar
Chile	Republic of Korea
China	Singapore
Croatia	The former Yugoslav Rep. of Macedonia
Denmark	United Arab Emirates
Japan	United Kingdom
Kuwait	

Multichannel approaches support delivery of services to the poor and increase participation of socially disadvantaged groups in government policy-making.

Traditional channels can include face-to-face contact, telephone or postal mail. Digital channels encompass websites, mobile-based services and public access points such as kiosks. Public agencies can also make use of existing physical and virtual networks managed by private sector or non-governmental organizations. To facilitate higher penetration of e-government and to advance efficiency and effectiveness in public service delivery, it is necessary that the use of all available channels be considered.

Multichannel service delivery can contribute to sustainable development by delivering public services to those who most need them, that is for the people. Poverty and isolation are closely related in many parts of the world and result from the lack of access to markets, emergency health services, education, the ability to take advantage of government services and so on.[3] Multichannel service delivery supports the provision of accessible services needed by the poor and increases the inclusion and participation of socially disadvantaged groups in government policies and decisions. For example, public access Internet points in rural areas, supported by intermediaries, can bring the benefits of public services to poor people who would otherwise need to make tremendous efforts to reach them, such as travelling to the nearest city.

Multichannel public service delivery can also be used to deliver sustainable services to socially excluded groups. Research shows that these groups require an intermediary person or organization to enable them to benefit from a combination of information and transactions to meet their highly specific and complex needs. In multichannel delivery, public services can be delivered by using a mix of channels, complemented by human interaction and networks. The intermediaries can be from any sector – public, private, or a social enterprise or community support group. Multichannel service delivery is thus defined as involving the organizational interactions that make up the network, rather than as just a collection of access routes for delivering the service.[4]

Among the channels within multichannel platforms, mobile-based technologies hold tremendous promise, especially in developing countries, and can be expected to play a leading role in multichannel constellations going forward. Research suggests that the economic and social benefit of mobile technologies will be highest in rural areas, which currently have less telephony services.[5] Mobile phones allow rural citizens access to information, whether for business, medical, or educational purposes. For those without fixed addresses and without bank accounts, a cell phone provides a place where they can be contacted and a means through which they can pay bills. Unlike other forms of communication, including most web technologies, mobile phones do not require literacy, although they can play a role in its development, at the same time contributing to a kind of sustainable development that is people-centred and inclusive.[6]

This chapter reviews the usage of multichannel service delivery mechanisms by national governments and specifically highlights mobile-based technologies, due to their pervasiveness and agility. It then presents some of the major challenges and opportunities that are faced by public officials responsible for implementation of multichannel service delivery platforms and concludes with major findings and policy recommendations.

4.1 **Global and regional trends**

The 2012 Survey finds that the majority of countries are not fully utilizing the opportunities provided by multichannel delivery mechanisms. Australia, Bahrain, Canada, Denmark, France, the Netherlands, Qatar, the Republic of Korea, Saudi Arabia, Singapore, Sweden, the United Arab Emirates, the United Kingdom, and the United States rank high in multichannel service delivery because they provide services in various channels such as traditional ones supported by intermediaries, free access to public services through kiosks or WiFi, and mobile-based channels such as mobile web or applications. As seen from the list, these are all high income countries, suggesting that financial capacity is one of the main factors in implementing multichannel service delivery mechanisms.

4.1.1 **Channel selection**

As seen in figure 4.1, 190 countries are using web channels to deliver public services, which are by far the most common means used across United Nations Member States. Seventy-one countries utilize public-private partnership, 32 use kiosks and 60 provide services via mobile-based channels. There are 19 countries which utilize all channels listed in figure 4.1, 15 being high-income countries and, the remaining four (Chile, China, Malaysia and the former Yugoslav Republic of Macedonia), upper middle income economies.

Figure 4.1 **Overview of channels for public service delivery**

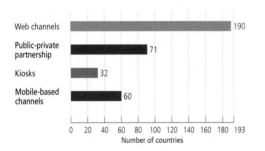

Figure 4.2 shows the regional breakdown of channels in percentages. As seen, public-private partnership is the second most utilized channel in all regions except the Americas, where Member States make use of kiosks more than public-private partnership and mobile-based channels. In Oceania, utilization of kiosks is much lower (14 per cent) and there is no single country in Africa that lists usage of kiosks in its national portal. Delivering services through public-private partnership is utilized most in Europe and Asia, 56 and 53 per cent, respectively. Public-private partnership is significantly lower in other regions and lowest in Africa (17 per cent). Asia and Europe are also the leaders in the usage of mobile-based channels, 47 and 51 per cent, respectively. Utilization of mobile technologies by governments is lowest in Africa with only 7 per cent of countries providing services to citizens' mobile devices.

Figure 4.3 shows the breakdown of channels based on income level. As seen, usage of kiosks and mobile-based channels is very low in lower middle income

Figure 4.2 **Breakdown of channels by region**

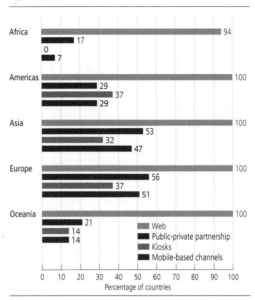

and low income countries. This finding implies that countries with limited resources do not invest in mobile-based technologies and kiosks. However, public-private partnership is the second most used channel in low income and lower middle income countries, which implies that countries with limited resources can still make use of the private sector to deliver public services. The figure confirms previous findings that countries with limited resources are not able to invest in kiosks and mobile-based channels.

Figure 4.3 **Breakdown of channels by income level**

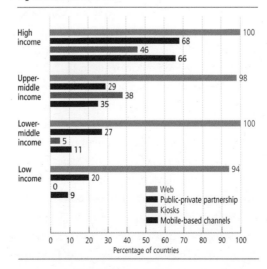

Partnerships in which public services are provided using private infrastructure are increasingly common in low and lower-middle income countries where many people cannot afford or do not have access to the Internet.

Mobile devices are among the most widespread personal technologies in the world yet m-service delivery lags behind web channel development in many countries.

4.1.2 Integration of mobile services

Mobile phones are becoming the most rapidly adopted technology in history and the most popular and widespread personal technology in the world.[7] Mobile government (or m-government for short), as one of the channels in multiservice delivery, has tremendous benefits for public agencies.[8] M-government can help modernize the public sector organizations – hence the business process, work and interactions between citizens and government – using mobile-based services. Mobile phone penetration extends outreach and access to often difficult-to-reach groups such as seniors, people with disabilities and persons living in rural areas. Citizens have access to government information and services anytime and anywhere using wireless networks through their mobile and wireless devices. As mobile phones are typically personal, the possibility of locating an individual's exact physical location ensures that governments can directly provide services to each person. Empowerment of field workers and cross-agency interactions can reduce requirements and costs for time, travel and staffing, as well as eliminate redundant data entry. Mobile crews with mobile devices can increase unit availability. Real-time and location-based processes result in quick and easily accessible data and communications, information consistency, responsive case management and seamless information exchanges.

Figure 4.4 summarizes the findings of the 2012 Survey on selected mobile channels. Compared to the 2010 Survey, there is little difference in the number of countries that provide SMS notification services. In 2010, 25 Member States provided SMS service while in 2012, 27 out of 193 Member States had initiated the service of sending messages and alerts via SMS to citizens' mobile phones. The 2012 Survey started looking at the availability of a separate m-government site in 2012 and noted that 25 Member States have a website specifically designed for mobile phones. Noticeable increases in mobile applications (from 14 Member States in 2010 to 29 in 2012) and in mobile payment transactions (from 17 countries in 2010 to 33 in 2012) were also noted. Bahrain,

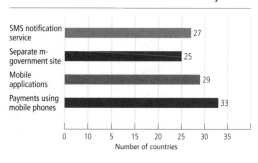

Figure 4.4 **Selected mobile-based channels for multiservice delivery**

Qatar, the Republic of Korea, Saudi Arabia, Singapore, the United Kingdom, and the United States are the only countries utilizing all channels depicted in figure 4.4.

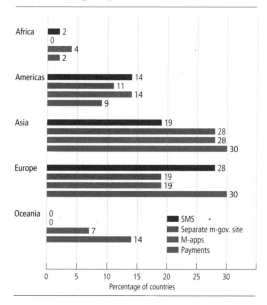

Figure 4.5 **Breakdown of mobile-based channels by region**

Figure 4.5 shows the regional breakdown of mobile-based channels. As seen, there is little information about mobile-based channels in the national portals of countries in Africa. While there are many innovative and widespread uses of mobile phones by the private sector in Africa,[9] the finding above implies that African governments are running behind compared to the private sector in utilizing mobile-based channels. Madagascar is the only country in Africa – and

Box 4.1 **Malta MyAlerts[12]: Notifications through multiple delivery channels**

As part of the e-government strategy to enhance citizen communication with the government, Malta provides timely notifications and alerts citizens to government services of interest through multiple delivery channels. Malta myAlerts provides citizens with a one-stop-shop for all notifications by email and SMS, allowing citizens to be notified about various government services instantly. These services are updated continuously to provide the latest information on governmental notifications, while myAlerts also provides citizens with news regarding ongoing and new e-government initiatives.

Using mobile channels makes sense in Malta in particular, as mobile cellular subscriptions per 100 inhabitants were 109.34 while internet users per 100 inhabitants totalled 63 in 2010 according to ITU. As the numbers reveal, the penetration of mobile phones is much higher and public agencies can reach the majority of the population by using mobile-based services. ◆

---

also the only low income country – with a website offering a service to send SMS messages to the citizen's mobile phone.

Asia is the leading region in utilization of mobile-based channels, specifically in providing mobile applications and a separate mobile government site. In Singapore,[10] citizens can receive timely and personalized SMS alerts and notifications for various services such as passport renewals and road tax renewals. In Malaysia,[11] the Ministry of Agriculture and Agro-based Industries enables farmers to lodge reports on problems of paddy attacks, including assaults by pests and diseases, through SMS, which will enable fast and immediate action to be taken by the Department of Agriculture. The Republic of Korea provides a national mobile portal service (http://m.korea.go.kr) through which citizens can use the m-government services of each government organization and receive customized national policy information at once. Bahrain's mobile portal, a mobile version of the national portal, enables anyone with a mobile phone to communicate with all government entities and access their services, in addition to other services, via text message.

Figure 4.6 shows the breakdown of mobile-based channels based on income level. As seen in the figure, high income countries are much more active in delivering public services through mobile-based channels compared to other countries. It is also important to note that payment

Figure 4.6 **Breakdown of mobile-based channels by income level**

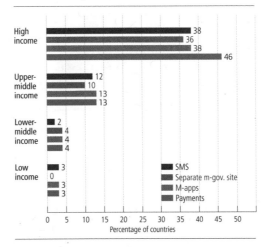

transactions via mobile phones are the mobile channel functions most utilized by high income countries. Less than 5 per cent of lower middle-income and low income countries provide public services through mobile-based channels while the ratio hardly exceeds 10 per cent in upper middle income economies.

4.1.3 **Public service access points**

Public agencies are using public-private partnership, kiosks, and free wireless access to services to provide additional access points to citizens.

Box 4.2 Turkey: UYAP SMS information system[13]

The SMS judicial information system, developed by the IT Department of the Ministry of Justice of Turkey, provides a legal notification service for its citizens and lawyers. This system automatically informs all related parties who have cases before the Turkish courts by short message service (SMS), also known as text message, when any legal event, data or announcement related to their case needs to be sent. Thanks to this system, the parties no longer have to go to the courts to collect this information. This service also provides improved access for the disabled and elderly and enhances overall e-accessibility. The SMS service does not replace official notifications, as it only intends to provide up-to-date basic information. ◆

As the private sector can bridge the gap between public agencies' offers and citizens' wishes and requests, public-private partnerships can result in both increased efficiency and better customer-oriented service delivery.[14] An important role private organizations can perform is to create multifunction access points for citizens (e.g., when a citizen purchases a car, the dealer does all the necessary work instead of the citizen having to visit different government offices).[15] The private sector's comparative advantage can be its flexible labour force, lower cost through competition, and wide distribution network, which results in services that are more accessible and acceptable to citizens. However, it should not be forgotten that the nature and scale of private sector provision is often greatly dependent on how well public sector services are performing.

A review of cases suggests that more and more governments are now using public-private partnership to provide services. In India, citizens can visit 51 e-seva centres (community one-stop-shops) with 400 service counters spread over the state of Andhra Pradesh where they can pay taxes and utility bills, register births and deaths, and apply for driver licenses and passports, among other transactions. The e-seva centres are formed as a result of partnerships between the government and private firms with government providing staff and firms providing hardware and software in return for transaction

Box 4.3 Italy: Reti Amiche for multichannel public service delivery

In Italy, Reti Amiche (User-friendly Networks) is an initiative adopted with the aim of bringing the public administration closer to the citizen by offering as many channels as possible that provide access to the various services and by adopting a user-friendly rationale in interacting with the citizens. The Reti Amiche utilizes the networks and channels existing in the private sector (Post Office, Tobacconists, large-scale retail trade outlets, ATMs, etc.) to provide information and deliver services through points of access that are easily found and close to the citizens.

More than 70 per cent of the front desks are Lottery and Betting Offices and Tobacconists, activated by Reti Amiche on the basis of memorandums of understanding signed with the Italian Tobacconist Federation and with Lottomatica. Two types of transaction that are the most frequently used are requests for the issuing of documents such as passports, birth, marriage and death certificates and residence permits; and payment transactions such as social contributions for domestic help, taxes, and fines. Reti Amiche is an initiative of the Ministry for Public Administration and Innovation. ◆

fees. In Mexico, delivery of public services such as social subsidies in remote areas is achieved through banking correspondents.[16]

The 2012 Survey assesses the availability of free access to government services through kiosks or free wireless networks and finds that 24 countries provide free access. In Estonia, free WiFi implemented by public agencies not only provides wider access to government services but also helps the economy by attracting global conference and event organizers.[17] In the United States, San Francisco's Department of Technology is expanding public WiFi in a variety of neighbourhoods as part of the city's community broadband network. In Mexico, digital community centres aim to reduce the digital divide among adults, while also offering advanced tools, training and entrepreneurial support to younger generations who are already "wired." In New Zealand, the city of Wellington has launched cbdfree,[18] which is a public access WiFi network that allows WiFi enabled devices to freely connect with the Internet from anywhere outdoors within the designated area. It is important to note that there is no low income country offering free access to government services and that only three lower-middle income countries do so: El Salvador, Guatemala, and the Republic of Moldova.

4.1.4 Channel coordination

While previous sections analyzed availability of multiple channels, it should be noted that multichannel public service delivery means more than just using multiple channels. In multichannel service delivery, all channels are integrated and coordinated. Front office applications communicate to each other and support the service provision with centrally stored and accessible data. Citizens always receive the same response and see the same information no matter which channel they use to access public services. They can select their preferred channels given their needs and circumstances and, especially with the availability of mobile channels, they can reach governments anytime, anywhere, anyhow. Central data storage and reuse of data increase governments' performance

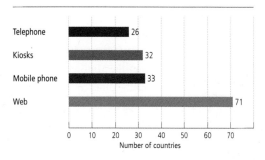

Figure 4.7 **Availability of payment transactions in different channels**

and responsiveness on the supply side. Storing data centrally means that data need to be collected only once and that they can be accessed (reused) by back office applications.

The 2012 Survey assesses whether countries are coordinating delivery of public services across channels. In order to do this, the Survey checks availability of payment transactions in different channels. As seen in figure 4.7, 26 Member States allow citizens to complete payment transactions by calling the respective agency. There are 33 countries that accept payments via mobile phones and 71 countries that accept payments via government portals, and 32 countries have implemented self-service kiosks for citizens to complete payment transactions. For a positive user experience, it is important for public agencies to unify information delivery and transactions across channels and deliver the same message in all channels regardless of citizens' channel preferences.

4.2 Challenges and opportunities of multichannel service delivery

While there are tremendous benefits associated with multichannel public service delivery, realizing these benefits is not easy. Multichannel provisioning requires substantial institutional change as well as coordination within government agencies and in some cases with outside organizations. The complexity of multichannel projects further increases when considering the challenges that public agencies

Box 4.4 ServiceOntario of Canada[19]

ServiceOntario is currently a programme within the Ministry of Government and Consumer Services. It has the support of the Cabinet, the Minister, a Board comprised of Deputy Ministers from other ministries providing service, and key corporate stakeholders. ServiceOntario delivers information and transactional services through four channels: online, in-person, kiosk, and telephone. Mechanisms used to encourage the use of the online channel are service guarantees (e.g., a two-day service guarantee for an electronic master business license), and expedited services. ServiceOntario has built partnerships with the private sector to assist with service delivery (e.g., Teranet, a private sector company, provides access to the Ontario land registration system).

The historical roots of ServiceOntario go back to the year 2000, when the Integrated Service Delivery Division was created within the Ministry of Consumer and Business Services. The focus of the organization was on working with ministries to develop a multichannel service delivery system, with particular emphasis on the electronic channel. The involvement of partner ministries was on a voluntary basis at that time. However, in 2006, the Cabinet approved a revitalized vision and mandate for ServiceOntario, which then became the government's primary public-facing service delivery organization. Ministries then ceased providing those services that are delivered on their behalf by ServiceOntario. ◆

sometimes face in e-government implementation. These include a bureaucratic culture, outdated policies, budgetary constraints, inadequate technical skills and lack of leadership.

4.2.1 Strengthening service delivery frameworks

Public officials responsible for multichannel service delivery have a variety of channels at their disposal. Once government agencies can answer why they want to offer new channels, they can make properly motivated choices in terms of which channels to implement and how to redesign services to reap the optimal benefits from them.[20] It is also important that these channels be part of a multichannel strategy and that their impact and role are assessed within the context of that strategy overall. Introducing new channels without clear goals may result in separate channels that are neither integrated nor coordinated. Channels that "do not talk to each other" would result in negative user experience and eventually cause project failure due to low utilization.

Allocating adequate resources for multichannel public service delivery projects is a must. Initial costs can be quiet high since undertaking these projects would require a review of existing systems and infrastructure, including legacy applications. Introducing new channels in the front office would also require creating a back office that is able to handle these new channels in an efficient way. Since multichannel provisioning requires collaboration within and between agencies, it is important to create a fair financing methodology to accommodate each agency. This can be achieved by taking into consideration agency size, budget and referrals for its services. Although a multichannel approach can, in principle, enable an "anytime, anywhere, anyhow" policy of e-service delivery and increase efficiency, most government agencies, especially those operating on a shoestring, may not be able to afford to develop and maintain such sophisticated networks.

Multichannel public service delivery can contribute to sustainable e-government development by enhancing the allocative efficiency[21] of public administration. It is naïve to assume that new channels will always lead to cost savings and increased efficiency for public agencies. Instead, new channels should always be introduced to deliver a better quality of public service to citizens. If a personal ID can be issued within one hour on the basis of new channels, whereas before it took 30 days and required citizens to queue up for two days in different public agencies, the allocative efficiency may be considerably higher even if the government spends more on the delivery of that specific service.[22]

Competencies of the personnel involved in multichannel service delivery projects are extremely crucial. Strong project management and coordination skills as well as technical knowledge are required. To address these needs, implementing a training and development plan in conjunction with all the agencies involved in multiservice channel delivery would be helpful. The plan needs to start with different job streams, skill sets and competencies required for successful delivery of public services in a multichannel platform. Programmes may be implemented where skills and behaviours essential to service excellence are emphasized. Staff members working in different channels need to be trained in the specifics of that channel, such as telephone skills for call centre agents and cash handling and dealing for front-office agents. Once new technologies are used in the new channels, increasing personnel comfort with the new technology and increasing their perception of its ease of use are the best ways to prepare staff for technology acceptance.[23]

Public officials need to take into consideration access and affordability issues while designing multichannel service delivery platforms. Age, gender, income, educational background and level of disadvantage affect citizens' attitudes towards their channel choice. Public agencies can tackle these challenges in different ways. Implementing a regulatory policy that favours competition can bring the prices down so that more citizens can afford access to the Internet. Implementing social coverage policy, which can aim at providing basic telephony and Internet access to the disadvantaged groups, can be another effective measure.

Internet access and cellular subscription continue to rise worldwide but the existence of the digital divide is also well documented. While governments encourage the use of electronic and mobile channels over traditional channels for efficiency gains, many disadvantaged groups do not have access to these channels. According to the ITU, in 2011, 73.8 per cent of the population in developed countries, 26.3 per cent in developing countries and 34.7 per cent of the entire world population were able to access the Internet. This means that nearly 65 per cent of citizens worldwide do not use the Internet at all. There is no access for 99 per cent of the population in Ethiopia, 95 per cent in Eritrea and Iraq, and 90 per cent in Mongolia, Nicaragua, and Angola. While mobile subscriptions have increased dramatically in recent years, mobile broadband subscriptions are still very low even in developed economies and less than 5 per cent in most of Africa.[24]

Many citizens worldwide still cannot afford to access e-services. Fixed broadband prices have dropped significantly in recent years but there are still huge differences among countries when it comes to affordability. ICT services continue to be more affordable in high income economies and less affordable in low income economies. According to ITU, the cost of ICT services averaged 1.5 per cent of GNI per capita in developed countries, compared with 17 per cent of GNI per capita in developing countries in 2010. This obviously has significant implications for the uptake of ICT services for people in developing countries.[25]

4.2.2 Responding to changes in technology

Fast moving technology creates another challenge for public officials implementing multichannel platforms. Web 2.0 technologies such as social media, e-participation tools and recent paradigms such as open data have only added to these challenges, and public agencies have been slow to adjust to these new concepts of openness and interaction. There are also growing numbers of available devices, especially mobile ones such as smart phones and tablets that citizens are using. Finding the right balance between applications and devices and investing wisely on technical platforms in an era of rapidly changing technology is a difficult task that public officials face in the design of multichannel service delivery systems.

Public officials tasked with designing multichannel service delivery systems must have knowledge of the availability of different devices and their bandwidth requirements. For example, the proportion of mobile phones to personal computers can be a deciding factor on the type of channel to be implemented. In countries with low computer penetration, public agencies can consider providing services through kiosks or mobile-based channels.

Limitations of mobile devices and adaptation of information and services that can be provided by these devices should also be considered while designing new channels. During the assessment of government portals, it has been noted that many portals are laid out for presentation on desktop-size displays and exploit capabilities for desktop browsing software. Accessing such a web page on a mobile device often results in a poor or unusable experience. Contributing factors include pages not being laid out as intended. Because of the limited screen size and the limited amount of material that is visible to the user, context and overview are lost.[26] Mobile phones, therefore, may not be appropriate for submission of long forms such as those needed for filing taxes. Instead, phones can be used for provision of emergency and other time-critical public information to citizens.

To overcome limitations of mobile devices and offer a better user experience, it is important for governments to utilize mobile-based technologies such as SMS, a separate m-government site or mobile applications.

SMS is one of the most widely used data applications in the world. Research shows that the main reason why citizens use SMS-based e-government services is because they believe that these services are easy to use.[27] The total number of SMS sent globally tripled between 2007 and 2010, from an estimated 1.8 trillion to 6.1 trillion. In other words, close to 200,000 text messages are sent every second. In developing countries, seven out of ten people have access to SMS,[28] which means that people are more familiar with SMS than the Internet. As simple and cost-effective as it is, SMS is not widespread globally. SMS can complement e-government services where it is deemed that they are more appropriate, for example, providing a

channel for reaching people in areas with only mobile phone access.

A new wave of development is happening in mobile technologies with the use of smart phones and web enabled phones. Mobile phones have begun to turn into do-it-all devices that can act like portable computers. This is completely changing the way in which citizens interact with governments. People now can access public services by using applications in their smart phones that are downloaded from commercial platforms. As additional channels, these applications offer a variety of useful tools, from finding the nearest tax office to reporting problems.

4.2.3 Expanding delivery options through partnerships

Multichannel public service delivery can be used to deliver sustainable services to socially excluded groups. Technology alone cannot guarantee that the benefits of multichannel service delivery will reach large – and eventually all – parts of society. Disadvantaged groups maintain a strong preference for face-to-face channels and they are the biggest users (and people most in need) of public services.[29] In order to include these citizens in public service delivery, public agencies may consider utilizing and revitalizing traditional channels. Intermediaries such as those in the private sector and NGOs, supported by a robust layer of technology, can provide services to disadvantaged groups on behalf of, or in partnership with, government agencies. Intermediaries can assist citizens who cannot, or do not wish to access services themselves, but have access to them through these third parties, whether on an informal, professional or commercial basis. This would also offer opportunities for advisers and caretakers to offer personal services online and offline and use ICT support systems to improve the quality of service, either where a personal approach is more appropriate or to fulfil the needs of specific target groups.[30]

Multichannel platforms require a sound coordination framework in the public and third party organizations involved in service delivery. Services, information and processes in different channels need to be coordinated in such a manner that information is available on every channel.[31] A corporate culture with excellent coordination skills and a cooperative mind set is required for multichannel service delivery projects. Achieving this harmony without strong policy leadership and political support is nearly impossible.

4.3.4 Channel steering and e-government marketing

While physical access to ICT infrastructures is important for utilization of new channels, research shows that access alone is not enough.[32] Motivation and desire to use electronic and mobile channels, as well as having the necessary skills and confidence are other factors that prevent people from using online channels. Once new channels are implemented, certain user groups may need to be motivated to give up traditional channels in order to accomplish both a more efficient government and better user experience. Influencing citizens to use the most cost-effective channels may not always be straightforward. Raising awareness of citizens via communication campaigns about more cost efficient channels can help to influence citizen perception. In other cases citizens may need to be trained on how to effectively utilize the new channels. Frequently used channels can be used to inform the client on what other channels are available to satisfy their needs. For example, if somebody telephones a government call centre and the answer is on the web, the caller could be directed to the Internet via an interactive voice system before a contact is established between the citizen and the call centre agent.

Citizens are not homogeneous and they all have different needs. In order to increase user satisfaction, it is important that public services be tailored to the needs of individual users to the extent possible. Public agencies are in a better position to provide tailored services if they segment user populations, subdividing them into more or less homogeneous, mutually exclusive subsets of users who share an interest in the service(s).[33] In order to identify homogeneous subgroups such as younger clients who heavily use e-channels or less technically oriented older people who rely on traditional channels, public agencies need to analyze their constituents in detail. This requires understanding the social preferences of citizens, their habits of information consumption, as well as accessibility requirements, including people with disabilities..

Monitoring the usage of new channels is equally important for citizen uptake once new channels are implemented. Officials need to be able to answer questions such as how many people are using the new channel and through which types of devices; how much it costs the agency to run the new channel; how well the devices operate and under what conditions; what the basic usage trends and satisfaction levels of users are; and the demographics of citizens accessing the new channel. For instance, Directgov (http://www.direct.gov.uk) in the United Kingdom is available through the government's website, through any Internet enabled phone and through digital TV. It has been found that users of the Directgov TV service are more likely to be older (63 per cent over 35, 40 per cent over 45, and 17 per cent over 55, respectively); the majority are not working (67 per cent); and half (48 per cent) rarely or never use the Internet.[34] Such analysis would give further insight to public officials about the future direction of multichannel provisioning.

4.3 Conclusion and recommendations

Multichannel public service delivery and specifically usage of mobile-based channels will continue to be high on the e-government agenda in the coming years. Success factors in multichannel public service delivery depend on a vast range of parameters; there is no single formula or generic solution that fits all situations. In some circumstances, a wide variety of channels may be needed, whereas in other situations, a limited number or even a single channel will suffice. While designing multichannel service delivery systems, public officials should pay particular attention to the issues listed below:

> Mobile phones are now becoming do-it-all devices that act like portable computers, and can completely change the way people interact with government.

Have a well-established coordination framework across stakeholders involved in multichannel service delivery

Multichannel public service delivery is a complex process. It demands interrelated, intersectoral and integrated service delivery from the many sectors and government departments involved. Collaboration and coordination within and across government agencies are needed for success. All channels need to share a set of common principles and their data and a culture of cooperation among agencies must be in place. Effective coordination and cooperation call not only for technical interoperability but also strong political and top level management support. (See Chapter 3, Section 3.1.2 Public sector interoperability.)

Devote adequate resources to planning before implementing new channels

When new channels are designed, it is important that their impact and role be assessed within the context of an overall strategy. Seamless connectivity of different channels needs to be considered as part of service delivery and is increasingly important as an enabler of public sector productivity. New channels should be developed complementary to existing ones wherever possible. Therefore, an evolutionary approach which tries to align new channels with existing practices is more suitable.

Utilize the potential of all possible channels

Research shows that a combination of contact channels works best to increase e-government service adoption and public agencies should therefore provide multiple contact points.[35] The existence of one channel and its applications alone does not guarantee results. Each channel should focus on exploiting its specific characteristics, usually those that they possess as a comparative advantage to other channels, to reach larger groups of citizens. In this respect, traditional channels can focus on reaching a higher number of citizens by increasing access via kiosks or free wireless access points; mobile channels can target mobile citizens as a complementary channel for e-government; and e-channels can further strengthen their reach

by using the latest web technologies. While designing their e-government systems, public officials need to clearly define the objectives of each channel and proactively consult with citizens and stakeholders for successful multichannel public service delivery implementation.

Ensure that all groups and individuals, particularly those disadvantaged in some way, can access combined and flexible services using multichannel delivery systems

While aiming for high efficiency and effectiveness, public officials need to keep in mind that all citizens have equal rights to access public services, that is, all citizens should be able to access services even if they do not own or have access to the newest and most innovative platforms, such as a smart phone or tablet. Disadvantaged groups are the largest and most in need users of public services but also the least likely to be able to access or afford electronic and mobile channels. Public agencies can tackle access and affordability issues in different ways. Implementing a regulatory policy that favours competition can bring the prices down so that more citizens can afford access to the Internet. Implementing social coverage policy, which can aim at providing basic telephony and internet access to the disadvantaged groups, can be another effective measure. Kiosks and public access points are effective measures to overcome the digital divide and reach out to segments of the population that are entirely unfamiliar with Internet applications. (See Chapter 5, Section 5.1 for factors influencing e-service access and use.)

Pay particular attention to mobile-based services

Mobile government gives public agencies an opportunity to address the digital divide, especially in developing countries. M-government is expected to continuously expand due to the high penetration of mobile services, especially in developing countries. As a result of convergence, mobile devices such as tablets will become the primary and maybe the only connection tool to the Internet and therefore to e-government services. Hence, the enormous potential of mobile devices is still largely untapped and more innovative applications will be seen as mobile phones become powerful enough to run a full desktop operating system that can do virtually everything a computer can do.

Use existing networks and services of third party organizations in multichannel public service delivery

Technology alone cannot guarantee that the benefits of multichannel platforms will reach large – and eventually all – parts of the population. Technology needs to be socially and culturally embedded and understood in order to be used effectively to create value. Traditional channels, ideally supported by a robust layer of technology, are still the only option in most parts of the world. Public-private partnership and use of existing private sector channels can help governments to include more citizens in service delivery. Intermediaries can assist citizens who cannot, or do not wish to access services themselves, but have access to them through these third parties, whether on an informal, professional or commercial basis. The best recipe for success is a healthy mix of technology and services.   CB

UN Photo/Kibae Park

Chapter 5

Bridging the digital divide by reaching out to vulnerable populations

Sustainable development cannot be reduced to environmental protection alone.[1] Socioeconomic factors are just as important, and so are the institutional frameworks undergirding development and development management initiatives. Social exclusion and lack of adequate access to public services can significantly undermine sustainable development. E-government, in improving public service provision and delivery, and in promoting inclusion – with due regard to the needs of vulnerable populations – can be instrumental in mitigating the effects of exclusion and improving people's livelihoods. E-government, in this sense, is instrumental in promoting a sustainable development that is for the people.

Broadband Internet can help people in rural and remote areas interact with doctors online and facilitate education of young people where physical facilities are unavailable.

Just as clean environment alone cannot address sustainability, the availability of computers or the Internet does not in itself determine who can access and use ICTs and e-government services effectively. Also important are digital skills and an awareness, willingness and capacity to engage with ICTs and e-government. One illustration comes from broadband, which is not solely about high-speed Internet. Coupled with the right e-government strategies, it can be a very effective tool in fighting poverty, increasing literacy and protecting the environment.

For instance, e-government can deliver public services such as health and education more effectively through broadband, with e-health allowing people in rural and remote areas to access doctors online and e-education enabling youth to receive Internet-based education that would not be physically available. It can also contribute to the design, provision and delivery of more accountable services by incorporating the inputs of wider segments of society that otherwise would not have the means to contact their local or national representatives or representative institutions.

Research shows that every 10 per cent increase in broadband penetration accelerates economic growth by 1.38 per cent in low- and middle-income countries.[2] E-government, powered by broadband, can improve people's livelihoods while giving them a voice in decision-making processes through enabling literacy and education for the masses and fulfilling their local information needs.

Built on these premises, this chapter focuses specifically on vulnerable populations and tackles the challenges they face in accessing and using ICTs and e-services in the public sector. The challenges are presented along four lines of analysis: language and literacy, abilities and capacities, gender and income, and location and age. The e-government divide in the case of vulnerable populations is thus about how governments of the world fare in facilitating digital access for the illiterate and low-educated, persons with disabilities, the poor, women, children, the elderly, and communities living in rural and remote areas.

5.1 Factors affecting e-government access and use

There are many ways to define and understand the digital divide. The 4A perspective – Awareness, Access, Attitudes and Applications – emphasizes the need to examine the local/community-level digital gaps in addition to those at national/global levels.[3] The access-use definitions underline the socioeconomic factors such as income, gender, life stage and geographic location.[4] The phased-digitalization definitions focus on degrees of progress along infrastructure, skills and competition in the first phase, diffusion of devices in the second phase, and impact in the third and final phase of digitalization.[5] The business-model definitions concentrate on the difference between the productive assets or capital (info-density) and the consumables or labour (info-use) of ICTs,[6] and purpose definitions extend the scope of digital divide from equipment and skills to variables such as autonomy of use and social support, attributes of governance systems,[7] and reasons for using the Internet (social, political, economic versus entertainment).[8]

These and other definitional debates, as well as the parallel methodological quest for determining the adequate indicators of the digital divide, point to a trend that moves from the traditional technology-oriented measures of ICT tools and Internet usage in the 1990s to user-driven indicators of skills and purpose of information usage in the 2000s, to the most recent indicators of social learning and impact conjuring ICT as an enabler of development in 2010. It is this latter perspective that puts the greatest emphasis on targeted policy areas for specific at risk or vulnerable groups, such as education, health and digital literacy for women, youth, the elderly, the disabled, and the less educated and low income groups. Community involvement and the production of local content by local populations, including the vulnerable groups in particular, now gain increased significance and become some of the new parameters for assessing the digital divide and e-government's role in bridging it.[9]

The access of populations to ICTs and their effective engagement with e-government processes can be broken down to individual (micro), local-community (micro-meso), national-society (meso) and international (macro) levels of analysis.

Each level of analysis covers:

- ICT penetration or supply comprising material issues such as technology, infrastructure, equipment and ICT tools and policies;
- ICT take-up or demand including human issues such as skills, usage, and content; and,
- ICT environment or context such as the degree to which economic, political and civic liberties can interact to determine who will have better access to ICTs and e-government while getting the most out of them.

Vulnerable populations are particularly important in this comprehensive perspective because the standard ICT penetration, ICT take-up and enabling environmental conditions may not always be applicable to their specific attributes, needs and wants.[10] Thus, a specific focus on vulnerable populations is useful and necessary for overcoming the barriers that governments of the world face in their drive to ensure the digital inclusion of all citizens, thereby contributing to efforts towards ensuring sustainable development for all.

Table 5.1 summarizes some of the divide issues, indicators and policy areas contained under each one of the three pillars of ICT penetration or supply, ICT take-up or demand, and ICT environment or context, as well as the cross-pillar category of vulnerable populations.

An appropriate focus on extending e-government to vulnerable groups is critical to ensuring that e-government supports inclusion and development for all. Many countries have incorporated this inclusive e-government approach with special sections devoted to the marginalized groups on their websites offerings.

The United Nations E-Government Survey 2012 pays specific attention to vulnerable groups and how they are able to access and use e-information and e-services. An overall picture of how e-government across the world integrates vulnerable groups is provided in figure 5.1. The main question is whether the national government website contains specific sections on at least one of the vulnerable groups, namely the poor, the illiterate, the blind, the elderly, immigrants, women and youth.

Table 5.1 Components and subcomponents of the conceptual map of digital divide[11]

ICT penetration or supply	**Technology:**
	Desktop, laptop, smart phones, mobile computers, broadband, Internet service providers (ISP), cost, teledensity such as computers per household, number of Internet hosts, international telephone traffic, communications infrastructure, ICT infrastructure quality.
	Government policy:
	Government prioritization of ICT; policies regarding ICT and minorities, ethnic groups, other risk groups; telecommunications policy and joint government, private sector and civil society programmes; investment in ICT infrastructure, education, research and development; ICT expenditures, training and awareness-raising; quality of mathematics and science education; regulatory issues such as universal access, consumer advocacy, pricing policies, interconnection agreements, licensing for ISPs, spectrum licensing, infrastructure-sharing; use of social media to increase e-participation, foreign direct investment and openness to-trade, competition policy, restrictions on access or content.
ICT take-up or demand	**Access:**
	Network connectivity, affordability, reach, service provision, speed, broadband access
	Usage:
	Computer use, Internet use, time and frequency, skills (literacy, education, knowledge of hardware and software), capacity, creating a presence on the Internet; purposes of information use (health, politics, employment, entertainment), ability to extract information.
ICT environment	**Social-political-economic factors:**
	Legal and regulatory framework, regime type, governance system, macroeconomic environment, poverty, local economic environment, trust, political will, leadership, habituation (integration of technology and Internet into the culture), structural inequalities, stereotypes, cultural values, ratio of females in the labour force, availability of scientists and engineers.
	Vulnerable populations are part and parcel of the three main pillars. Socio-demographic factors (income, gender, age, occupation, geographic location, ethnicity and race, religiosity, language, physical capacity, affordability) arise under all three pillars above. Yet, they are particularly instrumental in situating the vulnerable groups on the map of the digital divide.
	Salient ICT issues specific to vulnerable groups include: indirect benefits of ICTs through intermediaries,[12] the rise of social media with lower technical skill requirements,[13] cell-only wireless users and the implications for the changing face of the digital divide.[14]

Figure 5.1 Inclusion of at least one of the vulnerable groups on the national website

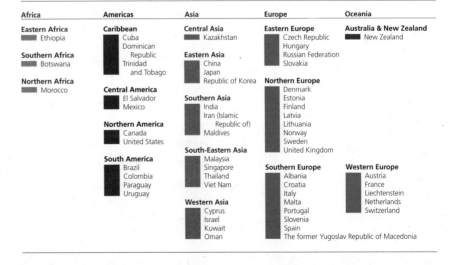

Africa	Americas	Asia	Europe	Oceania
Eastern Africa Ethiopia	**Caribbean** Cuba Dominican Republic Trinidad and Tobago	**Central Asia** Kazakhstan	**Eastern Europe** Czech Republic Hungary Russian Federation Slovakia	**Australia & New Zealand** New Zealand
Southern Africa Botswana	**Central America** El Salvador Mexico	**Eastern Asia** China Japan Republic of Korea	**Northern Europe** Denmark Estonia Finland Latvia Lithuania Norway Sweden United Kingdom	
Northern Africa Morocco	**Northern America** Canada United States	**Southern Asia** India Iran (Islamic Republic of) Maldives		
	South America Brazil Colombia Paraguay Uruguay	**South-Eastern Asia** Malaysia Singapore Thailand Viet Nam	**Southern Europe** Albania Croatia Italy Malta Portugal Slovenia Spain The former Yugoslav Republic of Macedonia	**Western Europe** Austria France Liechtenstein Netherlands Switzerland
		Western Asia Cyprus Israel Kuwait Oman		

Gaps in access to e-government services are often associated with connectivity hurdles such as the lack of affordable equipment, telephone lines and Internet connections.

The results show that, as of 2012, only 28 per cent of Member States (56 out of a total of 193 countries) have included such sections on their national websites. Within the group of 56 countries that do provide such information on vulnerability, Europe leads the way with about 50 per cent of them. Asia-Pacific and Latin America are the runners-up with 20 per cent each. Only Botswana, Ethiopia and Morocco make it to the list from Africa.

There are many issues that contribute to the digital exclusion of vulnerable groups culminating in the underutilization of e-government services by those who need them most. Among the important issues of digital exclusion are infrastructure and access. Gaps in citizens' access to and use of ICTs and e-government services often consist of connectivity hurdles, such as the lack of affordable access to PCs, Internet devices, modems, telephone lines, and Internet connections. One possible partial solution to this infrastructure hurdle could be to devise cheaper means of access such as the creation of publicly accessible kiosks in Internet community centres, which would also bring down the access price.[15] Another approach could emphasize users' attributes, needs, and wants since infrastructure and access are often mired in social, economic and political contexts including differences of language, literacy, education, age, disabilities, capacity, income, location and gender. In other words, even if Internet community centres and machinery are made available and affordable, large segments of populations across countries might still be unable to reach or use them effectively due to the need for extra or non-standard technical features, outreach policies and/or e-government skills sets.

Figure 5.2 **Multilingual national portals**

National Portals with content in more than one language

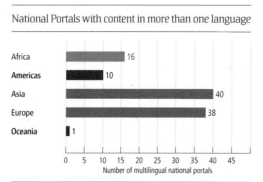

5.1.1 **Language and literacy**

One of the most important obstacles to e-inclusion, particularly among vulnerable groups with little education, is language. Today, more than 80 per cent of all websites are in English.[16] Yet only one third of the users worldwide speak English as their native language.[17] The illiterate poor seldom have the means to learn a foreign language.

Figure 5.3 **Multilingual European portals**

Percentage of countries in Europe with national portals having content in more than one language

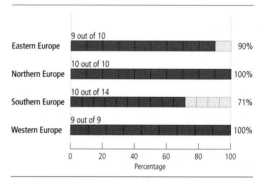

In this respect, both public education and local content production become paramount. The 2012 Survey finds cautiously optimistic rates regarding moves towards digital multilingualism, including local content production. As shown in figure 5.2, more than half (105 countries) of the

Figure 5.4 **Multilingual Asian portals**

Percentage of countries in Asia with national portals having content in more than one language

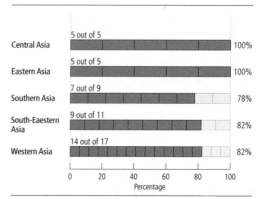

193 Member States are now offering their national websites in more than one language.

In using language to reduce the digital divide, Asia is the leader with 40 countries offering their national websites in more than one language. Asia is followed closely by Europe, with 38 such countries.

Tables 5.2 and 5.3 delve into the sub-regional trends of the leaders. Asia, East Asia and Central Asia are fully multilingual digitally. In Europe, Western and Northern European countries are.

Latin America and Oceania have room to make progress. Only eight countries in Latin America and Samoa in Oceania provide their national websites in more than one language.

Several African countries have already undertaken twin actions: to reach in – to their nationals in their official language(s)–, and to reach out – to the rest of the world through English and/or other commonly spoken languages worldwide. These countries are Algeria, Botswana, Cameroon, Cape Verde, Chad, Egypt, Equatorial Guinea, Ethiopia, Madagascar, Mauritania, Morocco, Somalia, Sudan, and Tunisia.

The fact that some countries do not yet offer their national websites in more than one language does not mean that that they are not making progress towards multilingualism on other grounds. Educational programmes and training in foreign languages and ICT literacy, particularly targeting the vulnerable groups, are widespread measures applied by countries to overcome the digital linguistic barrier. Some examples are provided in box 5.1.

The provision of government websites in the official national and local languages of minority and other groups, particularly through their direct involvement, could help in mitigating the e-government access and use divide by expanding reach, promoting awareness and instilling ownership in the design of e-services and products. These findings also imply that translating the national websites into English can be helpful in promoting inclusion in the broader information society at the global level.

5.1.2 Abilities and capacities

Education and digital literacy are particularly important for citizens with different physical and cognitive abilities. Considering that more than 18 per

---

Box 5.1 Selected examples of e-government initiatives of education to bridge the digital divide

Country	Initiatives

Uruguay: Plan Ceibal

- A laptop to every student enrolled in the public school system.
- Adaptive technology in the laptops for students with special needs.
- Co-ownership through engagement of students/parents in design.
- Aiming at adaptive technologies en masse and at reduced cost.

South Africa: Digital Doorway

- Network of robust computer systems in rural communities to interconnect them – among each other and to the Internet.
- Emphasis on awareness-raising and computer literacy with community-driven learning programmes.

Nepal: Coppades

- ICT infrastructure and connectivity to rural public schools.
- Solar Power enabled online education project for rural schools with no connectivity to electricity grid.
- Connecting schools and students through email and their newly created school websites.

France: Aijalcom

- Community technology learning centres for youth in underserved areas.
- Preparing youth to join the workforce, increasing computer literacy and supporting local socioeconomic development.

---

cent of the world's population is disabled in some way,[18] several countries have put forth innovative programmes of capacity-building that respond to the specific needs of these vulnerable groups.

Persons with disabilities face substantial barriers to access and use e-government. Web pages that use small fonts or particular colour combinations may be unreadable for the visually impaired. Similarly, audio or video content on web pages may not be useful for the hearing impaired. Those with motor impairments may require special features on websites so that they can be navigated without a pointing device.

Many persons with disabilities use adaptive technologies to overcome the challenges they face in consuming online content. Examples include screen readers and special pointing or input devices. The former are used by the visually impaired to render a written webpage as an audible description of the page. The latter enable those with motor disabilities who may not be able to manipulate a standard keyboard and mouse to interface with a computer and navigate online content.

While these technologies offer persons with disabilities tremendous opportunities, they can be sensitive to technical details of website implementation. Such technical flaws in implementation are typically not visible on a webpage as rendered by a standard browser. They can, however, be detected using automated tools that read the underlying HyperText Markup Language (HTML) in which web pages are actually stored and transmitted.

E-government can and often does represent a tremendous opportunity for persons with disabilities by bringing services to them in a way that cannot be accomplished effectively via physical delivery. Paradoxically however, insufficient attention to the needs of the disabled in e-government planning and implementation can actually disadvantage this vulnerable group even more.

Therefore, while capacity-building programmes of ICTs for persons with disabilities are important, they are not the only remedy. Often times, simple technical tweaks such as adding labelling to images on the web so that screen readers can find them, providing audio Captchas[19] for the visually impaired or designing devices with graphical interfaces or tactile inputs can be highly effective means for mitigating the digital divide faced by population groups with different visual, hearing and other abilities.

The 2012 United Nations E-Government Survey measures the digital divide faced by persons with disabilities through three questions:

- Does the site offer video of sign language?
- Does the website offer a service to read the content of pages aloud via a speaker or headphones?
- Can the design of the site allow for configuration of font size, font type, font colour and background colour?

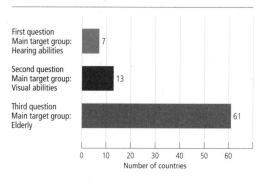

Figure 5.5 Assisted sites

Number of countries with national portals offering video of sign language, services to read the content of pages aloud, and configuration of font size, font type, font colour and background colour

The first question targets mainly those people with different hearing abilities. The second does the same for those with different visual abilities. The third question is also relevant for the visually challenged, as well as for the elderly.

Results show that the world is only beginning to tackle digital ability. Figure 5.3 and table 5.2 show the associated findings of this year's Survey.

Table 5.2 National websites with accessibility features

	Number of countries	Percentage
Read content aloud	13	7%
Video of sign language	7	4%
Configure fonts and/or colours	61	32%

The findings demonstrate that only seven countries offer video of sign language on their national government websites, and except for Canada, they are all situated in Europe. The trend-setters in digital ability are Austria, Finland, France, Portugal, Sweden and the United Kingdom.

The Survey also shows that only 13 countries offer services to read their national government web pages aloud via a speaker or headphones. One would have expected the previous seven to have undertaken this functionally equivalent step. Yet, surprisingly, except for France and Sweden, there is no overlap between the two groups.

Box 5.2 **Automated search for barriers to usage**[22]

An automated search for barriers to usage was carried out by the United Nations E-Government Survey 2012. E-accessibility checker software[20] was used to test the primary national website of each country to assess how well it conforms to the World Wide Web Consortium's (W3C) standards promulgated under the Web Accessibility Initiative (WAI) and embodied in the Web Content Accessibility Guidelines (WCAG),[21] version 1.0. The tool only tests those aspects of the guidelines that can be tested automatically. It searches, inter alia, for deprecated features, ambiguous links, graphical elements lacking descriptive elements, unlabelled form elements, and features that can only be navigated with a mouse.

Deprecated features are HTML statements that the W3C recommends avoiding and which may be dropped from future versions of HTML. Some features are deprecated specifically because they do not support accessibility or more current HTML functions.

Ambiguous links are multiple links that have the same text but point to different destinations. Screen reader users may not be able to differentiate such links. Similarly, graphical elements that lack descriptive text or proper labelling may be missed or rendered meaningless for them. Last but not least, features that require a mouse place users with different dexterity abilities and levels at a disadvantage.

The e-accessibility checker found that 98 per cent of the national web pages assessed across the

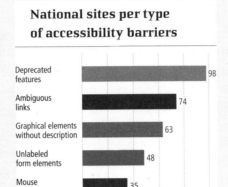

National sites per type of accessibility barriers

193 Member States had deprecated features, 74 per cent had ambiguous links, 63 per cent had graphical elements lacking descriptive text, 48 per cent had unlabelled form elements, and 35 per cent had features that could only be used with a mouse. The WCAG classifies requirements into priority 1 and priority 2. Priority 1 requirements must be met to comply with the WCAG. Priority 2 requirements should be met.[22] To put it differently, failure to meet priority 1 requirements renders a site "impossible" to access for some users. Failure to meet priority 2 requirements imposes "significant barriers" to access.

Depending on how many tests a website passed for priority 1 requirements, it was assigned from 0 to 3 points for priority 1, with higher numbers representing a higher

proportion of tests passed. Similarly, for priority 2, each website was assigned from zero to three points. The chart below shows how points were distributed among countries.

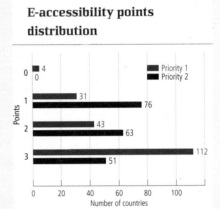

E-accessibility points distribution

As can be seen below, 112 countries' sites (58 per cent) scored 3 points on the priority 1 test, while only 51 countries' sites (26 per cent) scored 3 points on the priority 2 test. Conversely, only 31 countries' sites (16 per cent) scored only 1 point for priority 1, while 76 countries' sites (39 per cent) scored 1 point for priority 2. While countries are more successful at complying with the priority 1 than with the priority 2 requirements, one implication of this is that there is considerable room for improvement in rendering e-government services available to persons with disabilities.[23] ◆

When it comes to serving populations with different visual abilities through the ICTs, it is not just Europe that carries the torch of innovation. Other countries from several regions of the world also offer services to read their government websites aloud via a speaker or headphones. Among them are Bahrain, Oman and the United Arab Emirates in Western Asia, Japan in East Asia, Malaysia in Southeastern Asia, and Chile in South America.

The Caribbean stands out in Latin America. Although the region as a whole is only in 3rd place,

after Europe and Asia, 3 out of the 8 Latin American countries whose national websites have built-in mechanisms that enable the configuration of visual site characteristics come from the Caribbean. The forerunners are the Bahamas, Saint Vincent and the Grenadines, and Trinidad and Tobago.

Although these digital ability statistics point to an infancy stage at best, there is cause for hope. For instance, a promising 32 per cent of governments across the globe (61 Member States out of a total of 193) have already incorporated features that allow for the configuration of font size, font type, font colour and background colour into the design of their national websites. These advances facilitate the digital access, not only of those with different visual abilities, but also of the elderly.

The findings also point to an overall lack of structured national plans for the digital inclusion of persons with disabilities. As certain countries are taking initiatives to make Internet access a legal right,[24] planning and implementing structured digital inclusion programmes take on increased significance. The European Union's Web Accessibility Initiative (WAI) guidelines for public websites and universal design for e-accessibility are good starters. But there is a need to focus more on implementation.[25]

5.1.3 Gender and income

Regarding the gender dimension or the gender digital divide, women have been unreservedly associated with low Internet use and an overall disinterest in technology. They are underrepresented in their ownership and use of computers and mobile phones, and access the Internet less frequently than men even though once in the labour force, women tend to use the Internet more than men.[26]

The rising social media and networking tools show some promising gender trends. Women demonstrate higher levels of engagement with social networking sites than men. Although they account for 47.9 per cent of total visitors to the social networking sites, they consume 57 per cent of pages and spend significantly more time doing it: about five and a half hours per month compared to men's four hours.[27]

Table 5.3 shows that the most active women in social media are in Latin America, followed by North America and Europe. Women in Asia are relatively less interested in social media. In all regions, women are engaged more fully in social media than men.

Perspectives on the gender digital divide are provided by the E-Government Survey's data on countries that devote specific sections to vulnerable groups on their national websites. Figure 5.6 pictures the 55 countries that do so and categorizes them according to their female economic activity. All 55 of them, clustered into five regions, display

Table 5.3 **Access of females versus males to social media**[28]

Social Networking Category Reach by Worldwide Region for Females and Males, May 2010.
Total audience, age 15+ – Home & Work Locations*
Source: comScore Media Metrix

	Social networking % reach by region	
	Females %	Males %
Worldwide	75.8	69.7
Latin America	94.1	91.9
North America	91.0	87.5
Europe	85.6	80.6
Asia Pacific	54.9	50.7

*Excludes visitation from public computers such as Internet cafes or access from mobile phones or PDAs.

uniform levels of female economic activity[29] hovering around 50 per cent, which is very close to the world average.

The within-region distribution of these countries with regard to female economic activity also follows similarly uniform patterns with low degrees of standard deviation from their respective regional means. Thus, in the sample of 55 countries whose national websites mention vulnerable groups, there are not too many deviating countries within regions with respect to the ratios of women undertaking economic activities.[30]

Regarding the income dimension or the economic digital divide, research and experience have already shown that the poor – individuals,

Figure 5.6 **Female economic activity**

Levels of economic activity carried out by women in countries that mention vulnerable groups in their national websites

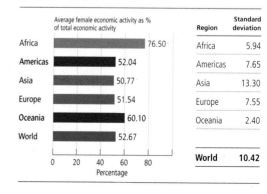

Average female economic activity as % of total economic activity		Region	Standard deviation
Africa	76.50	Africa	5.94
Americas	52.04	Americas	7.65
Asia	50.77	Asia	13.30
Europe	51.54	Europe	7.55
Oceania	60.10	Oceania	2.40
World	52.67		
		World	**10.42**

communities or nations – lack adequate access to ICT tools, including the Internet[31] and more recently to the faster and more convenient broadband technology.[32] The income gap is usually exacerbated by low levels of education, difficult access to technological and other amenities because of location in remote areas, and sometimes additional disabilities hampering the development of ICT skills.[33] Income is thus a factor, but not the only one in shaping the digital divide.

Figure 5.7 Broadband (2012) and GDP per capita (2010 or the latest figure)

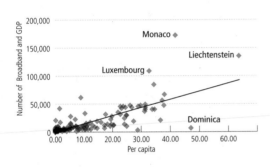

Source: ITU data used in the E-Government Survey Data (2012) for broadband (2011 values) and GDP/Capita (current US$, 2010) from World Bank (2012) found at (http://data.worldbank.org/indicator/NY.GDP.PCAP.CD). The following countries' broadband per 100 habitants is zero or very close to zero (<0.08): Afghanistan, Burundi, Cameroon, Chad, Congo, Eritrea, Ethiopia, Guinea, Guinea-Bissau, Iran (Islamic Republic of), Liberia, United Republic of Tanzania, and Zambia.

The emerging economies in the developing world are catching up fast. Internet users in developing countries increased from 44 per cent of the world's population in 2006 to 62 per cent in 2011. And 37 and 10 per cent of these users are in China and India, respectively.[34] The increasing income levels paralleled with the increasing take-up of ICTs in general underline once more the importance of infrastructure and access, including affordability in the digital divide.

A glance at the group of countries offering built-in, sophisticated software service for reading content aloud via a speaker or headphones shows that they are indeed all upper-middle or high-income countries.[35] Yet there are still considerable differences in the GDP/per capita levels of even this small cluster of twelve rich countries. The range stretches from the least rich, Malaysia (US$8,373) to the richest, Luxembourg (US$108,921).[36]

Expanding the income perspective from a simple GDP/per capita to the more comprehensive Human Development Index (HDI) yields similar results: Countries must be above a certain threshold of socioeconomic development to begin addressing the higher-end needs of their vulnerable populations, here between the HDI levels of 0.705 (Oman) and 0.943 (Norway).[37]

As simpler solutions for digital inclusion are explored, more countries from the lower income groups join the group of countries that address the needs of their citizens with different visual abilities. This is the case of the 60 countries whose national government websites allow changes in font size, font type, font colour and background colour. This number is a good contrast to the only seven and twelve countries that respectively offered more costly technological solutions to the visual and hearing needs of persons with disabilities. The ranges of GDP per capita and HDI levels in this larger and more diverse group are from Ethiopia (US$358.25) to Liechtenstein (US$134,914.67), and from Mozambique (0.322) to Norway (0.943), respectively.

One new development with the potential to counter the economic digital divide is what the International Telecommunications Union calls the "mobile miracle."[38] Putting connectivity and ICT services within reach of the vulnerable populations, least developed countries have seen their mobile data connectivity jump from a meagre 1.2 per cent of their population to 30 per cent in the last 10 years. Among the developing regions, Africa has the highest mobile growth rate. Mobile penetration has risen from just one in 50 people to over one quarter of the population there in the last decade.[39]

These trends in mobile connectivity are not just technology enhancements. They are used by governments to bring public services to their citizens, such as safe drinking water, healthcare services, online education, all provided through m-government. The 2012 United Nations E-Government Survey shows some convergence between those governments that are relatively advanced in m-government and those that have taken steps to integrate vulnerable groups.

Out of a total of 25 Member States that offer separate m-government sites, 14 also include specific sections on their national websites for vulnerable groups such as the poor, illiterate, blind, old, young, and women.

Figure 5.8 **M-government and vulnerable groups**

Countries that offer both a separate m-government and references to vulnerable groups on their national websites

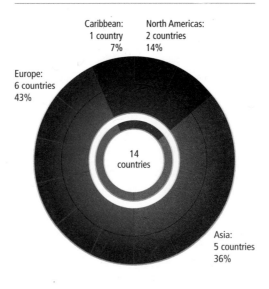

Caribbean: 1 country 7%

North Americas: 2 countries 14%

Europe: 6 countries 43%

14 countries

Asia: 5 countries 36%

Figure 5.9 **Broadband, m-government, and vulnerable groups**

Average broadband and infrastructure ratios of countries that both specify vulnerable groups in their national websites and offer a separate m-government portal

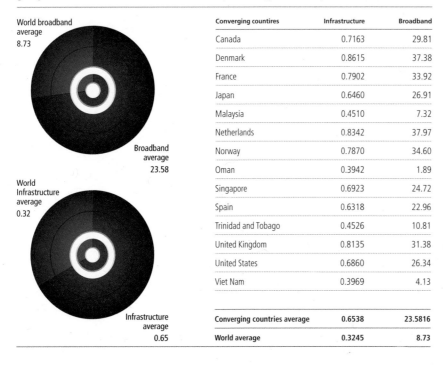

World broadband average 8.73

Broadband average 23.58

World Infrastructure average 0.32

Infrastructure average 0.65

Converging countires	Infrastructure	Broadband
Canada	0.7163	29.81
Denmark	0.8615	37.38
France	0.7902	33.92
Japan	0.6460	26.91
Malaysia	0.4510	7.32
Netherlands	0.8342	37.97
Norway	0.7870	34.60
Oman	0.3942	1.89
Singapore	0.6923	24.72
Spain	0.6318	22.96
Trinidad and Tobago	0.4526	10.81
United Kingdom	0.8135	31.38
United States	0.6860	26.34
Viet Nam	0.3969	4.13
Converging countries average	**0.6538**	**23.5816**
World average	**0.3245**	**8.73**

These countries are: Canada, Denmark, France, Japan, Malaysia, the Netherlands, Norway, Oman, Singapore, Spain, Trinidad and Tobago, the United Kingdom, the United States, and Viet Nam. From a regional perspective, Europe and Asia are again leaders, followed by North America and the Caribbean.

Relating the digital inclusion and m-government convergence to broadband and infrastructure data can yield interesting insights. The average broadband and infrastructure ratios of the converging countries over the respective world averages are high. Their infrastructure scores average about 49.6 per cent higher than the world average, and their broadband score averages about 37 per cent higher than the corresponding world average. These findings, illustrated in figure 9, point once more to the important factor of infrastructure and increased access through e- and m-government.

M-government is contributing to bridging the digital divide but is not a complete or sufficient answer per se. Access to a cell or a mobile phone is not the same thing as creating and managing one's own business or community, which a networked computer allows. Multichannel service delivery and m-government coupled with the right e-government strategies can together expand access and alleviate the challenges faced by the vulnerable groups.

5.1.4 **Location and age**

The income gap in ICT penetration and take-up parallels other parameters of digital exclusion. One of them is the rural/urban divide or the spatial digital divide. Most of the world's poor live in rural areas, and most of the world's rural populations tend to be poor. There are still about 1.4 billion people living on less than US$1.25 a day, and close to 1 billion people suffering from hunger. At least 70 per cent of them are rural.[40]

In the spatial digital divide, sectoral perspectives are particularly important. E/m-health and e/m-education in remote areas and distant markets with low population densities are more than technology upgrades. They can be effective tools in promoting sustainable development through increased access and community-oriented services that actively involve all segments of society in the formulation, design and provision of needed e-services.

The digital divide is also an age issue. Today, 45 per cent of Internet users worldwide are below the age of 25. This is equal to over one billion young women and men. Yet that leaves two billion young potential users still offline.[41] Considering the dexterity of youth in adapting to change and their propensity to innovation, they constitute a not-to-be-missed opportunity for policy makers whose aim is to build long-term digital literacy.

Connecting schools to the Internet and connecting them with each other via ICT tools are important means for getting youth on board. As the International Labour Organization warns of a global youth employment crisis, IT-based inclusion initiatives become even more critical.[42]

The elderly can also benefit from Internet training and access programmes. In their case, fighting computer anxiety and raising awareness of the benefits of usage are important. In general, medical information, tips on stretching a limited income, expansion of social support networks, and staying in touch with family[43] are among the advantages that senior citizens can seize to improve their well-being and help close the digital divide.

Online social activity is highest for teens and young adults. Currently, about 72 per cent of young adults and teens use social networking sites, compared to 40 per cent of adults age 30 and older. But even though social networking sites are still dominated by younger users, increasing trends showing more use by the elderly are promising. Lately, social media have been important tools for empowering older people. According to the Pew Research Center, the 74-plus demographic is the fastest growing user group of social networks and social networking among Internet users ages 65 and older grew 100 per cent between April 2009 and May 2010, jumping from 13 to 26 per cent.

5.2 Conclusions and policy recommendations

At the end of the day, social phenomena that can be advanced through the right economic models, political decisions and social policies include issues in sustainable development such as energy access and

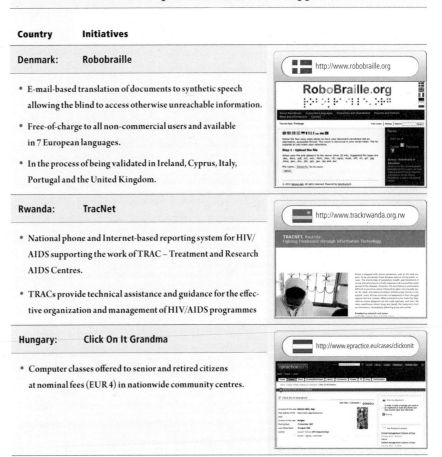

Box 5.3 Selected examples of initiatives in support of access/use

Country	Initiatives
Denmark:	**Robobraille**

- E-mail-based translation of documents to synthetic speech allowing the blind to access otherwise unreachable information.
- Free-of-charge to all non-commercial users and available in 7 European languages.
- In the process of being validated in Ireland, Cyprus, Italy, Portugal and the United Kingdom.

Rwanda:	**TracNet**

- National phone and Internet-based reporting system for HIV/AIDS supporting the work of TRAC – Treatment and Research AIDS Centres.
- TRACs provide technical assistance and guidance for the effective organization and management of HIV/AIDS programmes

Hungary:	**Click On It Grandma**

- Computer classes offered to senior and retired citizens at nominal fees (EUR 4) in nationwide community centres.

efficiency, food security and sustainable agriculture; sound water management and healthy oceans; balanced urbanization; improved resilience; and disaster management. Likewise, myriad dimensions of the digital divide, including the spread, density, use and applications of information and communication technologies are social in their construct for they often overlap with the existing socioeconomic inequalities in societies.[44] In fact, even technology itself is social because it is shaped by human action and applied in social contexts – not in a vacuum.[45]

The social nexus between the digital divide and sustainable development evokes the necessity for scholars and policy makers to consider ways of feeding one into the other in order to address the challenges facing both. For instance, if by bridging the gender digital divide, structural gender inequality can be reduced, then policy makers would have achieved two aims with a single effort.

Transforming the digital divide into digital dividends for development for the people necessitates a direct and targeted focus on vulnerable groups by e-government. Such a focus repudiates one-sided or piecemeal e-government policy-making. As also corroborated by the evidence presented in chapter 5 on usage and user needs, it requires comprehensive and hybrid approaches with integrative, multi-stakeholder and multichannel implementation frameworks.

The digital divide in e-government can best be addressed through multiple dimensions. Below is a short summary of these and associated policy recommendations:

- Access to ICTs holds educational advantages, prospects for future employment and earnings, opportunities for social and civic involvement, and potentials for increases in civic equity. The ICT advantage can be multiplied through policies targeting vulnerable groups. This implies consideration of linking e-government strategies with sustainable development policies.
- The United Nations E-Government Survey shows that governments of the world are only starting to include their vulnerable groups digitally. Such inclusion initiatives should be enhanced and spread to all levels, eventually including the local level.
- Many factors are important for overcoming the digital divide: adequate financial resources, commitment by the top leadership, a national ICT workforce, open competitive and transparent economic and political environments, education, technology transfers, and innovation. Two particularly essential issues are infrastructure and access, both within the framework of efficient, effective and citizen-centric e-government. Two related issues of importance here are broadband and m-government.
  - Broadband involves the effective use of the speed and connectivity advantages offered by technology and putting them at the service of sustainable development initiatives.
  - M-government is instrumental in increasing access to and effective use of ICTs and e-government services but hardly provides a complete answer to the digital divide. Access to a cell or a mobile phone is not the same thing as creating and managing one's own business or community, for which

a networked computer is essential. Yet, m-government is crucial in expanding the number of users and diversifying the channels for service delivery, particularly in the public sector, as documented in chapter 6.

- Three salient ICT issues specific to vulnerable groups are:
  - Indirect benefits of ICTs through intermediaries such as traditional media channels, which can access the Internet while vulnerable groups cannot;
  - The rise of social media with their more inclusive tendencies and lower technical skill requirements, which are opening up new horizons for the inclusion of vulnerable groups; and
  - The emergence of cell-only wireless users within the vulnerable groups.

All three must be on the radar screens of governments – in terms of the right infrastructure, adequate training, effective regulation and inclusive policy making.

- New skills are gaining importance. Among them are fast retrieval of information; threading between legitimate and illegitimate sources; assessing usefulness, validity and relevance of data; and use of social media and multimedia. New skills create a new type of social capital.
- The new skills and the new social capital being created are very much associated with the rising influence of online social media. Social media include and engage more diverse social groups into policy making. The lower technical know-how required to tap into these media can be an advantage for the vulnerable groups. They can be employed in the new government organizations created to manage e-participation. Prospective data analysts can be recruited from amongst the vulnerable populations.
- Connecting schools to the Internet and connecting them with each other via ICT tools are important in getting youth on board. Fighting computer anxiety is more important in the case of the elderly. Developing e-learning and suitable ICT contents for target populations is key. The right infrastructure and technology can support this process. A good example is a

device called "Simputer," which is simple and can be used by the illiterate.[46]

- Education and training in ICTs for persons with disabilities are important but not the only remedies. Often times, simple technical tweaks can be useful: adding labelling to images on the web so that screen readers can find them, or providing audio Captchas for those with different visual abilities, including the elderly.[47]

The digital divide is no longer confined to counting telephone lines or cellular subscriptions per 100 inhabitants. It is about who has the skills and the means to access information, and then uses it to create new content and engage with other citizens to better respond to their needs and aspirations. For this kind of divide to be bridged, strong economies and healthy governance systems need to encompass a direct and targeted focus on vulnerable groups, including the specific disadvantages that they face and the unique contributions that they can make in bridging the digital divide. E-government should take into account the panoply of abilities of citizens toto to effectively address this issue with an eye on supporting sustainable development for the people. ᴈ

Italianestro/Shutterstock.com

Chapter 6
**Expanding usage to realize the full
benefits of e-government**

Chapter 6

Expanding usage to realize the full benefits of e-government

Availability of online public services ('supply-side') has been the primary focus of e-government studies and policymaking, but over the past years, citizen usage of e-government services ('demand-side') has also become a priority issue. An increasing number of governments, mostly in developed countries, are making greater efforts to increase usage of services. They start by recognizing that the benefits of e-government services are very much determined by the number and type of users of these services, and the frequency of their use.

There is also mounting pressure for performance reporting on taxpayer-funded e-government investments in some countries (e.g., the United Kingdom and Canada). Measuring and reporting the usage level have become important for assessing and demonstrating the benefits of e-government initiatives and ensuring continued support.

However, the overall level of usage remains relatively low compared to traditional service delivery methods, even in countries that are making greater efforts to enhance take-up, and notwithstanding continued progress in the provision and sophistication of e-government services. Many potential benefits of e-government are thus concealed and have not been fully realized. This presents a major challenge for policymakers, who need to rethink how public services can be taken up more by citizens so as to help realize their full potential benefits, and therefore, to contribute to sustainable development for the people.

This chapter will provide an overview of the level and trends of e-service usage in countries around the world, identify key policy issues and challenges, describe recent efforts by governments as well as regional and international organizations to increase usage, identify recent efforts and emerging practices, and draw some policy conclusions.

With a view to the Rio +20 Conference in 2012, this chapter will also explore e-service usage in the particular context of sustainable development. The notion of sustainable development entails intra-generational and intergenerational equity and integration and a balanced consideration of social, economic and environmental objectives.[1]

- In connection with the environmental dimension of sustainable development, there is a rather straightforward way of connecting e-service usage and sustainable development, for example, through the environmental impact of e-service take-up. While ICT is considered to pose some risk for the environment,[2] e-government service usage is found to have positive impacts on it.[3]
- In connection with the social dimension of sustainable development, e-government usage can also be analyzed through its connection with usage differences across countries and usage divide within countries.
- Furthermore, e-service usage can be analyzed through some other less immediately discernible connections with social media as well as open government data provision and service.

First, social media presents a new avenue of not only e-service delivery but also usage. With its active use by minorities and other groups usually not active in consuming e-services delivered through other channels, it helps reduce e-service usage divide within countries, hence fostering socially inclusive development.

Second, open data is an increasingly important source of information service provided by governments and other entities and presents opportunities for everyone to freely use, reuse and integrate various data pertaining to socio-economic and environmental dimensions of sustainable development.

6.1 E-service usage: The current landscape

This section describes the level of usage and its development trends and highlight different growth rates between e-government availability and take-up. It will also outline current levels and trends of citizen take-up of e-government services, as well as types and stages of services used.

6.1.1 Low level of usage

There is no comprehensive data available to assess citizen usages at the global level. Data are not yet systematically collected and uniformly available across countries around the world. There are only a few studies of some developing countries (e.g., Bahrain, Pakistan, Nigeria, Saudi Arabia, gulf region countries, and Bangladesh).[4] According to them, the level of e-government usage is generally low, even as it is in most advanced countries. In EU27 countries, the average usage rate is 32 per cent, and in OECD countries, the average usage rate in 2010 was only around 40 per cent, notwithstanding recent increases in citizen take-up of e-services.[5]

That said, in some countries, the Internet has become a frequently used channel of public service take-up. For example, in Australia it has even become the channel most often used. Two in five citizens are using Internet to contact government. Moreover, given a choice, four in five citizens would prefer to contact government by Internet instead of by phone.[6] Still, this is more the exception than the norm. For example, in Lithuania, a country with Internet penetration of almost 70 per cent in e-service usage, e-government usage is not growing all that fast. Two thirds (66 per cent) of the country's residents have never used e-government services.[7]

The realities and challenges of measurement are that outcome and usage indicators are more difficult to develop than e-government access and readiness indicators. Nevertheless, the United Nations E-Government Survey 2012, with its global data, presents valuable indications on the level of usage. Though only from the perspective of potential – not actual – use by citizens, the Survey can help estimate the extent to which e-government service is used.

Since it is not always possible to measure actual usage, the Survey assesses how many non-government websites link to the government portal. According to the Survey data, 144 countries (75 per cent of 193 United Nations Member States) have more than 10 websites that link to the government portal. This is an indirect measurement of the usage of these countries' government portal by non-government or private sector entities.

6.1.2 Gap between e-service availability and usage

E-government usage has thus far been limited and has not kept up with the fast growing provision and availability of e-services. According to recent research commissioned by the European Commission, the different speed and growth rate between e-service availability and e-service take-up is substantial (see figure 6.1).[8]

Low usage limits the reach and impact of e-government services, and more needs to be done if governments are to successfully leverage e-government to improve efficiency and effectiveness and realize other benefits. The recent financial and economic crisis has also shown that e-government projects and realization of their benefits are important for effective crisis response.[9]

The indicator of e-government availability shows the percentage of the 20 basic services, as

Figure 6.1 E-government usage growth rate lagging behind e-government availability growth rate (2005 – 2010)

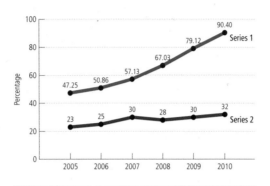

Source: Eurostat data on e-government usage by individuals (October, 2007); The User Challenge Benchmarking — The Supply of Online Public Services, 7th Measurement (September 2007), prepared by Cap Gemini for European Commission.

identified by the EU (see series 1), which are fully available in EU27 countries. E-government usage is measured by the percentage of individuals aged 16 to 74 who have used the internet for interacting with public authorities (see series 2).

6.1.3 Limited types of e-services used

The most frequently provided (as well as used) types of services are information services, which are the first step of sophistication of e-government initiatives. Many countries remain at this initial stage of e-government provision and usage. Online transactional services, whether they involve payment or not, are being provided less often – and are much less used.

As far as provision of e-services is concerned, the United Nations E-Government Survey 2012 data show the limited extent of e-transactional service availability. All 193 United Nations Member States provide some information services – except for Libya, Central African Republic and Guinea. But a much smaller number of countries provide transactional services with regard to environment, labour, social welfare, finance, health, education, and other sectors (see figure 6.2). It was not

Box 6.1 **Benefit of e-tax payment: Convenience and ease of paying taxes**

One good example of tangible and substantial benefits that may accrue from using e-services is online tax payment, which is convenient and easy to do. E-payment of taxes is growing in popularity. According to the United Nations E-Government Survey 2012 data, citizens in 77 countries (40 per cent of United Nations Member States) can now pay income taxes online.

Many countries around the world suffer from extremely long tax processing time (e.g., nearly ten weeks in Kenya). But the report, *Paying Taxes 2011: The Global Picture* found that those countries that are advanced in using e-payment do well on a number of tax payment indicators, improving their ease of paying taxes. Recently, developing countries have also benefited, with Tunisia, Cape Verde and Sao Tome and Principe having improved most in the ease of paying taxes through e-tax payment.[10] ◆

unexpected to find that many transactional services are concentrated in finance and other sectors rather than the other five analyzed.

However, in some of these countries (e.g., Mexico), citizen take-up of e-transaction services is rapidly increasing. According to the 2012 Survey, 66 countries, approximately one third of United Nations Member States, even provide an online tracking system to ascertain the status of online transactions such as grant applications, which indicates that they acknowledge the importance of transactional services and their monitoring.

> The current situation is characterized by a substantial gap between e-government supply and demand, and generally low levels of e-service take-up.

Figure 6.2 **Transaction services: Countries providing online payment facilities in different sectors**

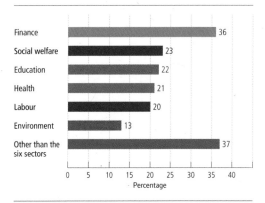

Sector	Percentage
Finance	36
Social welfare	23
Education	22
Health	21
Labour	20
Environment	13
Other than the six sectors	37

That said, it is important to note that even in countries such as the United States, where e-transaction services are growing rapidly, citizens still use the government website much more for information than for transactions.[11] Thus, the current situation is characterized by the generally low e-service usage level, a substantial gap between the e-government 'supply' side and 'demand' side, and the limited types of e-services used.

This presents a major challenge for policymakers in their efforts to improve citizens' take-up of e-services and user satisfaction. They not only need to increase the overall level of e-service usage, but also to close existing gaps and significantly move usage beyond the realm of information to more complex transactions and services such as e-consultation. According to the United Nations e-Government Survey 2012, online e-consultation features provided most by countries are: discussion forums (78 countries), bulletin boards (76 countries), petition tools (42 countries) and voting tools (18 countries). But as far as the demand side is concerned, there are no comprehensive data.

6.2 Challenges, recent efforts and opportunities

This section builds on identification and analysis of these overall challenges and explore more specific sets of challenges and policy implications related to sustainable development by:

- Examining factors affecting usage and multi-facetted challenges (section 6.2.1);
- Analyzing the current e-government usage differences and divides across and within countries for an inclusive approach (section 6.2.2);

Box 6.2 **311 Service: Trust, transparency and service request map of New York City**

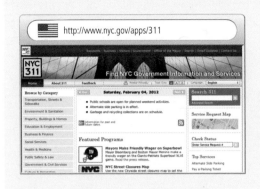

This kind of positive cycle of interaction may stand the 311 service request map of New York City in good stead, as well as other initiatives that aim to increase transparency and public service usage. The foremost objective of this recently launched map is increased transparency. It is identified as "probably the most aggressive" in the United States in this regard and also as offering the most detailed information about 311.[14] It has interactive mapping capabilities and provides information on and access to location-specific service requests made through 311. Most importantly, it enables real-time tracking of handling of service requests, thereby enhancing transparency and accountability of public service delivery.[15] ◆

- Exploring the potential of social media, in particular, to foster social inclusion and increase usage (section 6.2.3); and
- Exploring the opportunities for integration of economic, social and environmental data through governments' open data services and their take-up by citizens for engagement in better and more integrated public service delivery (section 6.2.4).

6.2.1 **Multifaceted challenges of e-service usage**

There are wide-ranging factors affecting usage and challenges that policymakers need to identify and address in their efforts to increase citizen take-up of e-government services. These factors affect user motivations and satisfactions underlying intentions to use e-government services, and hence affect the level of usage.

The important factors range from convenience to concerns over trust, security and privacy. And the same factors may have different impacts in different country situations. Based on this recognition, policymakers need to develop a concrete operational strategy in a manner that maximizes positive and minimizes negative usage factors.

Convenience is the dominant factor and generally understood as enjoying 24-7 accesses and saving travel. Convenience is often found as a stronger incentive than mere cost-saving, even in developing countries (e.g., Malaysia, India, and Albania).[12]

Privacy and security concerns are also important. They potentially work as barriers impeding e-service usage as they prevent users from trusting and therefore using e-government services.[13] In fact, they are often mentioned as a major reason for non-usage of e-government services.

Lack of clear policy statements on privacy and security are likely to discourage citizens from using e-government services. The problem is that, according to United Nations E-Government Survey 2012 data, less than half of the United Nations Member States provide such statements. Government websites of 79 countries (41 per cent of 193 United Nations Member States) provide a privacy statement (including developing countries). Only 39 countries (20 per cent of United Nations Member States) have a visible security policy with a secure link feature clearly indicated on their government website (see figure 6.3).

This presents a problem, as usage of e-services is often associated with security and privacy assurances provided to users, as shown in several empirical studies in both developed and developing countries (e.g., Australia, Germany, Mauritius, Jordan, Saudi

> Online privacy and security concerns may be preventing users from trusting and therefore using e-government services.

Figure 6.3 **Number of countries with privacy statement and security policy online**

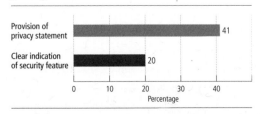

The more citizen-centric online and mobile services are, the higher the level of uptake.

Arabia [city of Medina], and United Republic of Tanzania).[16] In Australia, security presents a critical issue for those using e-services. The majority (83 per cent) of Australian citizens contacting the government by Internet would even prefer to re-enter their personal information each time they use a website rather than have their details stored by the government agency.[17]

Besides privacy and security, trust in using e-government services is also critical. And there is a positive and important cycle of interaction between trust and transparency. As online transparency leads to greater trust, citizens are likely to use e-government more often.[18]

Furthermore, usability is a factor that has important bearings on e-service usage. Good usability and perceived ease of use increase e-service usage. Usability can be indicated by questions such as whether the site is easy to find and use, well maintained, up-to-date and robust. Government websites with poor technical design often present usability problems in terms of the initial search and the internal navigation. Having robust search engines is particularly important, as they are the most common entry point for government website interactions.[19]

Organizing and updating government websites are also important and at the same time challenging, especially in developing countries, even though several basic changes to the layout of government websites could improve their organization. At present, the level of usability is generally low, at least as measured by some indicators such as availability of a glossary of words helping users understand the content of government websites, and tutorials guiding users to access e-services. The United Nations E-Government Survey 2012 data show, for example, that websites of only 28 countries (15 per cent of 193 United Nations Member States) contain a glossary of words. The situation is somewhat better with respect to the availability of a tutorial: 52 countries (27 per cent of United Nations Member States) provide a tutorial on their national portal guiding users to access to e-services.

In addition, citizen-centricity and focus on user needs are highly relevant to e-service usage. The more citizen-centric personalized e-government services are, with strong user focus, the more their uptake is likely to increase.[20] Citizens tend to prefer

services focused on their personal needs. Interest among different citizens and citizen groups in using specific e-services depends on their personal situation. For example, e-services needed by unemployed people are very different from those services needed by retirees.

To make e-services more relevant to citizens, some governments have begun to identify and segment their base and group their services around citizens' needs and situations based on a life-event or themed approach. For example, the Norwegian Agency for Public Management and e-Government integrates the personalized, one-stop self-service portal 'Miside' with the existing 'Noreg.no'. The new Noreg.no (http://www.noreg.no) aims to present information and e-services based on the "life event approach."[21] The Singaporean Government uses a proactive "sense and respond" approach to anticipate citizens' demands and provide integrated services geared towards users' needs.[22] *OneStopGov*, an important, high impact pilot project funded by the European Commission, aims to integrate disparate e-government services around life events for more personalized services.

These initiatives indicate a shift towards a user or citizen-centric approach to e-government service – from what services governments can provide to what citizens really need.[23] The resulting important aspect of citizen centricity in e-government is usefulness and relevance to citizens' needs. Another aspect is usability, again, whether the site is designed for easy use by citizens.

Citizen-centric service delivery with user focus is a complex issue with many perspectives that need to be analyzed. For example, its implementation requires back-office integration of various government agencies and a whole-of-government perspective (see chapter 3 on whole-of-government). It also requires a well-designed multichannel service delivery strategy that offers a choice of online or offline channels and the possibility of using the appropriate channel to access e-services (see chapter 4 on multichannel service delivery)

Closely related issues are citizen satisfaction and feedback incorporation. According to a comprehensive study and statistics on United States e-government satisfaction, citizen-centric and user needs focussed services will improve citizen satisfaction. Satisfaction then increases the likelihood that the citizen will return to the website (by 51 per cent), use it as a primary resource as opposed to utilizing more costly channels (by 79 per cent), or recommend the site to others (by 81 per cent).[24] Government agencies therefore need to make explicit efforts to increase citizen satisfaction and incorporate this as an important factor in policy design for usage increase.

The Dubai Government's recent launch of an online customer satisfaction survey is a step in the right direction. This is particularly encouraging, as there is limited user satisfaction monitoring in many countries. Even in Europe, not even one third of government websites can be rated and commented upon by the user.[25]

At the global level, United Nations E-Government Survey 2012 data provide some further insights into the limited efforts made by governments to garner and report on feedback by citizens on e-service usage. The national websites of 25 countries (13 per cent of 193 United Nations Member States) provide outcome on feedback received from citizens concerning the improvement of their services, whereas the website provides information on citizen usage in the form of basic web statistics, like hits or views, in 47 countries (24 per cent of United Nations Member States). In 18 countries, citizens can tag, assess and rank content on the website, which feeds back to government or to other users. Governments report on citizen website usage in the form of online services in the same number of countries (see figure 6.4).

6.2.2 Usage divide across and within countries

A real risk of divide exists – not only in Internet usage but also in e-government service usage. Governments need to effectively address these divides and differences for an inclusive approach and socially sustainable development.

Usage divide across countries: The differences in e-service usage among countries seem very much driven by infrastructure and connectivity, as citizen uptake of e-government services heavily depends

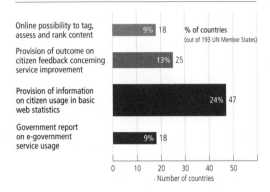

Figure 6.4 Governments' efforts to garner and report on usage feedback

on broadband Internet connectivity. Research conducted by OECD indicates the importance of broadband access for e-government usage. Figure 6.5 shows broadband-dependent e-government usage in 2008.

When it comes to e-government, broadband connectivity is critical, even in the most highly developed countries such as those in Europe. Government service usage is found to be very much contingent on fast and reliable Internet connection.[26]

Developing countries (e.g., Malaysia, Viet Nam) have shown that a higher level of broadband penetration is a pre-requisite for any governmental effort to increase citizen usage of e-government service.[27] This presents an important challenge for developing countries, where broadband penetration remains limited.

A real risk of divide exists, both in Internet access and e-service usage, which governments need to address for the sake of inclusive and socially sustainable development.

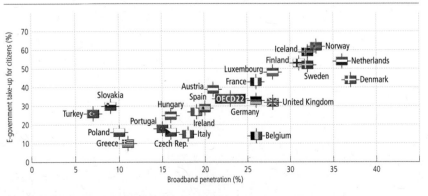

Figure 6.5 Relationship between broadband penetration and citizen uptake of e-government services (2008)

Source: OECD Broadband statistics (http://www.oecd.org/sti/ict/broadband) and Eurostat (2008)

Box 6.3 United States: Fostering social inclusion and increasing e-service usage through social media

Nearly one third of United States Internet users are using social media to access e-services. According to the latest United States study, "embrace" of social media by the United States government seems to have "particular appeal" to minority groups, low-income individuals, women and other groups that have historically lagged behind in their use of e-services. These groups all use social media at a rate similar to that of other citizens, leading to a smaller gap among different socio-economic groups than through other forms of online information and service delivery.[29] ◆

At the same time, the power of widespread mobile technology offers a good opportunity to extend public services to citizens, especially in developing countries. It is also likely to increase usage of public services, as they can be accessed and used by citizens everywhere and at all times. Mobile technology is also becoming increasingly important in the multichannel mix available to citizens. But at the same time, it is important to note that there are technical constraints that can limit m-service usage, and that mobile broadband technology is still in its early stages.

Thus, the winning approach is getting the right mix and balance of mobile technology and broadband Internet connectivity – with a clear focus on the next major step, namely, putting a broadband vision in place and "repeating the 'mobile miracle' for broadband Internet,"as stated in the latest ITU report.[28]

Usage divide within countries: Unequal access is likely to limit and fragment e-government usage, which is the case in many countries around the world. In the face of this reality, an important challenge of e-service take-up for sustainable development is to ensure that e-service actually reaches and is used by as many citizens as possible and minimizes marginalization of certain groups. This requires effectively increasing usage of e-services by all, including the poor and disadvantaged groups. After all, sustainable development is as much about economic and social inclusion as about environment and natural resource conservation and preservation.

E-government services are often used to a different extent by different citizens. For example, average usage of online information services in European countries is 28 per cent. The divergence is most pronounced between citizens with high education (53 per cent) and those with no or low education (12 per cent), followed by age, occupation and finally, living area. The most active e-government users are those with high education, living in densely populated areas, self-employed and aged 24-30. It is interesting to observe that members of the youngest group (aged 16-24), which are usually the most active in Internet use, are not the most active users of e-services, perhaps because they have less need for public administrative procedures.[30]

The least active user groups also include people living in sparsely populated areas, retired and other inactive and/or elderly citizens, and disabled persons. The problem is further compounded by the fact that these disadvantaged groups are often the very ones that require much interaction with government (e.g., to obtain social welfare benefits), but are likely to miss out on what e-government has to offer.[31] It is therefore all the more important to urgently address the usage gap. (For a related theme, see chapter 5 on bridging the digital divide.)

6.2.3 Expanding usage through social media

There has been a drastic rise of social media (e.g., Facebook, Twitter, Micro Blog, VK), which continue to grow rapidly, including through the use of mobile technology. In the United States, social media usage has reached a milestone in 2011; two-thirds of adult Internet users (65 per cent) were using a social networking site, which means that half of all adults (50 per cent) do so.[32] In this regard, the United States is the top-ranking country, followed by Poland, the United Kingdom and the Republic of Korea, where at least four in ten adult citizens use such sites.[33]

At the regional level, in Asia and the Pacific, social media have seen unprecedented growth, dominating the region's internet usage.[34] In the European Union, more than one third of all citizens use a social networking site. This is true both for countries with high (e.g., the Netherlands) and low (e.g., Latvia) internet take-up.[35] However, social media usage in some other regions is still low. For example, the country average for Facebook user penetration in the Arab region was only 5.94 per cent at the end of 2010.[36]

Government use of social media – though not a prerequisite for open government – is often highlighted as a good example of open government, which builds on principles of citizen centricity and information transparency.[37]

Government agencies are now using social media to improve public services, reduce costs and increase transparency. Through these media, they can inform citizens, promote their services, seek public views and feedback, and monitor satisfaction with the services they offer so as to improve their quality. As social media enable two-way communication in real time, government agencies can quickly engage citizens as co-producers of services, not just passive recipients. The latest study found that 66 per cent of all United States Government agencies currently use some form of social networking.[38]

At the global level, assessing the presence of social media in government portals of 193 United Nations Member States, the United Nations E-Government Survey 2012 finds that government websites of 78 Member States (40 per cent) provide a statement "follow us on Facebook or Twitter." The survey data also show that 14 country government websites (7 per cent) provide tools to obtain raw (non-deliberative) public opinion through chat rooms or an IM feature (see figure 6.6).

More than half of 78 countries providing a statement 'follow us on Facebook or Twitter' are from the developing world and from different regions, even in most underdeveloped region like Africa. Table 6.1 shows the list of these countries.

Figure 6.6 **Government websites and social media**

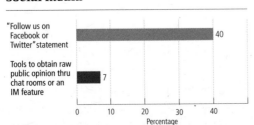

	Percentage
"Follow us on Facebook or Twitter" statement	40
Tools to obtain raw public opinion thru chat rooms or an IM feature	7

Table 6.1 **List of countries with government websites providing a statement 'follow us on Facebook or Twitter'**

Africa	Americas	Asia	Europe	Oceania
Côte d'Ivoire	Antigua and Barbuda	Afghanistan	Andorra	Kiribati
Democratic Republic of the Congo	Argentina	Azerbaijan	Austria	Vanuatu
Equatorial Guinea	Belize	Bahrain	Belgium	
Ethiopia	Brazil	Brunei Darussalam	Croatia	
Ghana	Canada	Georgia	Finland	
Guinea-Bissau	Chile	Iraq	France	
Morocco	Colombia	Israel	Germany	
Nigeria	Cuba	Japan	Greece	
Somalia	Dominican Republic	Malaysia	Hungary	
South Africa	Ecuador	Mongolia	Italy	
Sudan	El Salvador	Oman	Latvia	
Tunisia	Grenada	Pakistan	Liechtenstein	
	Guatemala	Philippines	Lithuania	
	Honduras	Qatar	Luxembourg	
	Mexico	Republic of Korea	Netherlands	
	Panama	Saudi Arabia	Norway	
	Paraguay	Singapore	Portugal	
	Peru	Thailand	Russian Federation	
	United States	United Arab Emirates	Spain	
	Uruguay	Uzbekistan	Sweden	
	Venezuela		Switzerland	
			Ukraine	
			United Kingdom	

Table 6.2 shows which 14 countries provide the tools in order to obtain raw public opinion through chat rooms or an IM feature.

Social media hold much potential for generally increasing citizen usage of e-services. In some countries, social media has actively been used by citizens to keep themselves informed about government. Moreover, these media help to foster social inclusiveness by reducing the e-service usage divide among different socio-economic groups.

How to effectively leverage these opportunities that social media provide is now becoming an important public service issue. This is all the more important, as social media provide new, additional avenues for the delivery of governments' information and other public services and can also amplify their impact.

Table 6.2 **List of countries providing chat rooms or an IM feature**

Bolivia (Plurinational State of)	Qatar
Canada	Republic of Korea
Chile	Saudi Arabia
Colombia	United Arab Emirates
Mexico	United Kingdom
Netherlands	United States
Poland	Uruguay

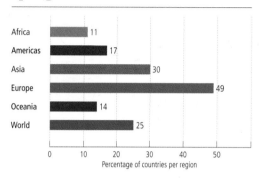

Figure 6.7 Government websites providing a statement that promotes open government data initiative

Percentage of countries per region

Even in developing countries (e.g., Nepal) embrace of and active engagement by government agencies in social media, and citizens' positive response, can help increase citizen take-up of e-services, which helps to create the critical mass required to generate momentum.[39] Furthermore, it is interesting to note the indirect effect of social media on e-service usage. It seems that greater social media usage (through increased transparency) may increase trust, and thus also increase e-service take-up.

6.2.4 Use of open data and public service co-production

A number of governments around the world (e.g., United Kingdom, United States and increasingly developing countries) have been opening previously 'locked-up' government-held data sets, providing raw data to their citizens. And citizens have actively taken up and made use of these data.

Open data is becoming an important government-provided raw information service that citizens can freely use, repurpose, create value out of and even co-produce.

Open data offers new opportunities for integration of economic, social and environmental data – often in an easily accessible, localized and visualized format. In the end, sustainable development is all about integration, with balanced consideration of these three pillars, and open data can facilitate this integration.

The likely integration effect comes from breaking down proprietary silos, freely available data users examine, combine and overlay maps. The recently launched Kenyan Government's open data website (http://www.opendata.go.ke), which is one of the most comprehensive portals in sub-Saharan Africa, holds the potential to generate this integration. Its data are drawn from several sources (e.g., Ministries of Finance, Planning, Health and Education and the Kenya National Bureau of Statistics). The website is organized by six sectors – education, energy, health, water and sanitation, population and poverty.

The new, consolidated and combined database, based on data from these sectors and layered over a map, can yield useful insights into understanding complex issues, often requiring the integration of different sustainable development data sets. A good example is the examination of the effect of access to drinking water on children's school attendance, which requires the integration of data pertaining to social and environmental pillars of sustainable development, at the least.[40]

Open data furthermore offers opportunities for citizen input, feedback and transparency, which will increase the chances for success of improved public services and service uptakes under the right circumstances. There are cases of the transparency of data driving productivity and service improvements.

For example, open data and transparency were instrumental in reducing costs of employment services in Germany and restoring public confidence in the relevant agencies, where lack of comprehensive data on customer histories and the labour market had hitherto prevented understanding of the impact of services and their value. The challenge was to integrate 11 datasets of different structure, format and data quality into one.[41] *Openly Local* in the United Kingdom is another good example of how open data can motivate citizens to engage with their local public services and government, enabling more efficient, better quality services with more choices (as described in the British Open Public Services White Paper).[42]

In this connection, preliminary, ongoing research by the United Nations Department of Economic and Social Affairs provides a quick, initial picture of open government initiatives in countries around the world. According to the research, Europe is the leader well above the world average. Africa, and then Oceania are well below the world average.

Beyond transparency and service improvement, open data affords the possibility to users to co-produce e-government information and services. Users of the service are here considered not just mere consumers and passive recipients of services but valuable assets and resources that can collaborate with government providers to produce services that are in their interest.[43]

From the usage point of view, this has an important implication. Co-production has the effect of ultimately blurring the distinction between service providers and user communities. In fact, it is even argued that co-production can transform mainstream public services into more effective ones as it offers a radically new approach by sharing the design and delivery of services with users.[44]

Figure 6.8 **FOI laws in countries around the world: Global view**

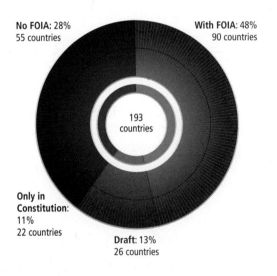

No FOIA: 28%
55 countries

With FOIA: 48%
90 countries

193 countries

Only in Constitution: 11%
22 countries

Draft: 13%
26 countries

Source: UNDESA (2011), Future Government: Global Perspective in Connection to Open Government. UNPACS data.

Clear examples of co-produced services come from emergency situations with crisis mapping (e.g., OpenStreetMaps, Sinsai.Info). Here, a mash-up map with aggregated data enables users to view and add data. The rise of open data has created e/m-services for assisting with public emergencies, accelerating the ability of communities of volunteers to

Figure 6.9 **Freedom of Information in different regions of the world**

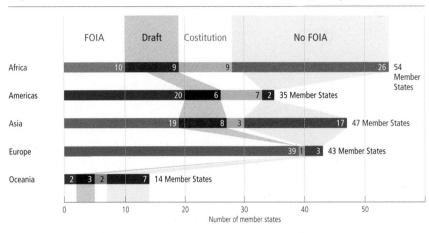

Source: UNDESA (2011), Future Government: Global Perspective in Connection to Open Government. UNPACS data.

co-produce public services, which tend to be faster and more responsive in emergency situations than those provided by government agencies alone.

In this context, freedom of Information (FOI) legislation warrants attention. FOI is an important cornerstone of open data use because the latter can only take place when there is a right to access government information. FOI laws provide for the disclosure of government-held information. They define the ways in which the public may access information – namely that citizens may gain access in principle, but with some specific exemptions set forth in the statute.

According to initial and ongoing UNDESA research, over the past 10 years, an increasing number of countries, including developing countries, have recognized the right to information through the adoption of a wave of FOI laws.

In 1990, only 13 countries had adopted national FOI laws, whereas there are currently 90 countries out of 193 United Nations Member States (48 per cent) that have adopted such laws around the world. At the same time, 55 countries (28 per cent) have no FOI legislation. There are 22 countries (11 per cent) with only an FOI article in the constitution, and 26 countries (13 per cent) with relevant draft legislation.

FOI laws vary in scope from country to country. Most of them do not contain specific legislation for providing open government data catalogues. Europe is the leader in terms of open data legislation as seen in figure 6.9, depicting the regional breakdown.

6.3 Increasing e-service usage: Policy conclusions

In their efforts to increase e-government usage and citizen satisfaction, policy makers are faced with multi-faceted policy challenges, issues and opportunities underlying e-government usage. Without a doubt, there is increasing policy emphasis on take-up of e-services.

Notwithstanding the many efforts made in this direction, there is still a general lack of a clear strategy to facilitate e-government service usage as well as evaluation frameworks to assess citizens' needs and expectations. To effectively increase usage of e-services, particularly in the context of sustainable development, more effective policies and strategies need to be put in place to help overcome usage differences and divides, increase awareness and promotional activities, focus on user needs, further explore and exploit the potentials of social media and open data, and provide additional incentives for e-service usage.

Designing and providing citizen-centric services with user focus

Users and their needs must be placed at the centre of e-service design and delivery to improve usage. E-services can be better tailored to meet the specific needs and priorities of different users. To this end, governments should enhance their capacity to garner, monitor and incorporate users' feedback, satisfaction and needs.

In particular, in order to foster personalized e-services and identify needs and gaps in e-service delivery, it is important to collect disaggregated data on different citizen groups, analyze and monitor their specific usage patterns, and share the data with citizens. This analysis should form the basis for resource allocation and the development of more personalized e-services for greater usage opportunities. A study on ICT access centres in Armenia found that lack of such data collection and monitoring, indeed, impedes additional interventions that could have addressed gender, income and other barriers to access and usage.[45]

Narrowing usage divide across and within countries

E-service usage difference across countries: Even the strong broadband dependency of e-service usage, governments should pay much more attention to broadband infrastructure development. This would help overcome usage divide across countries. They should also fully utilize mobile technology prevalent in developing countries, recognizing that mobile networks also help expand broadband Internet access in the developing world.

In this connection, it is important to highlight ongoing work of the United Nations Broadband Commission for Digital Development, which has set a target of connecting half the world's poor citizens to broadband Internet by 2015.

Many relevant organizations are involved in this work. In particular, UNDESA contributes to the Commission's work on broadband and e-government as a member of its Working Group on E-government and Public-Private Partnerships. The objective of the group is to highlight the opportunities associated with e-government and PPPs in the future development of broadband. UNDESA supports broadband deployment, diffusion and promotion as a medium that will usher in greater efficiency and effectiveness in e-government, which will then ultimately make possible the faster diffusion and utilization of broadband by all citizens in the world.

E-service usage divide within countries: Similarly, governments also need to actively explore ways to make broadband Internet more widely available to their citizens so as to increase their e-service usage within countries. However, according to the United Nations E-Government Survey 2012 data, only a limited number of countries (24) promote free access to government services via the Internet through means such as kiosks or free Wi-Fi. Some countries, such as Brazil, make a concerted effort to address this problem. The Treasury of the State of Bahia successfully provides public access points (pontos de autoatendimento) to enable some citizens without private Internet access to use the whole range of its online tax services.[46] This shows that there are effective ways to make broadband Internet more widely available to citizens, so as to increase their e-service usage.

At the operational level, prioritization and promotion of some services (which are potentially more conducive to sustainable development than others) will help to narrow the divide within countries. For example, broad based services are likely to have greater sustainable development impact (through greater socio-economic inclusion) than those catering to needs of a few privileged citizens or driven primarily by short-term economic efficiency considerations. These services include fields such as agriculture (e.g., Online Delivery of Land Titles to Rural Farmers in Karnataka, India) and health (e.g., Electronic Birth Registration in Rajshahi, Bangladesh).

In particular, effective provision and promotion of citizen uptake of e-government services related to agriculture will have a more direct and substantial impact on inclusion for a vast majority of citizens in poor countries. For example, in sub-Saharan Africa, 65 per cent of the population relies on subsistence farming but has little access to vital, agricultural information.

Seen from the social inclusiveness perspective, it is also vital for governments not to disenfranchise a large number of citizens; various channels for a multitude of access possibilities for different groups, such as senior citizens, need to be provided. There is also a need to strike the right balance between online and offline service delivery, and to ensure that there are parallel service channels – at least until the access and usage gap is narrowed. The idea is to provide multiple access possibilities (see chapter 4 on multichannel service delivery). Some governments, such as that of Slovenia, have successfully explored multichannels for accessing e-services. Employment Service of Slovenia is a multichannel e-counselling service that helps individuals make decisions about career paths and job search activities.

User segmentation as a related practice: To address existing usage divides among different groups, it is useful to separate citizens and potential e-service users into groups and sub-groups according to their specific usage gaps, needs and concerns. Such segmentation is needed for implementation of a socially inclusive strategy aimed at increasing uptake of e-services by as many citizens as possible.

The starting point for policy makers is to conduct a deeper analysis and identify actual needs of different groups and sub-groups, and then move on to devise measures taking into account

specific needs. This means that such differentiation measures need to be in place in addition to general measures (e.g., Internet literacy promotion) for the general, low-usage groups. For example, according to an empirical study conducted in Germany, service complexity and concerns about data security are most critical for e-service usage by the elderly and this necessitates the design of less complex e-government services along with general measures.[47]

Leveraging social media for greater e-service take-up

Governments need to make concerted efforts to exploit the full potential of social media to deliver messages and information services, promote awareness for greater citizen e-service take-up, and garner valuable user feedback and suggestions for service improvements.

This implies that governments need to leverage social media for greater e-government service usage by citizens, including in particular, the poor, the elderly and other disadvantaged groups. As social media become widespread and mainstream, the strategic engagement of all groups in this new e-service usage channel becomes even more important.

Governments should therefore strengthen their presence on existing social media sites and promote e-services, particularly those particularly conducive to sustainable development, while also trying out new channels and sources of feedback, and new platforms and networks to bring together citizens and stakeholders. Thereby, governments can also share information about successful e-service take-up and utilization to further encourage citizens' usage of e-services.

Using open data for better public service and greater usage

Open data and integration of three pillars: Exploiting open data for sustainable development (particularly as applied to the environment) is challenging. Sustainable development is about the integration of economic, social and environmental dimensions, but the problem is that e-government applications are still not used in an integrated fashion. Governments need to actively make available to the public, more data that are related to all three pillars of sustainable development, encourage an integrated analysis and creative use and reuse of government information.

Getting the co-production right: Getting the co-production right will help develop better public services. Governments thus need to make space for co-production in government services and focus on creating a framework within which all citizens can become both users and producers of e-services. It would also be useful to find examples of co-production to see how open data is used in practice.

Issues to address: Among the realities of open data availability is the fact that some governments are slow to provide essential information. Important issues that warrant a lot of attention from policy makers striving to get the most out of open data and facilitate e-service usage include: copyright protection, privacy law, existence of quality data standardization, digitization of data, basic collection and standardization of data practices across a country, and FOI legislation.

Increasing public awareness and promoting e-services

Governments should pro-actively engage themselves in activities to increase awareness of, promote and popularize e-service usage. Otherwise, despite the high number of e-services available, their usage levels may remain below expectations.

How many and to what extent do governments around the world make efforts to increase e-service usage through such activities? Implementation of such public awareness is increasing and promotional activities are relatively easy. Nevertheless, according to United Nations E-Government Survey 2012 data, only a limited number of governments have portals with a self-promotional section (e.g., one that asks users to link to the site or provides information on events related to promoting the portal (43 countries or 22 per cent of United Nations Member States).

Against this background, practices are emerging among e-government policy makers in some countries to increase public awareness and promote e-services. These include the Dubai Government's various channels and mechanisms for e-service awareness,[48] the Republic of Korea's effort to use and promote the "Pororo" figure as

an "e-government publicity ambassador," and the United States Department of the Interior's e-government strategy.[49] However, as far as current promotional activities are concerned, the situation is generally not very good. In fact, even developed countries lack marketing and promotion strategies and only about half of government institutions communicate their e-government goals and benefits to citizens and businesses.[50]

Some countries go beyond promotion of their e-services and offer additional, sometimes substantial, incentives. Several countries (e.g., France, Ireland and Singapore) offer an extended filing period for users of online tax filing services. In the United States, the *Free File* website allows most taxpayers to prepare and file their taxes online for free and get their refunds in half the time it would take to process their paper returns.[51]

Dealing with measurement difficulties

In general, measuring usage is hard and obtaining pertinent data is much more difficult than measuring the supply side of e-government. Collecting comparable usage data across countries is very difficult. The Task Group on e-Government of Partnership on Measuring ICT for Development, launched in 2004, coordinates international efforts in this area, sets standards and harmonizes ICT statistics at the global level.

In order to capture, at least in part, the extent to which citizens actually use e-services and achieve internationally comparable statistics, the Task Group is currently working on e-government usage indicators. The Economic Commission for Africa, Economic Commission for Latin America and the Caribbean, and International Telecommunication Union have prepared a framework for developing e-government indicators along with a set of globally comparative e-government core indicators and statistical standards.

Measurements need to reflect more accurately citizens' experience and satisfaction. Some governments use web analytics, customer views and customer experience replication, but there is not yet any international consensus on how these measures could be applied.[52] In view of this difficulty, governments need to urgently improve on usage-related data and measurement (including user satisfaction measurement in particular), and build capacity by providing training on how to assess and measure user take-up of e-services and develop assessment frameworks. They can benefit from cross-learning opportunities and good practices for more accurate measurement.

Measuring e-government take-up is no doubt challenging, but also very important. Why? After all, without a clear understanding of how to measure e-government usage, it is difficult to measure the impact of e-government. Increasing efforts to measure usage therefore constitutes a good step forward towards gauging the extent of e-government success and failure, and evaluating progress towards development for the people. ଔ

Annexes

Eliot Sela

Annexes

Annexes

Survey methodology

The United Nations e-government development index (EGDI) is a composite indicator measuring the willingness and capacity of national administrations to use information and communication technology to deliver public services. It is based on a comprehensive survey of the online presence of all 193 Member States, which assesses the technical features of national websites as well as e-government policies and strategies applied in general and by specific sectors for delivery of essential services.

The assessment conducted by UNDESA rates the e-government performance of countries relative to one another as opposed to being an absolute measurement. The results are tabulated and combined with a set of indicators embodying a country's capacity to participate in the information society, without which e-government development efforts are of limited immediate utility.

Although the basic model has remained consistent, the precise meaning of these values varies from one edition of the Survey to the next as understanding of the potential of e-government changes and the underlying technology evolves. This is an important distinction because it also implies that it is a comparative framework that seeks to encompass various approaches that may evolve over time instead of advocating a linear path with an absolute goal.

Mathematically, the EGDI is a weighted average of three normalized scores on the most important dimensions of e-government, namely: scope and quality of online services, development status of telecommunication infrastructure, and inherent human capital. Each of these sets of indexes is itself a composite measure that can be extracted and analyzed independently.

$$EGDI = (\tfrac{1}{3} * online\ service\ index) +$$
$$(\tfrac{1}{3} * telecommunication\ index) +$$
$$(\tfrac{1}{3} * human\ capital\ index)$$

Prior to the normalization of the three component indicators, the Z-score standardization procedure is implemented for each component indicator to ensure that the overall EGDI is equally decided by the three component indexes, i.e. each component index presents comparable variance subsequent to the Z-score standardization. In the absence of the Z-score standardization treatment, the EGDI would mainly depend on the component index with the greatest dispersion. After the Z-score standardization, the arithmetic average sum becomes a good statistical indicator, where "equal weights" truly means "equal importance."

For standard Z-score calculation of each component indicator:

$$z = \frac{x - \mu}{\sigma}$$

where:

x is a raw score to be standardized;

μ is the mean of the population;

σ is the standard deviation of the population.

The composite value of each component index is then normalized to fall between the range of 0 to 1, and the overall EGDI is derived by taking the arithmetic average of the three component indexes.

As indicated, the EGDI is used as a benchmark to provide a numerical ranking of e-government development across United Nations Member States, yet this approach has its own weaknesses. Minor changes in EGDI index value could induce ranking list reshuffling, which may mask the changes in the sophistication of e-government programmes.

7.1 Online service index

To arrive at a set of online service index values, the researchers assessed each country's national website, including the national central portal, e-services portal and e-participation portal, as well as the websites of the related ministries of education, labour, social services, health, finance, and environment as applicable. In addition to being assessed for content and features, the national sites were tested for a minimal level of web content accessibility as described in the Web Content Accessibility Guidelines of the World Wide Web Consortium.

The assessment questionnaire consists of four sections corresponding to the four stages of e-government development. The first of these includes questions relating to attributes that would be considered typical of an emerging presence, providing information that is limited and basic. The second stage is enhanced presence, in which the government provides greater public policy and governance sources of current and archived information, such as policies, laws and regulation, reports, newsletters, and downloadable databases. The third stage attributes to a transactional presence, allowing two-way interaction between the citizen and his/her government. It includes options for paying taxes and applying for ID cards, birth certificates/passports, license renewals and other similar C2G interactions by allowing citizens to submit these online 24-7. The fourth and final stage is labelled connected presence, which represents the most sophisticated level in the online e-government initiatives. It can be characterized by an integration of G2G, G2C and C2G (and reverse) interactions. The government encourages participatory deliberative decision-making and is willing and able to involve the society in a two-way open dialogue. Through interactive features such as the web comment form, and innovative online consultation mechanisms, the government actively solicits citizens' views on public policy, law making, and democratic participatory decision making. In the 2012 Survey, almost all questions call for a binary response of yes (1 point) or no (0 points). Exceptions include a small number of questions designed to capture data, on the number of forms and transactions for example. These could be worth up to 3 points.

Researchers were instructed and trained to assume the mind-set of an average citizen user in assessing each site. Thus, responses were generally based on whether the relevant features could be found and accessed easily, not whether they in fact exist. While it is possible, although implausible, to search the sites meticulously for all content and features, this approach misses the key point that the average user needs to find information and features quickly and intuitively for a site to be "usable" with content readily discoverable by the intended beneficiaries. Even if researchers had the resources to search for hours to locate a specific feature or function at a given site, no average citizens or government website users would expend that kind of time or effort.

The actual time spent for any given country review varies widely depending on how extensive the online presence is, and generally how "good" or "bad" the actual websites are, both in terms of design and user-friendliness, as well as in the extent of the content offered. The United Nations always puts great emphasis on accuracy over speed. Once its review is completed by the original reviewer/translator, a country is subject to complete re-review by a senior researcher (along with a translator when necessary) who re-verifies all answers and, if applicable, compiles outstanding judgment calls that are determined in conjunction with the lead researcher. Through this method, all surveyed sites are thoroughly assessed by at least two people, at least one of whom has years of experience in assessing online services of the public sector.

The total number of points scored by each country is normalized to the range of 0 to 1. The online index value for a given country is equal to the actual total score less the lowest total score divided by the range of total score values for all countries. For example, if country "x" were to score 114, with the lowest score of any country equal to 0 and the highest equal to 153, then the online services value for country "x" would be:

$$\text{Online service index (country "x")} = \frac{(114-0)}{(153-0)} = 0.7451$$

7.2 Challenges in reviewing a country's online presence

Selecting the appropriate site/ URL at the national level

One of the essential decisions for researchers when undertaking this survey is to identify the specific site(s) to review as the national government site for each country. Regardless of the sophistication of e-government in a specific country, the priority for users is to find a clear indication as to which of the many potentially government sites available could be deemed as the "official" national government site – in a sense, the gateway or starting point for national users. Not only is this fairly easy to do – a simple, clear statement at the chosen website is sufficient to start – but also an important step towards providing government information and services to the public in an integrated, usable and easy-to-find manner. Many countries have in fact engaged in the procedure of actually noting on their national site that it is their "official" Government site, or "Gateway to Government," or other such statement.

All Member States were invited to supply the addresses of their own top-level national and e-services/ministerial websites, and researchers generally take those URLs as a starting point. Yet not all countries provided the appropriate URLs. Thus, some discretion is exerted when deciding whether to use the country-provided websites. What is noteworthy in this Survey is that the researchers not only review the national portals but also undertake exhaustive research on e-services or e-participation portals when they exist.

One dilemma facing researchers is that a number of countries provide more than one apparently legitimate national access point. While some have simply not consolidated their government entry points into a single site or portal that could be clearly distinguished, others have actually taken this approach on purpose – offering different access points to different audiences. Considering that the use of integrated portals or websites is emerging as an increasing – and apparently effective – trend in e-government strategies worldwide, researchers would have to select the primary site as a National Portal or other portal if it were deemed to be the official homepage of the government. However, to accommodate the strategy of developing one-stop-shop services, more than one site could be scored if it were clearly part of a tightly integrated "network" of national sites. Nevertheless, it should be noted that for those countries for which more than one site was assessed, having more than one national entry is neither a disadvantage nor a benefit.

If no site were found that could reasonably be classified as the national site, then the country receives no points for the "Emerging Presence" section of the Survey because it is deemed that there is no "true" national site; rather, a substitute national site has to be used. While it has become less and less common since the Survey was introduced in 2003, when applicable this typically involves countries that have only one government site online, which usually turns out to be a pure Ministry of Information or Ministry of Tourism site. In such cases, the Ministry site was reviewed as a substitute national site.

Some countries do not offer certain public services at the federal level, but rather at the subnational or local level. No country is penalized for offering a service at the sub-national level as opposed to the federal level per se. In fact, when the issue arises researchers tend to be inclusive in assessing the matter as long as the information and/or service can be found from the national level.

A more difficult problem arises when not only a specific service is located at the local level but when the entire ministerial functions are altogether missing at the national level. If researchers are unable to locate a ministry as per the above described method, then the final step is to find out whether the country in question actually has such a ministry at the national level or whether the functions might be locally administered.

Identifying ministerial websites

Finding and selecting the appropriate site(s) at the ministerial level is typically an easier task because most national sites provide links to the ministries, often under a clearly defined header or subsection. Such an approach not only encourages citizen utilization and enhances the delivery of information across government but should, in fact, be considered a standard feature of any national site. Obviously, where this practice is in place, ministerial sites are easily identified by researchers.

In instances where this is not the case, researchers consult the data collection database with ministry URLs from the previous years' reports and/or check with the supervisor. If unavailable, researchers attempt to locate the ministerial URLs at other national government sites that might provide them. If still unsuccessful, the researchers continue by trying to find them through the most common search engines. The final step is to consult independent online collections of government URLs. If none of these methods result in finding the appropriate ministry it is determined to be unavailable. Similarly to locating a national site URL, if a meticulous search by researchers could not locate the site, then it is unlikely a citizen would expend the time and effort to do so.

Language limitations

The research team was fully equipped to handle the six official languages of the United Nations, namely Arabic, Chinese, English, French, Russian and Spanish. However, as in previous survey cycles, the team went beyond this mandate and made an effort to review each website in the official language of the country or, where that was not possible, in another of the languages available on the site. Translators provided assistance as necessary so that possible errors based on language have been reduced to a minimum.

The methodological framework for the United Nations e-government development index has remained consistent across survey periods. At the same time, the questionnaire has been adjusted to reflect emerging trends of e-government strategies, evolving knowledge of best practices in e-government, changes in technology and other factors, and data collection practices have been periodically refined.

With a view to the new and emerging trends since United Nations E-Government Survey 2010, the 2012 Survey questionnaire was improved to encompass the new developments with a focus on: the rising importance of a whole-of-government approach and integrated online service delivery; the use of e-government to provide information and services to citizens on environment related issues; e-infrastructure and its increasing role in bridging the digital divide, with a particular emphasis on the provision of effective online services for the inclusion of vulnerable and marginalized groups, such as the poor, the disabled, women, children and youth, the elderly, minorities, etc.; the increasing emphasis on service usage; and multichannel service delivery. The outcome was an enhanced survey instrument with a wider range of point distributions reflecting differences in levels of e-government development among countries.

Data quality checks

In order to ensure the data quality, UNDESA has put survey procedures under close monitoring including developing a standard web-based application platform for data collection and storage, preparing the methodological and training guidelines for researchers, and instituting a training programme for either group training or individual hands-on support to resolve thorny issues. Among other tasks, team members were asked to justify the selection of URLs and indicate whether the URLs had been reviewed in past surveys. Regular meetings were held to discuss concerns and ensure consistency of evaluation methods UNDESA applied the survey scores to generate an ordering of online service presence of all United Nations Member States and compared them with the historical results in previous surveys so as to detect possible shortcomings in the process. The team was assisted in the research by United Nations interns with languages skills not otherwise covered by the core group.

Towards a more citizen-centric approach

In line with the global trend towards a more citizen-centric approach as driven by the demand for greater efficiency and cost-effectiveness of the public sector, the questionnaire has been designed to reflect this paradigm of e-government. As mentioned above, user take-up has been included as one special subject in the 2012 Survey, which encourages the governments to take account not only of the supply side but also the demand side of e-services. Accordingly, the research team was instructed to enforce this approach consistently throughout the whole survey. If features could not be found easily, quickly and intuitively, then a site would score poorly.

Assessment of large countries

With a view to identifying differences in the determinants of e-government development between large and small countries, and in recognition of the additional challenges large countries face, an

Box 7.1 **The four stages of online service development**

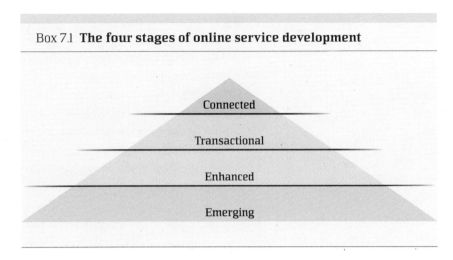

assessment was undertaken of the effects of population and land area in countries with a population of at least 100 million.

Stage 1:

Emerging information services: Government websites provide information on public policy, governance, laws, regulations, relevant documentation and types of government services provided. They have links to ministries, departments and other branches of government. Citizens are easily able to obtain information on what is new in the national government and ministries and can follow links to archived information.

Stage 2:

Enhanced information services: Government websites deliver enhanced one-way or simple two-way e-communication between government and citizen, such as downloadable forms for government services and applications. The sites have audio and video capabilities and are multi-lingual, among others.

Stage 3:

Transactional services: Government websites engage in two-way communication with their citizens, including requesting and receiving inputs on government policies, programmes, regulations, etc. Some form of electronic authentication of the citizen's identity is required to successfully complete the exchange. Government websites process non-financial transactions, e.g. e-voting, downloading and uploading forms, filing taxes online or applying for certificates, licenses and permits. They also handle financial transactions, i.e. where money is transferred on a secure network to government.

Stage 4:

Connected services: Government websites have changed the way governments communicate with their citizens. They are proactive in requesting information and opinions from the citizens using Web 2.0 and other interactive tools. E-services and e-solutions cut across the departments and ministries in a seamless manner. Information, data and knowledge are transferred from government agencies through integrated applications. Governments have moved from a government-centric to a citizen-centric approach, where e-services are targeted to citizens through life cycle events and segmented groups to provide tailor-made services. Governments create an environment that empowers citizens to be more involved with government activities so as to have a voice in decision-making.

7.3 Telecommunication infrastructure index

The telecommunication infrastructure index is an arithmetic average composite of five indicators: estimated internet users per 100 inhabitants, number of main fixed telephone lines per 100 inhabitants, number of mobile subscribers per 100 inhabitants, number of fixed internet subscriptions per 100 inhabitants, and number of fixed broadband facilities per 100 inhabitants. The International Telecommunication Union is the primary source of data in each case. Thanks to the improvement of ITU data quality and coverage, data gaps that appeared in prior surveys have been eliminated, ensuring that all countries have a telecommunication infrastructure index.

Each of these indicators standardized via the Z-score procedure to derive the Z-score for each component indicator. The telecommunication infrastructure composite value for country "x" is the simple arithmetic mean of each of the five standardized indicators derived this way:

Telecommunication infrastructure composite value=
Average   (Internet user Z-score
*   +   telephone line Z-score*
*   +   mobile subscription Z-score*
*   +   fixed internet subscription Z-score*
*   +   fixed broadband Z-score)*

Then, the telecommunication infrastructure composite value is normalized by taking its value for a given country, subtracting the lowest composite value in the survey and dividing by the range of composite values for all countries. For example, if country "x" were to have the composite value of 1.3813, with the lowest composite value for all countries equal to -1.1358 and the highest equal to 2.3640, then the normalized value of telecommunication infrastructure index for country "x" would be given by:

$$\text{Telecommunication infrastructure index} = \frac{[1.3813-(-1.1358)]}{[2.3640-(-1.1358)]} = 0.7192$$

7.4 Human capital index

The human capital index is a weighted average composite of two indicators: adult literacy rate and the combined primary, secondary, and tertiary gross enrolment ratio, with two thirds weights assigned to adult literacy rate and one third weight assigned to the gross enrolment ratio. The United Nations Educational, Scientific and Cultural Organization is the main source of data for both indicators. All data gaps were filled either using data from the 2010 UNDP Human Development Report or using proxy indicators from other authoritative sources such as official UNICEF figures from its public report or World Bank figures on its website.

Similar to calculating the telecommunication infrastructure index, each of the two component indicators is first standardized via the Z-score procedure to derive the Z-score value for each component indicator. The human capital composite value for country "x" is the weighted arithmetic mean with two thirds weights assigned to adult literacy rate and one third weight assigned to the gross enrolment ratio derived this way:

Human capital composite value =
⅔ x adult literacy Z-score
+ ⅓ x gross enrolment Z-score

Then, the human capital composite value is normalized by taking its composite value for a given country, subtracting the lowest composite value in the Survey, and dividing by the range of composite values for all countries. For example, if country "x" were to have the composite value at 0.8438, with the lowest composite value for all countries equal to -3.2354 and the highest equal to 1.2752, then the normalized value of human capital index for country "x" would be given by:

$$
\textit{Human caoital index}
$$
$$
(\textit{country "x"}) = \frac{[0.8438-(-3.2354)]}{[1.2752-(-3.2354)]} = 0.9044
$$

7.5 Supplementary e-participation index

The e-participation questions, as part of the e-government questionnaire, extend the dimension of the Survey by emphasizing quality in the connected presence stage of e-government. These questions focus on the use of the Internet to facilitate provision of information by governments to citizens ("e-information sharing"), interaction with stakeholders ("e-consultation"), and engagement in decision-making processes ("e-decision making"). A country's e-participation index value reflects how useful these features are and how well they have been deployed by the government compared to all other countries. The purpose of this measure is not to prescribe any particular practice, but rather to offer insight into how different countries are using online tools to promote interaction between citizen and government, as well as among citizens, for the benefit of all.

The e-participation index is normalized by taking their total score values for a given country subtracting the lowest total score for any country in the Survey and dividing by the range of total score values for all countries. For example, if country "x" were to have an e-participation score of 29, with the lowest value of any country equal to 0 and the highest equal to 38, then the normalized index value for country "x" would be given by:

$$
\textit{E.participation index}
$$
$$
(\textit{country "x"}) = \frac{(20-0)}{(38-0)} = 0.7632
$$

7.6 Country classifications and nomenclature in the Survey

Regional groupings are taken from the classification of the United Nations Statistics Division. For details, see http://unstats.un.org/unsd/methods/m49/m49regin.htm.

'There is no established convention for the designation of "developed" and "developing" countries or areas in the United Nations system. In common practice, Japan in Asia, Canada and the United States in northern America, Australia and New Zealand in Oceania, and Europe are considered "developed" regions or areas. In international trade statistics, the Southern African Customs Union is also treated as a developed region and Israel as a developed country; countries emerging from the former Yugoslavia are treated as developing countries; and countries of Eastern Europe and of the Commonwealth of Independent States in Europe are not included under either developed or developing regions.' For details on geographical groupings see the United Nations Statistics Division website at http://unstats.un.org/unsd/methods/m49/m49regin.htm.

According to the World Bank, 'Economies are divided according to 2010 GNI per capita, calculated using the World Bank Atlas method. The groups are: low income, $1,005 or less; lower middle income, $1,006 – $3,975; upper middle income, $3,976 – $12,275; and high income, $12,276 or more'. See http://data.worldbank.org/about/country-classifications.

This report uses the terminology 'developed' and 'developing' countries in line with the United Nations practice and keeping in mind the familiarity of the average reader with common usage. Wherever data and statistics are reported by income groups the report classifies countries according to the World Bank income classification of high, middle and low income groups. ⁓

Data tables

Table 7.1 **E-government development index**

Rank	Country	Index value	Online Service Component	Telecomm. infrastructure component	Human Capital Component		Rank	Country	Index value	Online Service Component	Telecomm. infrastructure component	Human Capital Component
1	Republic of Korea	0.9283	1.0000	0.8356	0.9494		54	Brunei Darussalam	0.6250	0.5948	0.4550	0.8253
2	Netherlands	0.9125	0.9608	0.8342	0.9425		55	Mexico	0.6240	0.7320	0.3104	0.8295
3	United Kingdom	0.8960	0.9739	0.8135	0.9007		56	Argentina	0.6228	0.5294	0.4352	0.9038
4	Denmark	0.8889	0.8562	0.8615	0.9489		57	Montenegro	0.6218	0.5098	0.5375	0.8182
5	United States	0.8687	1.0000	0.6860	0.9202		58	Andorra	0.6172	0.3137	0.7315	0.8063
6	France	0.8635	0.8758	0.7902	0.9244		59	Brazil	0.6167	0.6732	0.3568	0.8203
7	Sweden	0.8599	0.8431	0.8225	0.9141		60	Bulgaria	0.6132	0.4902	0.5006	0.8486
8	Norway	0.8593	0.8562	0.7870	0.9347		61	Belarus	0.6090	0.4118	0.5033	0.9120
9	Finland	0.8505	0.8824	0.7225	0.9467		62	Romania	0.6060	0.5163	0.4232	0.8783
10	Singapore	0.8474	1.0000	0.6923	0.8500		63	Kuwait	0.5960	0.5817	0.4179	0.7885
11	Canada	0.8430	0.8889	0.7163	0.9238		64	Oman	0.5944	0.6667	0.3942	0.7224
12	Australia	0.8390	0.8627	0.6543	1.0000		65	Bahamas	0.5793	0.4706	0.4554	0.8120
13	New Zealand	0.8381	0.7843	0.7318	0.9982		66	Panama	0.5733	0.4641	0.4408	0.8151
14	Liechtenstein	0.8264	0.5882	1.0000	0.8910		67	Trinidad and Tobago	0.5731	0.4837	0.4526	0.7830
15	Switzerland	0.8134	0.6732	0.8782	0.8888		68	Ukraine	0.5653	0.4248	0.3535	0.9176
16	Israel	0.8100	0.8497	0.6859	0.8945		69	Republic of Moldova	0.5626	0.5163	0.3586	0.8129
17	Germany	0.8079	0.7516	0.7750	0.8971		70	The former Yugoslav Rep. of Macedonia	0.5587	0.4510	0.4135	0.8115
18	Japan	0.8019	0.8627	0.6460	0.8969		71	Venezuela	0.5585	0.4837	0.3215	0.8705
19	Luxembourg	0.8014	0.6993	0.8644	0.8404		72	Georgia	0.5563	0.6013	0.2328	0.8348
20	Estonia	0.7987	0.8235	0.6642	0.9085		73	Dominica	0.5561	0.2941	0.6221	0.7520
21	Austria	0.7840	0.7451	0.6977	0.9091		74	El Salvador	0.5513	0.6732	0.2638	0.7169
22	Iceland	0.7835	0.5425	0.8772	0.9310		75	Grenada	0.5479	0.3529	0.4014	0.8895
23	Spain	0.7770	0.7582	0.6318	0.9409		76	Mongolia	0.5443	0.5882	0.1758	0.8688
24	Belgium	0.7718	0.6471	0.7420	0.9264		77	Costa Rica	0.5397	0.4967	0.3135	0.8089
25	Slovenia	0.7492	0.6667	0.6509	0.9300		78	China	0.5359	0.5294	0.3039	0.7745
26	Monaco	0.7468	0.3595	0.9370	0.9439		79	Bosnia and Herzegovina	0.5328	0.3725	0.3917	0.8341
27	Russian Federation	0.7345	0.6601	0.6583	0.8850		80	Turkey	0.5281	0.4641	0.3478	0.7726
28	United Arab Emirates	0.7344	0.8627	0.5568	0.7837		81	Saint Kitts and Nevis	0.5272	0.1830	0.5648	0.8338
29	Lithuania	0.7333	0.6993	0.5765	0.9240		82	Peru	0.5230	0.5163	0.2585	0.7942
30	Croatia	0.7328	0.6405	0.6965	0.8615		83	Viet Nam	0.5217	0.4248	0.3969	0.7434
31	Hungary	0.7201	0.6863	0.5677	0.9065		84	Seychelles	0.5192	0.3333	0.4037	0.8204
32	Italy	0.7190	0.5752	0.6697	0.9120		85	Saint Vincent and the Grenadines	0.5177	0.3137	0.4697	0.7696
33	Portugal	0.7165	0.6536	0.6028	0.8931		86	Albania	0.5161	0.4248	0.3370	0.7863
34	Ireland	0.7149	0.5359	0.6553	0.9535		87	Lebanon	0.5139	0.4771	0.2728	0.7917
35	Malta	0.7131	0.6144	0.7192	0.8057		88	Philippines	0.5130	0.4967	0.2082	0.8341
36	Bahrain	0.6946	0.8627	0.4183	0.8028		89	Dominican Republic	0.5130	0.5359	0.2632	0.7398
37	Greece	0.6872	0.5752	0.5531	0.9332		90	Saint Lucia	0.5122	0.3464	0.3814	0.8089
38	Kazakhstan	0.6844	0.7843	0.3555	0.9134		91	Uzbekistan	0.5099	0.4967	0.2075	0.8255
39	Chile	0.6769	0.7516	0.4001	0.8788		92	Thailand	0.5093	0.5098	0.2361	0.7819
40	Malaysia	0.6703	0.7908	0.4510	0.7691		93	Mauritius	0.5066	0.4314	0.3296	0.7588
41	Saudi Arabia	0.6658	0.7974	0.4323	0.7677		94	Armenia	0.4997	0.3268	0.3217	0.8505
42	Latvia	0.6604	0.5882	0.5051	0.8879		95	Maldives	0.4994	0.3268	0.3599	0.8114
43	Colombia	0.6572	0.8431	0.2894	0.8391		96	Azerbaijan	0.4984	0.3660	0.3033	0.8259
44	Barbados	0.6566	0.3725	0.6740	0.9232		97	Indonesia	0.4949	0.4967	0.1897	0.7982
45	Cyprus	0.6508	0.5621	0.5153	0.8751		98	Jordan	0.4884	0.3922	0.2717	0.8013
46	Czech Republic	0.6491	0.5425	0.5151	0.8898		99	Kyrgyzstan	0.4879	0.4248	0.1903	0.8485
47	Poland	0.6441	0.5359	0.4921	0.9044		100	Iran (Islamic Republic of)	0.4876	0.4902	0.2638	0.7089
48	Qatar	0.6405	0.7386	0.4513	0.7316		101	South Africa	0.4869	0.4575	0.2214	0.7817
49	Antigua and Barbuda	0.6345	0.3072	0.7192	0.8770		102	Ecuador	0.4869	0.4575	0.2482	0.7549
50	Uruguay	0.6315	0.5490	0.4442	0.9013		103	Tunisia	0.4833	0.4771	0.2886	0.6841
51	Serbia	0.6312	0.5752	0.4701	0.8484		104	Paraguay	0.4802	0.4575	0.1968	0.7862
52	San Marino	0.6305	0.2941	0.6794	0.9179		105	Fiji	0.4672	0.3595	0.2434	0.7986
53	Slovakia	0.6292	0.5033	0.5147	0.8696		106	Bolivia (Plurinational State of)	0.4658	0.4118	0.1786	0.8072

Table 7.1 **E-government development index** (cont.)

Rank	Country	Index value	Online Service Component	Telecomm. infrastructure component	Human Capital Component	Rank	Country	Index value	Online Service Component	Telecomm. infrastructure component	Human Capital Component
107	Egypt	0.4611	0.6013	0.2232	0.5588	160	Myanmar	0.2703	0.1046	0.0000	0.7064
108	Jamaica	0.4552	0.3072	0.2668	0.7916	161	Gambia	0.2688	0.3203	0.1344	0.3519
109	Guyana	0.4549	0.2549	0.2536	0.8562	162	Nigeria	0.2676	0.2222	0.1270	0.4535
110	Cuba	0.4488	0.3072	0.0709	0.9684	163	Senegal	0.2673	0.3464	0.1283	0.3271
111	Tonga	0.4405	0.2418	0.2069	0.8727	164	Nepal	0.2664	0.2876	0.0597	0.4521
112	Guatemala	0.4390	0.4641	0.2247	0.6284	165	Sudan	0.2610	0.2549	0.0725	0.4555
113	Palau	0.4359	0.1830	0.2802	0.8445	166	Côte d'Ivoire	0.2580	0.3333	0.1019	0.3388
114	Samoa	0.4358	0.2810	0.1927	0.8335	167	Yemen	0.2472	0.1765	0.1011	0.4642
115	Sri Lanka	0.4357	0.3791	0.1922	0.7357	168	Solomon Islands	0.2416	0.1307	0.0198	0.5743
116	Suriname	0.4344	0.1634	0.3578	0.7821	169	Liberia	0.2407	0.1895	0.0477	0.4849
117	Honduras	0.4341	0.3791	0.2173	0.7060	170	Timor-Leste	0.2365	0.2157	0.0649	0.4290
118	Cape Verde	0.4297	0.4379	0.2268	0.6245	171	Comoros	0.2358	0.0784	0.0436	0.5853
119	Kenya	0.4212	0.4314	0.1212	0.7109	172	Ethiopia	0.2306	0.4706	0.0093	0.2119
120	Morocco	0.4209	0.5425	0.2772	0.4430	173	Burundi	0.2288	0.1503	0.0173	0.5188
121	Botswana	0.4186	0.3595	0.1873	0.7091	174	Dem. Rep. of the Congo	0.2280	0.1765	0.0183	0.4893
122	Tajikistan	0.4069	0.2418	0.1474	0.8313	175	South Sudan	0.2239	0.1438	0.0725	0.4555
123	Namibia	0.3937	0.3007	0.1385	0.7419	176	Djibouti	0.2228	0.1961	0.0488	0.4236
124	Belize	0.3923	0.3987	0.1627	0.6155	177	Papua New Guinea	0.2147	0.2288	0.0411	0.3743
125	India	0.3829	0.5359	0.1102	0.5025	178	Togo	0.2143	0.1373	0.0744	0.4312
126	Turkmenistan	0.3813	0.1895	0.1139	0.8404	179	Benin	0.2064	0.1961	0.1118	0.3113
127	Micronesia (Federated States of)	0.3812	0.2092	0.1013	0.8332	180	Eritrea	0.2043	0.2092	0.0132	0.3907
128	Syrian Arab Republic	0.3705	0.2288	0.1952	0.6876	181	Mauritania	0.1996	0.0784	0.1123	0.4079
129	Gabon	0.3687	0.1895	0.1595	0.7572	182	Guinea-Bissau	0.1945	0.1046	0.0511	0.4278
130	Nicaragua	0.3621	0.3137	0.1194	0.6533	183	Mali	0.1857	0.3203	0.0645	0.1723
131	Dem. People's Rep. of Korea	0.3616	0.1176	0.0112	0.9560	184	Afghanistan	0.1701	0.2353	0.0573	0.2178
132	Algeria	0.3608	0.2549	0.1812	0.6463	185	Burkina Faso	0.1578	0.2941	0.0454	0.1338
133	Zimbabwe	0.3583	0.3007	0.1099	0.6644	186	Sierra Leone	0.1557	0.1699	0.0395	0.2576
134	Tuvalu	0.3539	0.0523	0.1866	0.8228	187	Haiti	0.1512	0.0915	0.0698	0.2922
135	Vanuatu	0.3512	0.2222	0.1783	0.6531	188	Niger	0.1119	0.1961	0.0293	0.1103
136	Lesotho	0.3501	0.3007	0.0499	0.6997	189	Chad	0.1092	0.0980	0.0291	0.2003
137	Iraq	0.3409	0.2876	0.1201	0.6151	190	Somalia	0.0640	0.1830	0.0090	0.0000
138	Sao Tome and Principe	0.3327	0.1176	0.1374	0.7432						
139	United Rep. of Tanzania	0.3311	0.3529	0.0839	0.5564	**Countries with no online serivces**					
140	Rwanda	0.3291	0.3399	0.0614	0.5861	Central African Republic		0.0000	0.0000	0.0297	0.3446
141	Nauru	0.3242	0.0980	0.1700	0.7047	Guinea		0.0000	0.0000	0.0491	0.2696
142	Angola	0.3203	0.3333	0.0892	0.5383	Libya		0.0000	0.0000	0.3743	0.8502
143	Uganda	0.3185	0.2941	0.0732	0.5883						
144	Swaziland	0.3179	0.1438	0.1125	0.6973						
145	Ghana	0.3159	0.3007	0.1111	0.5360	**Regional and Economic Groupings**					
146	Marshall Islands	0.3129	0.1373	0.0425	0.7590	Africa		0.2780	0.2567	0.1094	0.5034
147	Cameroon	0.3070	0.3007	0.0649	0.5554	Americas		0.5403	0.4648	0.3602	0.7958
148	Madagascar	0.3054	0.3203	0.0520	0.5438	Asia		0.4992	0.4880	0.2818	0.7278
149	Kiribati	0.2998	0.0654	0.0469	0.7871	Europe		0.7188	0.6189	0.6460	0.8916
150	Bangladesh	0.2991	0.4444	0.0641	0.3889	Oceania		0.4240	0.2754	0.2211	0.7754
151	Equatorial Guinea	0.2955	0.0980	0.0883	0.7001	World		0.4882	0.4328	0.3245	0.7173
152	Bhutan	0.2942	0.3529	0.1143	0.4153						
153	Lao People's Dem. Rep.	0.2935	0.2157	0.0998	0.5651	Developed countries		0.7329	0.6503	0.6509	0.8974
154	Zambia	0.2910	0.3137	0.0601	0.4993						
155	Cambodia	0.2902	0.1895	0.0814	0.5997	Developing countries other than LDCs		0.4865	0.4311	0.2860	0.7553
156	Pakistan	0.2823	0.3660	0.1239	0.3572						
157	Congo	0.2809	0.0784	0.1275	0.6369	Least developed countries		0.2420	0.2143	0.0685	0.4575
158	Mozambique	0.2786	0.3660	0.0443	0.4255						
159	Malawi	0.2740	0.2157	0.0321	0.5741	Small island developing States		0.4328	0.2821	0.2758	0.7406

Table 7.2 **Online service index and its components**

Country	Online Service Index Value *(in order of decreasing value)*	Stage % 7%	Stage II % 24%	Stage II % 30%	Stage IV % 39%	Total % 100%	Country	Online Service Index Value *(in order of decreasing value)*	Stage % 7%	Stage II % 24%	Stage II % 30%	Stage IV % 39%	Total % 100%
Relative Weight of Stages							Relative Weight of Stages						
Republic of Korea	1.0000	100%	79%	92%	87%	87%	Czech Republic	0.5425	100%	60%	25%	48%	47%
Singapore	1.0000	100%	79%	94%	86%	87%	Iceland	0.5425	92%	69%	38%	33%	47%
United States	1.0000	100%	90%	88%	83%	87%	Morocco	0.5425	100%	62%	29%	43%	47%
United Kingdom	0.9739	100%	95%	79%	81%	85%	Dominican Republic	0.5359	92%	50%	31%	49%	47%
Netherlands	0.9608	100%	88%	71%	88%	84%	India	0.5359	100%	64%	33%	38%	47%
Canada	0.8889	100%	83%	81%	68%	78%	Ireland	0.5359	75%	62%	44%	35%	47%
Finland	0.8824	100%	90%	75%	67%	77%	Poland	0.5359	100%	67%	42%	29%	47%
France	0.8758	100%	79%	85%	65%	77%	Argentina	0.5294	92%	60%	31%	42%	46%
Australia	0.8627	100%	74%	79%	70%	75%	China	0.5294	92%	55%	40%	38%	46%
Bahrain	0.8627	100%	76%	81%	67%	75%	Peru	0.5163	83%	45%	31%	49%	45%
Japan	0.8627	100%	79%	75%	70%	75%	Republic of Moldova	0.5163	100%	50%	25%	48%	45%
United Arab Emirates	0.8627	100%	74%	83%	67%	75%	Romania	0.5163	100%	64%	29%	36%	45%
Denmark	0.8562	100%	86%	77%	62%	75%	Montenegro	0.5098	92%	64%	31%	35%	45%
Norway	0.8562	100%	71%	79%	70%	75%	Thailand	0.5098	100%	55%	31%	39%	45%
Israel	0.8497	100%	69%	73%	74%	74%	Slovakia	0.5033	92%	60%	27%	39%	44%
Colombia	0.8431	100%	76%	65%	74%	74%	Costa Rica	0.4967	92%	45%	31%	43%	43%
Sweden	0.8431	92%	90%	71%	62%	74%	Indonesia	0.4967	92%	60%	23%	41%	43%
Estonia	0.8235	100%	69%	65%	74%	72%	Philippines	0.4967	83%	52%	37%	36%	43%
Saudi Arabia	0.7974	92%	60%	77%	67%	70%	Uzbekistan	0.4967	100%	62%	21%	39%	43%
Malaysia	0.7908	100%	64%	79%	59%	69%	Bulgaria	0.4902	100%	57%	40%	26%	43%
Kazakhstan	0.7843	92%	64%	52%	80%	69%	Iran (Islamic Republic of)	0.4902	67%	40%	46%	38%	43%
New Zealand	0.7843	100%	79%	69%	57%	69%	Trinidad and Tobago	0.4837	92%	64%	23%	35%	42%
Spain	0.7582	92%	67%	71%	58%	66%	Venezuela	0.4837	100%	62%	19%	38%	42%
Chile	0.7516	100%	62%	67%	61%	66%	Lebanon	0.4771	100%	62%	17%	38%	42%
Germany	0.7516	92%	67%	56%	68%	66%	Tunisia	0.4771	92%	45%	29%	41%	42%
Austria	0.7451	100%	71%	67%	54%	65%	Bahamas	0.4706	100%	52%	29%	33%	41%
Qatar	0.7386	83%	64%	62%	64%	65%	Ethiopia	0.4706	83%	62%	10%	45%	41%
Mexico	0.7320	100%	69%	62%	57%	64%	Guatemala	0.4641	100%	55%	21%	36%	41%
Lithuania	0.6993	83%	67%	54%	59%	61%	Panama	0.4641	92%	60%	13%	41%	41%
Luxembourg	0.6993	100%	69%	62%	49%	61%	Turkey	0.4641	100%	62%	23%	30%	41%
Hungary	0.6863	100%	69%	54%	52%	60%	Ecuador	0.4575	92%	55%	23%	35%	40%
Brazil	0.6732	100%	64%	48%	57%	59%	Paraguay	0.4575	92%	55%	21%	36%	40%
El Salvador	0.6732	100%	71%	38%	59%	59%	South Africa	0.4575	100%	60%	17%	35%	40%
Switzerland	0.6732	100%	88%	46%	43%	59%	The former Yugoslav Rep. of Macedonia	0.4510	100%	57%	23%	30%	39%
Oman	0.6667	92%	64%	48%	57%	58%	Bangladesh	0.4444	100%	60%	21%	29%	39%
Slovenia	0.6667	100%	71%	56%	45%	58%	Cape Verde	0.4379	92%	48%	23%	35%	38%
Russian Federation	0.6601	100%	67%	35%	62%	58%	Kenya	0.4314	100%	62%	17%	28%	38%
Portugal	0.6536	100%	74%	42%	51%	57%	Mauritius	0.4314	92%	57%	19%	30%	38%
Belgium	0.6471	100%	64%	65%	38%	57%	Albania	0.4248	100%	50%	21%	30%	37%
Croatia	0.6405	100%	76%	44%	45%	56%	Kyrgyzstan	0.4248	83%	60%	4%	41%	37%
Malta	0.6144	100%	62%	48%	45%	54%	Ukraine	0.4248	83%	57%	8%	39%	37%
Egypt	0.6013	100%	64%	27%	57%	53%	Viet Nam	0.4248	100%	52%	17%	32%	37%
Georgia	0.6013	100%	55%	58%	39%	53%	Belarus	0.4118	100%	55%	25%	22%	36%
Brunei Darussalam	0.5948	100%	62%	35%	51%	52%	Bolivia (Plurinational State of)	0.4118	75%	43%	21%	36%	36%
Latvia	0.5882	100%	67%	35%	46%	51%	Belize	0.3987	92%	48%	12%	35%	35%
Liechtenstein	0.5882	92%	71%	48%	35%	51%	Jordan	0.3922	83%	48%	31%	20%	34%
Mongolia	0.5882	100%	52%	33%	57%	51%	Honduras	0.3791	92%	52%	15%	25%	33%
Kuwait	0.5817	100%	62%	48%	38%	51%	Sri Lanka	0.3791	92%	48%	13%	29%	33%
Greece	0.5752	100%	60%	40%	43%	50%	Barbados	0.3725	92%	52%	13%	25%	33%
Italy	0.5752	92%	57%	48%	41%	50%	Bosnia and Herzegovina	0.3725	100%	50%	15%	23%	33%
Serbia	0.5752	100%	64%	38%	42%	50%	Azerbaijan	0.3660	92%	38%	15%	30%	32%
Cyprus	0.5621	100%	62%	46%	35%	49%	Mozambique	0.3660	100%	45%	8%	30%	32%
Uruguay	0.5490	100%	60%	38%	39%	48%	Pakistan	0.3660	83%	45%	6%	35%	32%

Table 7.2 **Online service index and its components** (cont.)

Country / Relative Weight of Stages	Online Service Index Value (in order of decreasing value)	Stage % 7%	Stage II % 24%	Stage II % 30%	Stage IV % 39%	Total % 100%
Botswana	0.3595	100%	50%	10%	25%	31%
Fiji	0.3595	83%	55%	13%	22%	31%
Monaco	0.3595	92%	40%	15%	28%	31%
Bhutan	0.3529	92%	50%	10%	25%	31%
Grenada	0.3529	83%	50%	8%	28%	31%
United Rep. of Tanzania	0.3529	92%	55%	2%	28%	31%
Saint Lucia	0.3464	83%	50%	8%	26%	30%
Senegal	0.3464	75%	31%	12%	36%	30%
Rwanda	0.3399	92%	48%	8%	25%	30%
Angola	0.3333	100%	45%	6%	25%	29%
Côte d'Ivoire	0.3333	75%	31%	10%	35%	29%
Seychelles	0.3333	67%	45%	4%	32%	29%
Armenia	0.3268	100%	36%	12%	25%	29%
Maldives	0.3268	75%	55%	8%	20%	29%
Gambia	0.3203	83%	50%	2%	25%	28%
Madagascar	0.3203	92%	40%	13%	20%	28%
Mali	0.3203	75%	40%	12%	25%	28%
Andorra	0.3137	75%	40%	8%	26%	27%
Nicaragua	0.3137	83%	45%	17%	14%	27%
Saint Vincent and the Grenadines	0.3137	75%	38%	13%	23%	27%
Zambia	0.3137	83%	38%	8%	26%	27%
Antigua and Barbuda	0.3072	50%	50%	8%	23%	27%
Cuba	0.3072	75%	36%	10%	26%	27%
Jamaica	0.3072	67%	48%	19%	13%	27%
Cameroon	0.3007	83%	48%	4%	20%	26%
Ghana	0.3007	83%	38%	2%	28%	26%
Lesotho	0.3007	92%	38%	4%	25%	26%
Namibia	0.3007	75%	40%	2%	28%	26%
Zimbabwe	0.3007	67%	45%	4%	25%	26%
Burkina Faso	0.2941	75%	33%	4%	29%	26%
Dominica	0.2941	100%	43%	12%	13%	26%
San Marino	0.2941	83%	48%	8%	16%	26%
Uganda	0.2941	100%	33%	8%	22%	26%
Iraq	0.2876	75%	33%	6%	26%	25%
Nepal	0.2876	67%	43%	2%	25%	25%
Samoa	0.2810	67%	48%	2%	20%	25%
Algeria	0.2549	75%	48%	8%	9%	22%
Guyana	0.2549	58%	38%	12%	14%	22%
Sudan	0.2549	67%	31%	10%	19%	22%
Tajikistan	0.2418	67%	40%	2%	16%	21%
Tonga	0.2418	100%	33%	2%	14%	21%
Afghanistan	0.2353	50%	33%	19%	9%	21%
Papua New Guinea	0.2288	67%	36%	2%	16%	20%
Syrian Arab Republic	0.2288	58%	31%	4%	19%	20%
Nigeria	0.2222	58%	12%	10%	25%	19%
Vanuatu	0.2222	83%	21%	6%	17%	19%
Lao People's Dem. Rep.	0.2157	75%	31%	2%	14%	19%
Malawi	0.2157	50%	26%	10%	16%	19%
Timor-Leste	0.2157	50%	33%	6%	14%	19%
Eritrea	0.2092	83%	36%	0%	10%	18%
Micronesia (Federated States of)	0.2092	58%	26%	4%	17%	18%
Benin	0.1961	92%	17%	6%	13%	17%
Djibouti	0.1961	50%	19%	2%	22%	17%

Country / Relative Weight of Stages	Online Service Index Value (in order of decreasing value)	Stage % 7%	Stage II % 24%	Stage II % 30%	Stage IV % 39%	Total % 100%
Niger	0.1961	67%	19%	2%	19%	17%
Cambodia	0.1895	67%	21%	2%	16%	17%
Gabon	0.1895	42%	24%	10%	13%	17%
Liberia	0.1895	42%	21%	2%	20%	17%
Turkmenistan	0.1895	67%	19%	4%	16%	17%
Palau	0.1830	42%	29%	4%	13%	16%
Saint Kitts and Nevis	0.1830	75%	26%	4%	9%	16%
Somalia	0.1830	25%	21%	4%	20%	16%
Dem. Rep. of the Congo	0.1765	75%	24%	4%	9%	15%
Yemen	0.1765	33%	7%	8%	23%	15%
Sierra Leone	0.1699	42%	14%	8%	16%	15%
Suriname	0.1634	67%	31%	0%	6%	14%
Burundi	0.1503	42%	5%	8%	17%	13%
South Sudan	0.1438	58%	19%	2%	9%	13%
Swaziland	0.1438	50%	24%	2%	7%	13%
Marshall Islands	0.1373	25%	26%	2%	9%	12%
Togo	0.1373	42%	14%	6%	10%	12%
Solomon Islands	0.1307	42%	24%	4%	4%	11%
Dem. People's Rep. of Korea	0.1176	58%	12%	4%	6%	10%
Sao Tome and Principe	0.1176	58%	7%	4%	9%	10%
Guinea-Bissau	0.1046	33%	12%	2%	9%	9%
Myanmar	0.1046	50%	17%	0%	4%	9%
Chad	0.0980	25%	14%	2%	7%	9%
Equatorial Guinea	0.0980	25%	10%	4%	9%	9%
Nauru	0.0980	33%	14%	2%	6%	9%
Haiti	0.0915	33%	19%	0%	3%	8%
Comoros	0.0784	42%	7%	2%	4%	7%
Congo	0.0784	33%	14%	2%	1%	7%
Mauritania	0.0784	33%	7%	2%	6%	7%
Kiribati	0.0654	33%	5%	2%	4%	6%
Tuvalu	0.0523	17%	2%	2%	6%	5%
Countries with no online services						
Central African Republic	0.0000	0%	0%	0%	0%	0%
Guinea	0.0000	0%	0%	0%	0%	0%
Libya	0.0000	0%	0%	0%	0%	0%
Regional and Economic Groupings						
Africa	0.2567	66%	31%	7%	21%	22%
Americas	0.4648	86%	53%	27%	36%	41%
Asia	0.4880	85%	51%	32%	38%	43%
Europe	0.6189	96%	66%	45%	46%	54%
Oceania	0.2754	61%	34%	14%	20%	24%
World	0.4328	81%	48%	26%	33%	38%
Developed countries	0.6503	96%	68%	49%	49%	57%
Developing countries other than LDCs	0.4311	83%	48%	24%	34%	38%
Least developed countries	0.2143	60%	27%	5%	17%	19%
Small island developing States	0.2821	67%	37%	11%	20%	25%

Table 7.3 **Telecommunication infrastructure index and its components**

Country	Index value (in order of decreasing value)	Estimated Internet users per 100 inhabs.	Main fixed phone lines per 100 inhabs.	Mobile subscribers per 100 inhabs.	Fixed Internet subscriptions per 100 inhabs.	Fixed broadband per 100 inhabs.	Country	Index value (in order of decreasing value)	Estimated Internet users per 100 inhabs.	Main fixed phone lines per 100 inhabs.	Mobile subscribers per 100 inhabs.	Fixed Internet subscriptions per 100 inhabs.	Fixed broadband per 100 inhabs.
Liechtenstein	1.0000	80.00	54.40	98.52	47.35	63.83	Brunei Darussalam	0.4550	50.00	20.03	109.07	25.56	5.44
Monaco	0.9370	80.00	96.40	74.31	35.42	41.89	Trinidad and Tobago	0.4526	48.50	21.87	141.21	10.85	10.81
Switzerland	0.8782	83.90	58.56	123.62	36.74	38.16	Qatar	0.4513	69.00	16.95	132.43	9.13	9.17
Iceland	0.8772	95.00	63.72	108.72	35.96	34.65	Malaysia	0.4510	55.30	16.10	121.32	20.01	7.32
Luxembourg	0.8644	90.62	53.68	143.27	34.26	32.83	Uruguay	0.4442	43.35	28.56	131.71	8.96	11.37
Denmark	0.8615	88.72	47.26	124.41	39.13	37.38	Panama	0.4408	42.75	15.73	184.72	6.16	7.84
Republic of Korea	0.8356	83.70	59.24	105.36	34.08	36.63	Argentina	0.4352	36.00	24.74	141.79	11.72	9.56
Netherlands	0.8342	90.72	43.15	116.23	37.02	37.97	Saudi Arabia	0.4323	41.00	15.18	187.86	7.02	5.45
Sweden	0.8225	90.00	53.46	113.54	35.25	31.59	Romania	0.4232	39.93	20.94	114.68	13.00	13.96
United Kingdom	0.8135	85.00	53.71	130.25	31.14	31.38	Bahrain	0.4183	55.00	18.07	124.18	6.79	12.21
France	0.7902	80.10	56.06	99.70	32.57	33.92	Kuwait	0.4179	38.25	20.69	160.78	12.51	1.68
Norway	0.7870	93.39	34.85	113.15	35.78	34.60	The former Yugoslav Rep. of Macedonia	0.4135	51.90	20.05	104.51	10.78	12.47
Germany	0.7750	81.85	55.41	127.04	24.23	31.59	Seychelles	0.4037	41.00	25.48	135.91	6.60	7.26
Belgium	0.7420	79.26	43.31	113.46	30.06	31.49	Grenada	0.4014	33.46	27.15	116.71	10.48	10.12
New Zealand	0.7318	83.00	42.81	114.92	32.73	24.93	Chile	0.4001	45.00	20.20	116.00	9.76	10.45
Andorra	0.7315	81.00	44.98	77.18	38.26	28.87	Viet Nam	0.3969	27.56	18.67	175.30	7.80	4.13
Finland	0.7225	86.89	23.30	156.40	26.79	29.07	Oman	0.3942	62.60	10.20	165.54	2.88	1.89
Malta	0.7192	63.00	59.38	109.34	26.83	27.54	Bosnia and Herzegovina	0.3917	52.00	26.56	80.15	10.60	10.40
Antigua and Barbuda	0.7192	80.00	47.05	184.72	17.77	17.25	Saint Lucia	0.3814	36.00	23.58	102.89	10.79	10.67
Canada	0.7163	81.60	50.04	70.66	32.53	29.81	Libya	0.3743	14.00	19.33	171.52	12.33	1.15
Austria	0.6977	72.70	38.66	145.84	25.68	23.85	Maldives	0.3599	28.30	15.20	156.50	6.44	4.92
Croatia	0.6965	60.32	42.37	144.48	33.97	18.25	Republic of Moldova	0.3586	40.00	32.50	88.59	5.65	7.53
Singapore	0.6923	70.00	39.00	143.66	25.22	24.72	Suriname	0.3578	31.59	16.19	169.64	2.43	2.99
United States	0.6860	79.00	48.70	89.86	26.63	26.34	Brazil	0.3568	40.65	21.62	104.10	8.17	7.23
Israel	0.6859	67.20	44.16	133.11	24.17	25.14	Kazakhstan	0.3555	34.00	25.03	123.35	5.28	5.28
San Marino	0.6794	54.21	68.81	76.11	20.83	32.03	Ukraine	0.3535	23.00	28.47	118.66	5.80	8.06
Barbados	0.6740	70.20	50.30	128.07	22.35	20.56	Turkey	0.3478	39.82	22.27	84.90	8.90	9.75
Italy	0.6697	53.68	35.67	135.42	34.23	22.13	Albania	0.3370	45.00	10.35	141.93	3.29	3.43
Estonia	0.6642	74.10	35.96	123.24	25.55	24.34	Mauritius	0.3296	24.90	29.84	91.67	8.13	6.30
Russian Federation	0.6583	43.00	31.45	166.26	41.73	10.98	Armenia	0.3217	37.00	19.08	125.01	3.11	2.69
Ireland	0.6553	69.85	46.49	105.18	25.02	22.82	Venezuela	0.3215	35.63	24.44	96.20	5.20	5.37
Australia	0.6543	76.00	38.89	101.04	27.85	23.19	Costa Rica	0.3135	36.50	31.80	65.14	5.91	6.19
Slovenia	0.6509	70.00	45.01	104.55	23.66	24.39	Mexico	0.3104	31.00	17.54	80.55	8.97	9.98
Japan	0.6460	80.00	31.94	95.39	26.85	26.91	China	0.3039	34.30	21.95	64.04	8.35	9.42
Spain	0.6318	66.53	43.20	111.75	21.89	22.96	Azerbaijan	0.3033	35.99	16.33	99.04	5.75	5.44
Dominica	0.6221	47.45	22.85	144.85	8.72	47.14	Colombia	0.2894	36.50	14.71	93.76	4.96	5.66
Portugal	0.6028	51.10	42.01	142.33	18.54	19.44	Tunisia	0.2886	36.80	12.30	106.04	3.99	4.60
Lithuania	0.5765	62.12	22.08	147.16	19.03	20.58	Palau	0.2802	26.97	34.08	70.89	5.08	1.14
Hungary	0.5677	65.27	29.82	120.32	19.02	19.59	Morocco	0.2772	49.00	11.73	100.10	1.52	1.56
Saint Kitts and Nevis	0.5648	32.87	39.31	161.44	9.72	25.00	Lebanon	0.2728	31.00	21.00	68.00	7.56	4.73
United Arab Emirates	0.5568	78.00	19.70	145.45	20.24	10.47	Jordan	0.2717	38.00	7.84	106.99	4.06	3.18
Greece	0.5531	44.40	45.81	108.22	17.48	19.83	Jamaica	0.2668	26.10	9.60	113.22	4.20	4.26
Montenegro	0.5375	52.00	26.84	185.28	14.14	8.30	Iran (Islamic Rep. of)	0.2638	13.00	36.30	91.25	1.21	0.68
Cyprus	0.5153	52.99	37.58	93.70	17.51	17.62	El Salvador	0.2638	15.00	16.16	124.34	2.44	2.83
Czech Republic	0.5151	68.82	20.95	136.58	13.12	14.66	Dominican Republic	0.2632	39.53	10.17	89.58	4.38	3.64
Slovakia	0.5147	79.42	20.12	108.47	15.23	16.06	Peru	0.2585	34.30	10.87	100.13	2.86	3.14
Latvia	0.5051	68.42	23.63	102.40	14.05	19.31	Guyana	0.2536	29.90	19.86	73.61	6.43	1.59
Belarus	0.5033	31.70	43.13	107.69	16.92	17.36	Ecuador	0.2482	24.00	14.42	102.18	3.94	1.36
Bulgaria	0.5006	46.23	29.36	141.23	12.91	14.70	Fiji	0.2434	14.82	15.92	116.19	1.65	1.86
Poland	0.4921	62.32	24.69	120.18	14.53	13.18	Thailand	0.2361	21.20	10.14	100.81	3.34	3.87
Serbia	0.4701	40.90	40.52	129.19	10.99	8.50	Georgia	0.2328	27.00	13.72	73.36	4.04	5.09
Saint Vincent and the Grenadines	0.4697	69.59	19.85	120.54	11.68	11.43	Cape Verde	0.2268	30.00	14.51	74.97	2.63	3.04
Bahamas	0.4554	43.00	37.71	124.94	11.40	7.13	Guatemala	0.2247	10.50	10.41	125.57	0.77	1.80

Table 7.3 **Telecommunication infrastructure index and its components** (cont.)

Country	Index value (in order of decreasing value)	Estimated Internet users per 100 inhabs.	Main fixed phone lines per 100 inhabs.	Mobile subscribers per 100 inhabs.	Fixed Internet subscriptions per 100 inhabs.	Fixed broadband per 100 inhabs.	Country	Index value (in order of decreasing value)	Estimated Internet users per 100 inhabs.	Main fixed phone lines per 100 inhabs.	Mobile subscribers per 100 inhabs.	Fixed Internet subscriptions per 100 inhabs.	Fixed broadband per 100 inhabs.
Egypt	0.2232	26.74	11.86	87.11	2.94	1.82	Haiti	0.0698	8.37	0.50	40.03	1.04	0.00
South Africa	0.2214	12.30	8.43	100.48	7.55	1.48	Cameroon	0.0649	4.00	2.53	41.61	0.14	0.01
Honduras	0.2173	11.09	8.81	125.06	0.97	1.00	Timor-Leste	0.0649	0.21	0.21	53.42	0.07	0.02
Philippines	0.2082	25.00	7.27	85.67	3.93	1.85	Mali	0.0645	2.70	0.74	47.66	0.13	0.02
Uzbekistan	0.2075	20.00	6.79	76.34	10.09	0.32	Bangladesh	0.0641	3.70	0.61	46.17	0.11	0.04
Tonga	0.2069	12.00	29.79	52.18	4.33	0.96	Rwanda	0.0614	7.70	0.37	33.40	1.43	0.02
Paraguay	0.1968	23.60	6.27	91.64	2.47	0.61	Zambia	0.0601	6.74	0.69	37.80	0.14	0.08
Syrian Arab Republic	0.1952	20.70	19.94	57.30	3.92	0.33	Nepal	0.0597	6.78	2.81	30.69	0.28	0.38
Samoa	0.1927	7.00	19.28	91.43	0.74	0.11	Afghanistan	0.0573	4.00	0.45	41.39	0.01	0.00
Sri Lanka	0.1922	12.00	17.15	83.22	1.21	1.02	Madagascar	0.0520	1.70	0.83	39.79	0.04	0.02
Kyrgyzstan	0.1903	20.00	9.41	91.86	0.90	0.29	Guinea-Bissau	0.0511	2.45	0.33	39.21	0.05	0.03
Indonesia	0.1897	9.10	15.83	91.72	0.73	0.79	Lesotho	0.0499	3.86	1.79	32.18	0.12	0.02
Botswana	0.1873	6.00	6.85	117.76	0.60	0.60	Guinea	0.0491	0.96	0.18	40.07	0.13	0.01
Tuvalu	0.1866	25.00	16.49	25.44	8.20	3.26	Djibouti	0.0488	6.50	2.08	18.64	1.34	0.91
Algeria	0.1812	12.50	8.24	92.42	0.58	2.54	Liberia	0.0477	0.07	0.15	39.34	0.43	0.00
Bolivia (Plurinational State of)	0.1786	20.00	8.54	72.30	3.59	0.97	Kiribati	0.0469	9.00	4.12	10.05	0.87	0.90
Vanuatu	0.1783	8.00	2.09	119.05	1.11	0.13	Burkina Faso	0.0454	1.40	0.87	34.66	0.11	0.08
Mongolia	0.1758	10.20	7.01	91.09	1.81	2.31	Mozambique	0.0443	4.17	0.38	30.88	0.06	0.06
Nauru	0.1700	6.00	18.61	60.46	1.49	3.90	Comoros	0.0436	5.10	2.86	22.49	0.23	0.00
Belize	0.1627	14.00	9.72	62.32	2.92	2.86	Marshall Islands	0.0425	3.55	8.14	7.03	1.34	0.00
Gabon	0.1595	7.23	2.02	106.94	0.76	0.25	Papua New Guinea	0.0411	1.28	1.77	27.84	0.50	0.09
Tajikistan	0.1474	11.55	5.35	86.37	0.01	0.07	Sierra Leone	0.0395	0.26	0.24	34.09	0.02	0.00
Namibia	0.1385	6.50	6.66	67.21	4.17	0.42	Malawi	0.0321	2.26	1.07	20.38	0.75	0.03
Sao Tome and Principe	0.1374	18.75	4.63	61.97	1.61	0.35	Central African Republic	0.0297	2.30	0.27	23.18	0.06	0.00
Gambia	0.1344	9.20	2.82	85.53	0.22	0.02	Niger	0.0293	0.83	0.54	24.53	0.03	0.02
Senegal	0.1283	16.00	2.75	67.11	0.49	0.63	Chad	0.0291	1.70	0.46	23.29	0.04	0.00
Congo	0.1275	5.00	0.24	93.96	0.03	0.00	Solomon Islands	0.0198	5.00	1.56	5.57	0.40	0.37
Nigeria	0.1270	28.43	0.66	55.10	0.12	0.06	Dem. Rep. of the Congo	0.0183	0.72	0.06	17.21	0.11	0.01
Pakistan	0.1239	16.78	1.97	59.21	2.17	0.31	Burundi	0.0173	2.10	0.39	13.72	0.06	0.00
Kenya	0.1212	20.98	1.14	61.63	0.08	0.01	Eritrea	0.0132	5.40	1.03	3.53	0.14	0.00
Iraq	0.1201	5.60	5.05	75.78	0.01	0.00	Dem. People's Rep. of Korea	0.0112	0.00	4.85	1.77	0.00	0.00
Nicaragua	0.1194	10.00	4.46	65.14	0.43	0.82	Ethiopia	0.0093	0.75	1.10	7.86	0.09	0.00
Bhutan	0.1143	13.60	3.62	54.32	0.93	1.20	Somalia	0.0090	1.16	1.07	6.95	0.11	0.00
Turkmenistan	0.1139	2.20	10.31	63.42	0.05	0.01	Myanmar	0.0000	0.22	1.26	1.24	0.05	0.03
Swaziland	0.1125	8.02	3.71	61.78	1.88	0.14							
Mauritania	0.1123	3.00	2.07	79.34	0.29	0.19							
Benin	0.1118	3.13	1.51	79.94	0.23	0.29							
Ghana	0.1111	8.55	1.14	71.49	0.39	0.21	**Regional and Economic Groupings**						
India	0.1102	7.50	2.87	61.42	1.53	0.90	Africa	0.1094	9.85	3.93	56.45	1.26	0.66
Zimbabwe	0.1099	11.50	3.01	59.66	0.80	0.26	Americas	0.3602	36.63	21.26	107.53	8.06	9.08
Côte d'Ivoire	0.1019	2.60	1.13	75.54	0.10	0.04	Asia	0.2818	29.33	15.06	91.64	6.98	5.41
Micronesia (Federated States of)	0.1013	20.00	7.61	24.78	1.17	0.90	Europe	0.6460	66.01	40.40	119.52	24.06	23.63
Yemen	0.1011	10.85	4.35	46.09	1.95	0.33	Oceania	0.2211	21.26	17.22	59.06	6.25	4.41
Lao People's Dem. Rep.	0.0998	7.00	1.66	64.56	0.26	0.19	World	0.3245	32.79	18.87	88.53	9.33	8.73
Angola	0.0892	10.00	1.59	46.69	1.72	0.10							
Equatorial Guinea	0.0883	6.00	1.93	57.01	0.20	0.17	Developed countries	0.6509	67.45	40.69	117.24	24.60	23.92
United Rep. of Tanzania	0.0839	11.00	0.39	46.80	1.09	0.01							
Cambodia	0.0814	1.26	2.54	57.65	0.14	0.25	Developing countries other than LDCs	0.2860	28.62	16.11	98.11	5.90	5.24
Togo	0.0744	5.38	3.55	40.69	1.01	0.09							
Uganda	0.0732	12.50	0.98	38.38	0.09	0.06	Least developed countries	0.0685	5.75	2.13	40.04	0.60	0.23
South Sudan	0.0725	10.16	0.86	40.54	0.11	0.38							
Sudan	0.0725	10.16	0.86	40.54	0.11	0.38	Small island developing States	0.2758	26.62	17.77	85.77	5.77	6.37
Cuba	0.0709	15.12	10.34	8.91	0.35	0.03							

Table 7.4 Human capital index and its components

Country	Human Capital index (in order of decreasing value)	Adult Literacy (%)	Enrollment (%)	Country	Human Capital index (in order of decreasing value)	Adult Literacy (%)	Enrollment (%)
Australia	1.0000	99.00	112.07	Guyana	0.8562	99.00	78.58
New Zealand	0.9982	99.00	111.65	Armenia	0.8505	99.53	76.30
Cuba	0.9684	99.83	103.19	Libya	0.8502	88.86	95.75
Dem. People's Rep. of Korea	0.9560	100.00	100.00	Singapore	0.8500	94.71	85.00
Ireland	0.9535	99.00	101.24	Bulgaria	0.8486	98.32	78.08
Republic of Korea	0.9494	99.00	100.28	Kyrgyzstan	0.8485	99.24	76.36
Denmark	0.9489	99.00	100.17	Serbia	0.8484	97.77	79.01
Finland	0.9467	99.00	99.66	Palau	0.8445	91.90	88.87
Monaco	0.9439	99.00	99.00	Turkmenistan	0.8404	99.56	73.90
Netherlands	0.9425	99.00	98.68	Luxembourg	0.8404	99.00	74.90
Spain	0.9409	97.68	100.73	Colombia	0.8391	93.24	85.15
Norway	0.9347	99.00	96.86	Georgia	0.8348	99.72	72.28
Greece	0.9332	97.16	99.88	Bosnia and Herzegovina	0.8341	97.81	75.64
Iceland	0.9310	99.00	96.00	Philippines	0.8341	95.42	80.01
Slovenia	0.9300	99.68	94.52	Saint Kitts and Nevis	0.8338	97.80	75.58
Belgium	0.9264	99.00	94.94	Samoa	0.8335	98.78	73.71
France	0.9244	99.00	94.47	Micronesia (Federated States of)	0.8332	94.00	82.38
Lithuania	0.9240	99.70	93.10	Tajikistan	0.8313	99.67	71.57
Canada	0.9238	99.00	94.32	Mexico	0.8295	93.44	82.56
Barbados	0.9232	99.70	92.90	Azerbaijan	0.8259	99.50	70.61
United States	0.9202	99.00	93.50	Uzbekistan	0.8255	99.33	70.84
San Marino	0.9179	99.00	92.95	Brunei Darussalam	0.8253	95.29	78.17
Ukraine	0.9176	99.69	91.62	Tuvalu	0.8228	98.00	72.63
Sweden	0.9141	99.00	92.06	Seychelles	0.8204	91.84	83.38
Kazakhstan	0.9134	99.68	90.66	Brazil	0.8203	90.04	86.63
Italy	0.9120	98.87	91.82	Montenegro	0.8182	96.40	74.50
Belarus	0.9120	99.73	90.24	Panama	0.8151	93.61	78.88
Austria	0.9091	99.00	90.90	Republic of Moldova	0.8129	98.46	69.48
Estonia	0.9085	99.79	89.30	Bahamas	0.8120	95.80	74.15
Hungary	0.9065	99.37	89.63	The former Yugoslav Rep. of Macedonia	0.8115	97.12	71.61
Poland	0.9044	99.51	88.87	Maldives	0.8114	98.40	69.26
Argentina	0.9038	97.73	92.01	Costa Rica	0.8089	96.06	72.97
Uruguay	0.9013	98.27	90.43	Saint Lucia	0.8089	94.80	75.27
United Kingdom	0.9007	99.00	88.96	Bolivia (Plurinational State of)	0.8072	90.70	82.37
Germany	0.8971	99.00	88.10	Andorra	0.8063	99.00	66.98
Japan	0.8969	99.00	88.06	Malta	0.8057	92.36	78.99
Israel	0.8945	97.10	90.98	Bahrain	0.8028	91.36	80.15
Portugal	0.8931	94.91	94.67	Jordan	0.8013	92.20	78.27
Liechtenstein	0.8910	99.00	86.69	Fiji	0.7986	94.40	73.60
Czech Republic	0.8898	99.00	86.42	Indonesia	0.7982	92.19	77.55
Grenada	0.8895	96.00	91.85	Peru	0.7942	89.59	81.38
Switzerland	0.8888	99.00	86.18	Lebanon	0.7917	89.61	80.76
Latvia	0.8879	99.78	84.53	Jamaica	0.7916	86.36	86.68
Russian Federation	0.8850	99.56	84.27	Kuwait	0.7885	93.91	72.16
Chile	0.8788	98.55	84.68	Kiribati	0.7871	93.00	73.49
Romania	0.8783	97.65	86.20	Albania	0.7863	95.94	67.93
Antigua and Barbuda	0.8770	98.95	83.53	Paraguay	0.7862	94.56	70.43
Cyprus	0.8751	97.93	84.95	United Arab Emirates	0.7837	90.03	78.12
Tonga	0.8727	99.02	82.40	Trinidad and Tobago	0.7830	98.74	62.03
Venezuela	0.8705	95.15	88.96	Suriname	0.7821	94.62	69.35
Slovakia	0.8696	99.00	81.70	Thailand	0.7819	93.51	71.36
Mongolia	0.8688	97.49	84.30	South Africa	0.7817	88.72	80.08
Croatia	0.8615	98.76	80.27	China	0.7745	93.98	68.74

Table 7.4 **Human capital index and its components** (cont.)

Country	Human Capital index (in order of decreasing value)	Adult Literacy (%)	Enrollment (%)	Country	Human Capital index (in order of decreasing value)	Adult Literacy (%)	Enrollment (%)
Turkey	0.7726	90.82	74.10	Dem. Rep. of the Congo	0.4893	66.81	52.11
Saint Vincent and the Grenadines	0.7696	88.10	78.38	Liberia	0.4849	59.05	65.30
Malaysia	0.7691	92.46	70.29	Yemen	0.4642	62.39	54.35
Saudi Arabia	0.7677	86.13	81.55	South Sudan	0.4555	70.21	38.00
Marshall Islands	0.7590	94.00	65.10	Sudan	0.4555	70.21	38.00
Mauritius	0.7588	87.90	76.24	Nigeria	0.4535	60.82	54.76
Gabon	0.7572	87.71	76.20	Nepal	0.4521	59.14	57.48
Ecuador	0.7549	84.21	82.09	Morocco	0.4430	56.08	60.98
Dominica	0.7520	88.00	74.47	Togo	0.4312	56.89	56.74
Viet Nam	0.7434	92.78	63.71	Timor-Leste	0.4290	50.60	67.77
Sao Tome and Principe	0.7432	88.78	71.00	Guinea-Bissau	0.4278	52.20	64.55
Namibia	0.7419	88.51	71.20	Mozambique	0.4255	55.06	58.77
Dominican Republic	0.7398	88.24	71.18	Djibouti	0.4236	70.30	30.43
Sri Lanka	0.7357	90.56	65.99	Bhutan	0.4153	52.81	60.51
Qatar	0.7316	94.72	57.41	Mauritania	0.4079	57.45	50.30
Oman	0.7224	86.62	70.11	Eritrea	0.3907	66.58	29.57
El Salvador	0.7169	84.10	73.42	Bangladesh	0.3889	55.90	48.70
Kenya	0.7109	87.01	66.73	Papua New Guinea	0.3743	60.10	37.64
Botswana	0.7091	84.12	71.59	Pakistan	0.3572	55.53	42.01
Iran (Islamic Rep. of)	0.7089	85.02	69.89	Gambia	0.3519	46.50	57.32
Myanmar	0.7064	92.03	56.48	Central African Republic	0.3446	55.23	39.62
Honduras	0.7060	83.59	71.85	Côte d'Ivoire	0.3388	55.26	38.22
Nauru	0.7047	92.00	56.13	Senegal	0.3271	49.70	45.68
Equatorial Guinea	0.7001	93.33	52.64	Benin	0.3113	41.65	56.74
Lesotho	0.6997	89.66	59.24	Haiti	0.2922	48.69	39.40
Swaziland	0.6973	86.93	63.70	Guinea	0.2696	39.46	51.04
Syrian Arab Republic	0.6876	84.19	66.44	Sierra Leone	0.2576	40.92	45.58
Tunisia	0.6841	77.56	77.79	Afghanistan	0.2178	28.00	59.97
Zimbabwe	0.6644	91.86	47.01	Ethiopia	0.2119	29.82	55.25
Nicaragua	0.6533	78.00	69.79	Chad	0.2003	33.61	45.62
Vanuatu	0.6531	82.03	62.37	Mali	0.1723	26.18	52.71
Algeria	0.6463	72.65	77.96	Burkina Faso	0.1338	28.73	39.07
Congo	0.6369	81.10	60.30	Niger	0.1103	28.67	33.70
Guatemala	0.6284	74.47	70.47	Somalia	0.0000	24.00	16.58
Cape Verde	0.6245	84.80	50.65				
Belize	0.6155	70.30	75.11				
Iraq	0.6151	78.06	60.80				
Cambodia	0.5997	77.59	58.08	**Regional and Economic Groupings**			
Uganda	0.5883	71.37	66.80	Africa	0.5034	65.76	57.32
Rwanda	0.5861	70.67	67.59	Americas	0.7958	90.81	79.53
Comoros	0.5853	74.15	61.01	Asia	0.7278	86.34	71.87
Solomon Islands	0.5743	76.60	53.98	Europe	0.8916	98.51	87.72
Malawi	0.5741	73.69	59.27	Oceania	0.7754	90.85	74.72
Lao People's Dem. Rep.	0.5651	72.70	58.96	World	0.7173	84.43	72.93
Egypt	0.5588	66.37	69.11				
United Rep. of Tanzania	0.5564	72.90	56.59				
Cameroon	0.5554	70.68	60.41	Developed countries	0.8974	98.53	89.03
Madagascar	0.5438	64.48	69.07	Developing countries other than LDCs	0.7553	88.68	73.98
Angola	0.5383	69.96	57.76				
Ghana	0.5360	66.62	63.33	Least developed countries	0.4575	61.54	54.73
Burundi	0.5188	66.57	59.42				
India	0.5025	62.75	62.61	Small island developing States	0.7406	87.63	72.51
Zambia	0.4993	70.88	46.99				

Table 7.5 E-participation index

Rank	Country	Index value	Rank	Country	Index value	Rank	Country	Index value	Rank	Country	Index value
1	Netherlands	1.0000	21	Argentina	0.2895	28	Ghana	0.1053	31	Kiribati	0.0263
1	Republic of Korea	1.0000	21	Croatia	0.2895	28	Iraq	0.1053	32	Armenia	0.0000
2	Kazakhstan	0.9474	22	Czech Republic	0.2632	29	Belarus	0.0789	32	Bosnia and Herzegovina	0.0000
2	Singapore	0.9474	22	Italy	0.2632	29	Benin	0.0789	32	Burundi	0.0000
3	United Kingdom	0.9211	22	Malta	0.2632	29	Cyprus	0.0789	32	Cambodia	0.0000
3	United States	0.9211	22	Venezuela	0.2632	29	Romania	0.0789	32	Central African Republic	0.0000
4	Israel	0.8947	23	Cape Verde	0.2368	29	Seychelles	0.0789	32	Comoros	0.0000
5	Australia	0.7632	23	Guatemala	0.2368	29	Sri Lanka	0.0789	32	Congo	0.0000
5	Estonia	0.7632	23	Liechtenstein	0.2368	29	Trinidad and Tobago	0.0789	32	Dem. People's Rep. of Korea	0.0000
5	Germany	0.7632	23	Serbia	0.2368	29	Uganda	0.0789	32	Djibouti	0.0000
6	Colombia	0.7368	23	Uzbekistan	0.2368	29	United Rep. of Tanzania	0.0789	32	Gambia	0.0000
6	Finland	0.7368	23	Ecuador	0.2368	29	Bahamas	0.0789	32	Guinea	0.0000
6	Japan	0.7368	24	Bolivia (Plurinational State of)	0.2105	29	Bangladesh	0.0789	32	Guyana	0.0000
6	United Arab Emirates	0.7368	24	China	0.2105	29	Fiji	0.0789	32	Haiti	0.0000
7	Egypt	0.6842	24	Indonesia	0.2105	29	Mauritius	0.0789	32	Jamaica	0.0000
7	Canada	0.6842	24	Senegal	0.2105	29	Somalia	0.0789	32	Lao People's Dem. Rep.	0.0000
7	Norway	0.6842	24	Grenada	0.2105	29	Sudan	0.0789	32	Libya	0.0000
7	Sweden	0.6842	24	Latvia	0.2105	30	Algeria	0.0526	32	Malawi	0.0000
8	Chile	0.6579	24	Slovenia	0.2105	30	Kenya	0.0526	32	Mali	0.0000
8	Russian Federation	0.6579	24	Georgia	0.2105	30	Saint Kitts and Nevis	0.0526	32	Marshall Islands	0.0000
8	Bahrain	0.6579	24	Philippines	0.2105	30	Sierra Leone	0.0526	32	Mauritania	0.0000
9	Qatar	0.6316	25	India	0.1842	30	Swaziland	0.0526	32	Myanmar	0.0000
9	Saudi Arabia	0.6316	25	Monaco	0.1842	30	Togo	0.0526	32	Nauru	0.0000
10	Mongolia	0.6053	25	Poland	0.1842	30	Cuba	0.0526	32	Niger	0.0000
11	New Zealand	0.5789	25	Belize	0.1842	30	Guinea-Bissau	0.0526	32	Papua New Guinea	0.0000
11	France	0.5789	25	Iran (Islamic Republic of)	0.1842	30	Turkey	0.0526	32	Samoa	0.0000
11	Mexico	0.5789	25	Kuwait	0.1842	30	Vanuatu	0.0526	32	San Marino	0.0000
12	Denmark	0.5526	25	Nigeria	0.1842	31	Angola	0.0263	32	South Sudan	0.0000
12	El Salvador	0.5526	25	Uruguay	0.1842	31	Barbados	0.0263	32	Suriname	0.0000
13	Lithuania	0.5263	26	Burkina Faso	0.1579	31	Bhutan	0.0263	32	Tajikistan	0.0000
14	Brazil	0.5000	26	Iceland	0.1579	31	Botswana	0.0263	32	Timor-Leste	0.0000
14	Malaysia	0.5000	26	Paraguay	0.1579	31	Cameroon	0.0263	32	Turkmenistan	0.0000
14	Spain	0.5000	26	South Africa	0.1579	31	Chad	0.0263	32	Tuvalu	0.0000
15	Dominican Republic	0.4737	26	Ukraine	0.1579	31	Dominica	0.0263	32	Yemen	0.0000
15	Brunei Darussalam	0.4737	26	Andorra	0.1579	31	Eritrea	0.0263			
16	Hungary	0.4474	27	Ireland	0.1316	31	Lesotho	0.0263			
16	Oman	0.4474	27	Mozambique	0.1316	31	Liberia	0.0263			
17	Luxembourg	0.3947	27	Nicaragua	0.1316	31	Madagascar	0.0263			
17	Morocco	0.3947	27	Slovakia	0.1316	31	Maldives	0.0263			
17	Peru	0.3947	27	The former Yugoslav Rep. of Macedonia	0.1316	31	Micronesia (Federated States of)	0.0263			
17	Republic of Moldova	0.3947	27	Afghanistan	0.1316	31	Namibia	0.0263			
18	Austria	0.3684	27	Antigua and Barbuda	0.1316	31	Nepal	0.0263			
18	Portugal	0.3684	27	Côte d'Ivoire	0.1316	31	Palau	0.0263			
18	Tunisia	0.3684	27	Honduras	0.1316	31	Rwanda	0.0263			
19	Ethiopia	0.3421	27	Pakistan	0.1316	31	Sao Tome and Principe	0.0263			
19	Greece	0.3421	27	Azerbaijan	0.1316	31	Solomon Islands	0.0263			
19	Switzerland	0.3421	27	Belgium	0.1316	31	Syrian Arab Republic	0.0263			
20	Costa Rica	0.3158	28	Albania	0.1053	31	Tonga	0.0263			
20	Lebanon	0.3158	28	Gabon	0.1053	31	Zambia	0.0263			
20	Montenegro	0.3158	28	Jordan	0.1053	31	Zimbabwe	0.0263			
20	Panama	0.3158	28	Saint Lucia	0.1053	31	Bulgaria	0.0263			
20	Thailand	0.3158	28	Saint Vincent and the Grenadines	0.1053	31	Dem. Rep. of the Congo	0.0263			
21	Kyrgyzstan	0.2895	28	Viet Nam	0.1053	31	Equatorial Guinea	0.0263			

Regional and Economic Groupings

	Index value
Africa	0.0828
Americas	0.2579
Asia	0.2738
Europe	0.3482
Oceania	0.1147
World	0.2225
Developed countries	0.3990
Developing countries other than LDCs	0.2223
Least developed countries	0.0428
Small island developing States	0.0875

Table 7.6 **Environment Index**

Country	Index value	Country	Index value	Country	Index value	Country	Index value
Germany	1.0000	Slovakia	0.7059	Guyana	0.4118	Sao Tome and Principe	0.1176
Republic of Korea	1.0000	South Africa	0.7059	Samoa	0.4118	Seychelles	0.1176
Singapore	1.0000	Spain	0.7059	Saudi Arabia	0.4118	Somalia	0.1176
United States	1.0000	Costa Rica	0.6471	Senegal	0.4118	Sudan	0.1176
Austria	0.9412	Cyprus	0.6471	The former Yugoslav Rep. of Macedonia	0.4118	Zimbabwe	0.1176
Israel	0.9412	Czech Republic	0.6471	Bahamas	0.3529	Comoros	0.0588
Japan	0.9412	Georgia	0.6471	Barbados	0.3529	Congo	0.0588
Malta	0.9412	Hungary	0.6471	Cape Verde	0.3529	Lesotho	0.0588
Mexico	0.9412	India	0.6471	Côte d'Ivoire	0.3529	Malawi	0.0588
New Zealand	0.9412	Iran (Islamic Republic of)	0.6471	Ethiopia	0.3529	Timor-Leste	0.0588
Russian Federation	0.9412	Jamaica	0.6471	Lebanon	0.3529	Afghanistan	0.0000
United Kingdom	0.9412	Mauritius	0.6471	Montenegro	0.3529	Algeria	0.0000
Australia	0.8824	Namibia	0.6471	Morocco	0.3529	Burundi	0.0000
Canada	0.8824	Republic of Moldova	0.6471	Nigeria	0.3529	Central African Republic	0.0000
Finland	0.8824	Saint Vincent and the Grenadines	0.6471	Papua New Guinea	0.3529	Chad	0.0000
France	0.8824	Tunisia	0.6471	Qatar	0.3529	Dem. People's Rep. of Korea	0.0000
Mongolia	0.8824	Ukraine	0.6471	Suriname	0.3529	Equatorial Guinea	0.0000
Norway	0.8824	Viet Nam	0.6471	Zambia	0.3529	Guinea	0.0000
Portugal	0.8824	Armenia	0.5882	Belize	0.2941	Guinea-Bissau	0.0000
Belgium	0.8235	Belarus	0.5882	Bhutan	0.2941	Iraq	0.0000
Chile	0.8235	Brunei Darussalam	0.5882	Dem. Rep. of the Congo	0.2941	Liberia	0.0000
Denmark	0.8235	Bulgaria	0.5882	Djibouti	0.2941	Libya	0.0000
Netherlands	0.8235	Colombia	0.5882	Haiti	0.2941	Marshall Islands	0.0000
Peru	0.8235	Dominican Republic	0.5882	Lao People's Dem. Rep.	0.2941	Myanmar	0.0000
Poland	0.8235	El Salvador	0.5882	Nepal	0.2941	Niger	0.0000
Sweden	0.8235	Estonia	0.5882	Philippines	0.2941	Saint Kitts and Nevis	0.0000
Switzerland	0.8235	Gabon	0.5882	Saint Lucia	0.2941	San Marino	0.0000
Turkey	0.8235	Jordan	0.5882	Sri Lanka	0.2941	Sierra Leone	0.0000
Brazil	0.7647	Kenya	0.5882	Tonga	0.2941	Solomon Islands	0.0000
China	0.7647	Maldives	0.5882	Bahrain	0.2353	South Sudan	0.0000
Greece	0.7647	Rwanda	0.5882	Benin	0.2353	Swaziland	0.0000
Iceland	0.7647	United Arab Emirates	0.5882	Botswana	0.2353	Syrian Arab Republic	0.0000
Ireland	0.7647	Uzbekistan	0.5882	Burkina Faso	0.2353	Togo	0.0000
Italy	0.7647	Angola	0.5294	Egypt	0.2353	Tuvalu	0.0000
Kazakhstan	0.7647	Antigua and Barbuda	0.5294	Gambia	0.2353		
Latvia	0.7647	Azerbaijan	0.5294	Guatemala	0.2353		
Liechtenstein	0.7647	Bosnia and Herzegovina	0.5294	Kuwait	0.2353		
Lithuania	0.7647	Mozambique	0.5294	Monaco	0.2353	**Regional and Economic Groupings**	
Pakistan	0.7647	Panama	0.5294	Nicaragua	0.2353	Africa	0.2418
Slovenia	0.7647	Paraguay	0.5294	Oman	0.2353	Americas	0.5025
Thailand	0.7647	Vanuatu	0.5294	Turkmenistan	0.2353	Asia	0.4914
Trinidad and Tobago	0.7647	Venezuela	0.5294	United Republic of Tanzania	0.2353	Europe	0.7182
Albania	0.7059	Bolivia (Plurinational State of)	0.4706	Eritrea	0.1765	Oceania	0.3403
Andorra	0.7059	Fiji	0.4706	Grenada	0.1765	World	0.4633
Bangladesh	0.7059	Kiribati	0.4706	Honduras	0.1765		
Croatia	0.7059	Madagascar	0.4706	Nauru	0.1765		
Cuba	0.7059	Mali	0.4706	Yemen	0.1765	Developed countries	0.7443
Indonesia	0.7059	Tajikistan	0.4706	Cambodia	0.1176		
Kyrgyzstan	0.7059	Uganda	0.4706	Cameroon	0.1176	Developing countries other than LDCs	0.4455
Luxembourg	0.7059	Uruguay	0.4706	Dominica	0.1176		
Malaysia	0.7059	Argentina	0.4118	Mauritania	0.1176	Least developed countries	0.2120
Romania	0.7059	Ecuador	0.4118	Micronesia (Federated States of)	0.1176		
Serbia	0.7059	Ghana	0.4118	Palau	0.1176	Small island developing States	0.3355

Notes

Chapter 1

1 World Bank Institute (2010).

2 World Bank (2011c). As of July 2011 the World Bank classified a country with a gross national income per capita of greater than USD 12,276 as high income.

3 For details on the four stages, see the methodology section of the statistical annex.

4 Oceania's jump in the 2008 average was due to the exclusion of four countries from the ranking due to unavailability of key indicators, which pulled up the index.

5 Seychelles: National ICT Policy.

6 The usa.gov website is discussed in more detail in Chapter 3 on whole-of-government.

7 Egov Magazine (2011).

8 ictQatar Supreme Council of Information & Communication Technology (2011).

9 European Commission Community Research and Development Information Service (2011).

10 European Commission Information Society (2011).

11 Teisesforumas (2012).

12 United Nations Statistics Division grouping (2011c) (4 October) is basis for LDCs classification.

13 UNDP Crisis Prevention and Recovery Report 2008 (http://www.undp.org/cpr/content/economic_recovery/PCERreport.pdf).

Chapter 2

1 A transactional service is defined as a two-way interaction between the government and the citizen, for example involving online payments.

2 United Nations (2011a).

3 For a full list, see UNEP Ministries of Environment website at http://www.unep.org/resources/gov/MEnvironment.asp.

4 See in particular Agenda 21 (principle 10) and Report of the World Summit on Sustainable Development (paras. 110, 112 and 128).

5 UNEP (2005).

6 UNEP (2010).

Chapter 3

1 See Christensen and Laegried (2007).

2 OECD (2006).

3 Bharosa and others (2010).

4 LaVigne (2001) and Raffat (2006).

5 Busson and Keravel (2005).

6 United Nations (2008).

7 For the additional characteristics see Krenner, Johanna and others.

8 For the stages see Wimmer, Maria A. (2002).

9 W3C (2009).

10 Pascual (2003) on issues of how to build an appropriate government information and software architecture.

11 This section draws on Busson and Keravel (2005).

12 See Sethi and Sethi.

13 Ibid.

14 See Chatzidimitriou and Koumpis (2008).

15 Ibid.

16 See Kubicek and Hagen (2000).

17 Busson and Keravel.

18 See "Online Collaboration" in Fortune magazine, vol. 164, no. 6, 17 October 2011, special advertising section.

19 Ibid.

20 See Wimmer and Traunmüller (2002)

21 Roy and Longford (2008).

22 See Franzel and Coursey (2004).

23 Rabaiah, Abdelbaset and Vandijck (2009).

24 Ibid.

Chapter 4

1 Multichannel service delivery has been used by the private sector for more than 30 years (e.g., ATMs have been in use in the financial sector since the late 1960s.

2 European Commission (2008).

3 Voigt (2011).

4 Ecotec Research and Consulting (2009).

5 World Bank (2011a).

6 Justmeans (2010).

7 According to ITU, there are nearly six billion mobile cellular subscriptions worldwide and more than four billion of those are in developing countries. In addition, more than 90 per cent of the world's population now lives within range of a cellular network, a figure that has doubled in the past ten years. People are moving rapidly from 2G to 3G platforms in both developed and developing countries. In 2011, a total of 159 economies worldwide launched 3G services commercially and the number of active mobile-broadband subscriptions increased to almost 1.2 billion.

8 OECD and ITU (2011).

9 GSM Association (2011).

10 Singapore (2011).

11 Malaysia (2011).

12 Malta (2011).

13 Çam (2010).

14 Klievnik and Jannsen (2008).

15 Ibid.

16 Mexico (2011).

17 Bold (2011).

18 New Zealand, Citylink (2011).

19 Ontario Ministry of Government Services (2011).

20 European Commission (2004).

21 See Von and Haldenwang (2002).

22 Ibid.

23 Mahapatra and Sahu (2008).

24 ITU (2011a).

25 Ibid.

26 W3C (2008).

27 Susanto and Goodwin (2010).

28 ITU (2010).

29 Hall (2008).

30 See Botterman (2008) and Millard (2009).

31 van Veenstra and Janssen (2010).

32 See many studies and stories at http://www.ukonlinecentres.com.

33 European Commission. (2004).

34 W3C (2009).

35 See Singh and Sahu (2008); Chen, Huang, and Hsiao (2006); Ebbers, Pieterson, and Noordman (2008)

Chapter 5

1   Segger and Khalfan (2004).

2   See World Bank (2009).

3   Barzilai-Nahon (2006).

4   Chen and Wellman (2005).

5   Corrocher and Ordanini (2002).

6   Sciadas (2005).

7   Norris and others (Eds.) (2001) and Mossberger and others (2003). Reference is made to the different applications and uses of online information to engage and participate in public life.

8   DiMaggio and Hargittai (2001).

9   Modarres (2011); Segev and Ahituv (2010).

10   One common analogy is the 80/20 factor: 80 per cent of profit is made by serving the most affluent 20 per cent, thus pushing IT designers to create products specifically for the affluent. See, for example http://www.digitaldivide.org.

11   The content of table 1 is not exhaustive. It is based on Barzilai-Nahon (2006). For more on the theory of social construction of technology, see Pinch and Bijker (1984); Dijk and Hacker (2003); Corrocher and Ordanini (2002); Selhofer and Mayringer (2001); Sciadas (2005); Modarres (2011); and Segev and Ahituv (2010).

12   Pick and Azari (2008).

13   Charalabidis and Loukis (2011).

14   Modarres (2011).

15   Rao (2000).

16   Wolff and Castro (2003).

17   Torsen (2005).

18   Vicente and Lopez (2010).

19   A security feature consisting of a string of distorted letters and numbers that users are supposed to read and retype before they register for a new service or send an e-mail.

20   See http://accessibility.egovmon.no/en/pagecheck.

21   W3C launched the Web Accessibility Initiative in April 1997. WAI has developed a detailed set of Web Content Accessibility Guidelines – WCA Guidelines 1.0 and associated checklists, which aim to promote accessible designs and to make content understandable and navigable.

22   Ibid.

23   Ibid. A word of caution is in order. First, the actual number of tests carried out on each site varies widely from site to site due to the fact that the number of testable features varies from site to site. For example, a very complex, feature-rich website may have hundreds of testable features. A very simple site, by contrast, may have only a handful of testable features. Thus, all else being equal, it is likely that simple sites will pass a higher proportion of tests than more complex sites. This fact renders cross-country comparisons difficult. Second, websites are highly dynamic; they change frequently as content is updated, revised, and retired. Thus, to thoroughly assess a country's commitment to accessibility via the e-accessibility checker, it would be necessary to repeat test runs

through time – to minimize the effect of any occasional errors or oversight on the part of website maintainers.

24   Estonia, Finland and Spain have declared access to the Internet as a legal right of their citizens. See, for example, ITU (2010).

25   Web Accessibility Initiative.

26   Olaya (2010).

27   ComScore Press Release (2010).

28   Ibid.

29   Adult economic activity rate refers to the percentage of the population aged 15 and over that is economically active. See United Nations Statistics Division (2011b).

30   The higher average of female economic activity in Africa can be explained by the small-N factor: only two African countries, Ethiopia and Botswana, offer vulnerability sections on their national websites. These two countries have high degrees of female economic activity – 80.7 per cent and 72.3 per cent of their populations, respectively.

31   Dasgupta and others (2005).

32   Tolbert and Mossberg (2006).

33   For instance, a disability often results in poverty, and conversely, living in poverty increases the likelihood of acquiring a disability. See, for example, D'Aubin (2007).

34   ITU (2011b).

35   See World Bank data at http://data.worldbank.org/about/country-classifications.

36   See World Bank data at http://data.worldbank.org/indicator/NY.GDP.PCAP.CD.

37   UNDP (2011).

38   ITU (2011d).

39   ITU (2011e).

40   IFAD.

41   ITU (2011b).

42   ILO (2011).

43   Yung and others (2010).

44   Schluter and Kragelj (2007).

45   Barzilai-Nahon (2006). For more on the theory of social construction of technology, see Pinch and Bijker (1984).

46   Stoiciu (2011).

47   Vicente and Lopez (2010).

Chapter 6

1   United Nations (2010).

2   Ecole Polytechnique Fédérale de Lausanne (2002).

3   Society of IT Management (2008).

4   In Bahrain, e-government services are not used regularly by the respondents, and this can be clearly shown in their responses to the question. Most of them (75 per cent) choose the answer "when needed." See Alzaki (2009); Sahraoui (2005); and AlSobhi, Kamal and Weerakkody (2010).

5   Yih-Jeou Wang (2009).

6   Australian Government Information Management Office (2009).

7   Pavilenene (2011).

8   Deloitte (2010).

9   OECD (2009).

10   World Bank (2011b).

11   Smith (2010).

12   Norazah, Suk and Ramayah (2010).

13   European Commission (2010a).

14   Katims (2011).

15   Howard (2011).

16   Al-Jaghoub, Al-Yaseen and Al-Hourani (2010); Al-Sobi, Faris, Vishanth Weerakkody and Al-Shafi (2009); Yonazi, Jim, Sol and Boonstra (2010); Vencatachellum and Pudaruth (2010).

17   Australian Government Information Management Office (2008) and (2009).

18   Foresee (2011); Morris and Alawadhi (2009).

19   Smith (2010).

20   Wang (2009).

21   Norway (2011).

22   Ross, Hutton and Peng. (2004).

23   Yong (2004).

24   ForeSee Results, Inc. (2011).

25   Cap Gemini (2009).

26   EU (2009).

27   Dwivedi, Selamat and Lal (2011); Yeo (2011).

28   ITU (2011c).

29   Smith (2010).

30   European Commission (2010b).

31   Public Technology (2005)

32   Madden and Zickuhr (2011).

33   Pew Research Center (2010).

34   Nielsen Wire (2010).

35   European Commission, Directorate General Communication (2010).

36   Human Capital Institute (2010).

37   Social media strategy (2010).

38   Human Capital Institute (2010).

39   Shah (2010).

40   Hopkins (2011).

41   United Kingdom (2011).

42   United Kingdom, Cabinet Office (2011).

43   Pizzicannella (2010).

44   Boyle and Harris (2009).

45   UNDP (2008).

46   Bart (2011).

47   Niehaves (2008).

48   See Dubai Government.

49   Prima and Rolianabt (2011).

50   In comparison, only 43 countries (22 per cent) have a self-promotional section, such as asking users to link to the site or providing information on events related to promoting the portal. More than half of these 43 countries are developing countries and one (Sierra Leone) is even a least developed country.

51   See United States Internal Revenue Service website at http://www/irs.gov/efile/article/0,,id=11986,00.html.

52   World Economic Forum (2011).

References

Al-Jaghoub, S., Al-Yaseen, H. and Al-Hourani, M. (2010). Evaluation of Awareness and Acceptability of Using E-Government Services in Developing Countries: The Case of Jordan. *The Electronic Journal of Information Systems Evaluation*, vol. 13, issue 1, pp. 1-8.

Alzaki, Ali Aduljalil Abbas (2009). Evaluation of E-Government Services in Bahrain. Open University Malaysia, Centre for Graduate Studies.

Al-Sobi, Faris, Vishanth Weerakkody and Shafi Al-Shafi (2009). European and Mediterranean Conference on Information Systems (12-13 April), Abu Dhabi, United Arab Emirates.

Australian Government Information Management Office (2008). Interacting with Government – Australians' Use and Satisfaction with E-Government Services – 2009.

Bart, Sandra (2011). Electronic Government Equals Sustainable Development for Guyana, DiploFoundation, Internet Governamce Capacity Building Programme.

Barzilai-Nahon, K. (2006). Gaps and Bits: Conceptualizing Measurements for Digital Divide/s. The Information Society 22: pp. 269-278.

Bharosa, Nitesh, and others (2010). Guiding Integrated Service Delivery: Synthesizing and Embedding Principles Using Role-Playing Games. Delft University of Technology, Netherlands.

Boyle, David and David M. Harris (2009). The Challenge of Co-Production. New Economic Foundation discussion paper.

Busson, Alain and Alain Keravel (2005). Interoperable Government Providing Services: Key Questions and Solutions Analyzed through 40 Case Studies Collected in Europe. École des Hautes Études Commerciales de Paris.

Bold, Ben (2011). Estonia Enjoys IT Conference Boom. *Conference and Incentive Travel Magazine*. 6 September 2011. Available from http://www.citmaga-zine.com/news/1089374/Estonia-enjoys-conference-boom/. Accessed January 2012.

Çam, Ali Rıza (2010). SMS Information System: Mobile access to justice. *European Journal of ePractice*, no. 10 (September 2010). Available from http://www.sms.uyap. gov.tr/english/smsinfo.pdf. Accessed January 2012.

Cap Gemini, S.A., and others (2009). Smarter, Faster, Better eGovernment. 8th Benchmark Measurement, November 2009. Prepared for European Commission Directorate General for Information Society and Media.

Charalabidis, Y. and E. Loukis (2011). Transforming Government Agencies' Approach to E-participation through Efficient Exploitation of Social Media. ECIS 2011 Proceedings Paper 84. Available from http://aisel.aisnet.org/ecis2011/84.

Chatzidimitriou, Marios and Adamantios Koumpis (2008). Marketing One-stop E-Government Solutions: the European OneStopGov Project. *IAENG International Journal of Computer Science*, 35:1, IJCS_35_1_11. (Advance online publication: 19 February).

Chen, W. and B. Wellman (2005). Charting Digital Divides: Comparing Socioeconomic, Gender, Life Stage, and Rural-Urban Internet Access and Use in Five Countries. Transforming Enterprise, ed. by W. Dutton, and others. Cambridge, Massachusetts: MIT Press. Available from http://homes.chass.utoronto.ca/~wellman/publications/.

Christensen, Tom and Per Laegreid (2007). The Whole-of-Government Approach to Public Sector Reform. Public Administration Review (November/December): pp. 1059-1066.

ComScore Inc. (2010). Social Networking Sites Reach a Higher Percentage of Women than Men Worldwide, 28 July 2010. Available from http://www.comscore.com/Press_Events/Press_Releases/2010/7/Social_Networking_Sites_Reach_a_Higher_Percentage_of_Women_than_Men_Worldwide.

Corrocher, N. and A. Ordanini (2002). Measuring the Digital Divide: A Framework for the Analysis of Cross-country Differences. *Journal of Information Technology*, 17: pp. 9-19.

Dasgupta, S., and others. (2005). Policy Reform, Economic Growth and the Digital Divide. *Oxford Development Studies* 33, 2: pp. 229-243.

D'Aubin, A. (2007). Working for Barrier Removal in the ICT Area: Creating a More Accessible and Inclusive Canada. *The Information Society* 23: pp. 193–201.

Deloitte (2010). User Expectations of a Life Events approach for Designing E-Government Services: Final Report prepared for the European Commission, DG Information Society and Media.

Dijk, J.V. and Hacker, K. (2003). The Digital Divide as a Complex and Dynamic Phenomenon. *The Information Society*, 19, 4: pp. 315-356.

DiMaggio, P., and E. Hargittai. (2001). From the 'Digital Divide' to Digital Inequality: Studying Internet Use as Penetration Increases. Working paper 15, Princeton University, Princeton, New Jersey.

Dubai Government. Official Portal. Available from http://www.dubai.ae/.

Dwivedi, Yogesh K., Mohamad Hisyam Selamat and Banita Lal (2011). "Broadband Adoption and Usage Behavior of Malaysian Accountants. International Journal of Electronic Government Research, 7(2), (April-June 2011) pp. 1-14.

Ecotec Research and Consulting (2009). MC-eGov: Study on Multichannel Delivery Strategies and Sustainable Business Models for Public Services Addressing Socially Disadvantaged Groups (June 2009).

Egov Magazine (2011). Technology High on National Agenda. (September). Available from http://egovonline.net/articles/current-article.asp?fm=3&yy=2011.

École Polytechnique Fédérale de Lausanne (2002). Why and how the environment has to be taken into account at the World Summit on the Information Society, Geneva 2003 – Tunis 2005. Contribution to the WSIS Working Group on the Impact of ICT on the Environment. WSIS/PC-2/CONTR/43-E.

European Commission (2004). Multichannel Delivery of eGovernment Services. Interchange of Data between Administrators. (June 2004).

___ (2008). Study on Multichannel Delivery Strategies and Sustainable Business Models for Public Services Addressing Socially Disadvantaged Groups. Ecotec Research and Consulting Ltd. (August 2008).

___ (2010a). E-Government statistics, Eurostat, 2010.

___ (2010b). Eurostat, May 2010.

European Commission Community Research and Development Information Service (2011). Seventh Framework Program, ICT. Available from http://cordis.europa.eu/fp7/ict/home_en.html. Accessed January 2012.

European Commission, Directorate General Communication (2010). Digital Agenda: Household Survey Reveals more Europeans on-line but concerned about costs and security. Press release, 13 October 2010.

European Commission Information Society (2011). ICT and Society, E-Government, Policy Available from http://ec.europa.eu/information_society/activities/egovernment/policy/index_en.htm. Accessed January 2012.

European Union (2009). More effective e-services when Companies and Authorities Cooperate. *eGovmonitor*, 18 November 2009.

ForeSee Results, Inc. (2011). Federal Social Media Usage and Citizen Satisfaction Update: Foresee ACSI E-Government Satisfaction Index (Q3) 2011.

Franzel and Coursey (2004). Government Web Portals: Management Issues and the Approaches of Five States. In David G. Garson and Alexei Pavlichev, Digital Government: Principles and Best Practices. Hershey, PA 17033: Idea Group Publishing, p. 68.

GSM Association (2011). Africa Now the World's Second Largest Mobile Market, Reports GSMA. *GSM World*, 9 November 2011. Available from http://www.gsma.com/articles/africa-now-the-world-s-second-largest-mobile-market-reports-gsma/20866. Accessed January 2012.

Hall, Nicola (2008). How Do Socially Disadvantaged Citizens Prefer to Access Public Services? MC-eGov Study on Multichannel Delivery Strategies and Sustainable Business Models for Public Services Addressing Socially-Disadvantaged Groups, think paper 5, Autumn 2008. Prepared by ECOTEC Consulting Ltd. for the DG Information Society of the European Commission.

Hopkins, Curt (2011). Kenya Launches Sub-Saharan Africa's First National Open Data Initiative. *ReadWriteWeb*, 8 July 2011. Available from http://www.readwriteweb.com/archives/kenya_launches_africas_first_national_open_data_in.php.

Howard, Alex (2011). New York City launches 311 on-line service request. gov20.govfresh. (16 February 2011). Availablefrom http://gov20.govfresh.com/new-york-city-launches-311-online-service-request-map/.

Human Capital Institute (2010). Social Networking in Government: Opportunities and Challenges.

ictQatar Supreme Council of Information & Communication Technology (2011). National Programs, E-Government. Available from http://www.ictqatar.qa/en/department/national-programmes/e-government/hukoomi. Accessed January 2012.

International Fund for Agricultural Development (2011). Rural Poverty Report. Rome, Italy. Available from http://www.ifad.org/rpr2011/report/e/overview.pdf

International Labour Organisation (2011). ILO warns of a generation "scarred" by a worsening global youth employment crisis. Press release 19 October 2011. Available from http://www.ilo.org/global/about-the-ilo/press-and-media-centre/news/WCMS_165465/.

International Telecommunication Union (2010). The World in 2010. Available from http://www.itu.int/ITU-D/ict/material/FactsFigures2010.pdf. Accessed January 2012.

___ (2011a). Estimates – Key Global Telecom Indicators for the World Telecommunication Service Sector. (December 2011). Available from http://www.itu.int/ITU-D/ict/statistics/at_glance/KeyTelecom.html. Accessed January 2012.

___ (2011b). ICT Facts and Figures.

___ (2011c). Measuring the Information Society.

___ (2011d). Available from http://www.itu.int/ITU-D/sis/newslog/2011/05/13/MobileMiracleContinuesToTransformLivesInTheWorldsPoorestNations.aspx.

___ (2011e). Available from http://news.idg.no/cw/art.cfm?id=109F444A-1A64-67EA-E4688EC85C411727.

Justmeans (2010). Cell Phones and Sustainable Development: The Future Is Mobile. (9 April 2010). Available from http://www.justmeans.com/editorials?action=readeditorial&p=13113. Accessed January 2012.

Katims, Laura (2011). New York City Unveils Real-Time 311 Request Map. *Government Technology*, 17 February 2011.

Klievnik, Bram and Marijn Jannsen (2008). Improving Government Service Delivery with Private Sector Intermediaries. European Journal of ePractice, No. 5 (October 2008). Available from http://www.epractice.eu/files/5.2.pdf. Accessed January 2012.

Krenner, Johanna, and others. Reflections on the Requirements Gathering in a One-Stop Government Project. University of Linz, Institute of Applied Computer Science.

Kubicek, Herbert and Martin Hagen (2000). One-Stop Government in Europe: An Overview, University of Bremen.

LaVigne, M. (2001). Five Kinds of "Know-How" Make E-Government Work. State University of New York at Albany, Center for Technology in Government. Available from http://www.netcaucus.org/books/egov2001/pdf/e-govtkn.pdf.

Madden, Mary and Kathryn Zickuhr (2011). Sixty-five Per cent of Online Adults Use Social Networking Sites: Women Maintain their Foothold on SNS Use and Older Americans are Still Coming Aboard. Washington, D.C., Pew Research Center (26 August 2011).

Mahapatra, Ashis Kumar and Sukanta Kumar Sahu (2008). Challenges of Wireless and Mobile Technologies in Government. India – KIIT University (December 2008).

Malaysia, Ministry of Agriculture and Agro-based Industry (2011). MySMS Service. Available from http://www.doa.gov.my/web/guest/khidmat mysms. Accessed January 2012

Malta (2011). My Alerts. Available from https://mygov.mt/notify/. Accessed January 2012.

Mexico (2011). Mexico's E-Government Strategy. Available from http://unpan1.un.org/intradoc/groups/public/documents/un-dpadm/unpan047378.pdf. Accessed January 2012.

Modarres, A. (2011). Beyond the Digital Divide. *National Civic Review:* pp. 4-7 (Fall).

Morris, Anne and Suha Alawadhi (2009). Factors Influencing the Adoption of E-Government Services. Kuwait, *Journal of Software*, vol. 4 (August 2009).

Mossberger, K., and others. (2003). Virtual Inequality: Beyond the Digital Divide. Washington, DC: Georgetown University Press.

New Zealand, Citylink (2011). Cbdfree, Wellington's free Wifi. Available from http://cbdfree.co.nz/. Accessed January 2012.

Niehaves, Bjoern, and others. (2008). You Got E-Government?' A Quantitative Analysis of Social In- and Exclusiveness of Electronic Public Service Delivery. *ECIS 2008 Proceedings*. Paper 32.

Nielsen Wire (2010). Social Media Dominates Asia Pacific Internet Usage. (9 July)

Norazah, Mohd Suk and T. Ramayah (2010). User Acceptance of the E-Government Services in Malaysia: Structural Equation Modelling Approach. *Interdisciplinary Journal of Information, Knowledge, and Management*, vol. 5.

Norris, P., and others, (Eds.) (2001). On "democratic divide" as a type of "digital divide". Digital divide: Civic engagement, Information Poverty, and the Internet Worldwide. Cambridge, United Kingdom: Cambridge University Press

Norway (2011). Norway: Citizens have their say in development of new egovernment portal. eGov monitor (28 July).

Organization for Economic Cooperation and Development (2006). Whole-of-Government Approaches to Fragile States. Paris.

___ (2009). The Financial and Economic Crisis: Impact on E-Government in OECD Countries. 5th Ministerial eGovernment Conference. (19-20 November, 2009) Malmö, Sweden.

OECD and ITU (2011). M-Government: Mobile Technologies for Responsive Governments and Connected Societies. Paris, OECD Publishing.

Olaya, D. (2010). Gender and ICT. World Summit on the Information Society Forum. Geneva. Available from http://www.itu.int/ITU-D/ict/papers/2010/PresentationGender-WSIS.pdf

Ontario Ministry of Government Services (2011). Service Ontario. Available from http://www.ontario.ca/en/services_for_residents/. Accessed January 2012.

Pascual, Patricia J. (2003). E-Government. E-Asian Task Force, UNDP-ARDIP (May).

Pavilenene, Danuta. Over half Lithuanians still do not use e-services. *The Baltic Course*. 25 July 2011.

Pew Research Center (2010). Computer and Cell Phone Usage Up Around the World – Global Publics Embrace Social Networking. Global Attitudes Project (15 December).

Pick, J. B. and R. Azari (2008). Global Digital Divide: Influence of Socioeconomic, Governmental, and Accessibility Factors on Information Technology. *Information Technology for Development* 14, 2: pp. 91-115.

Pinch, T.J. and W.E. Bijker (1984). The Social Construction of Facts and Artifacts: Or How the Sociology of Science and the Sociology of Technology Might Benefit Each Other. *Social Studies of Science* 14: pp. 399-441.

Pizzicannella, Roberto (2010). Co-production and open data: the right mix for public service effectiveness? Paper submitted for consideration to 10th European Conference on E-Government (17-18 June 2010), Limerick, Ireland.

Prima, Silviana and Rolianabt Ibrahim (2011). Citizen Awareness to E-Government Services for Information Personalization. *International Journal of Innovative Computing*, vol. 1, no. 1, 2011.

Public Technology.Net (2005). E-Government needs to Reach Disadvantaged People – Planning is Needed, 13 October 2005. Available from http://www.publictechnology.net/content/3827.

Rabaiah, Abdelbaset and Eddy Vandijck (2009). A Strategic Framework of E-Government: Generic and Best Practice. *Electronic Journal of E-Government*. ETRO Research group, Virje Universitiet, Brussels, Belgium, vol.7, issue 3, pp. 241-258. Available from http://www.ejeg.com/.

Raffat, Rabee M. (2006). Developing a Successful E-Government. University of Sydney.

Rao, M. (2000). Struggling with the Digital Divide: Internet Infrastructure, Content, and Culture. Is a progressive Internet environment enough to close the gap between North and South? Internet Society. (October). Available from http://www.isoc.org/oti/articles/1000/rao.html.

Ross, N., L. Hutton and L. Peng (2004). Revolutionary E-Government Strategies across Asia-Pacific – Strategy White Paper. Alcatel Telecommunication Review (3rd Quarter).

Roy, Jeffrey and Longford, John (2008). Integrating Service Delivery across Levels of Government: Case Studies of Canada and Other Countries. IBM Center for the Business of Government.

Sahraoui, and others (2005). Current state of e-services in Saudi Arabia: The case of intermediaries in facilitating government services in Medina city. Information Systems Journal (2010), vol.: 2009, EMCIS (2009), pp. 1-15.

Schluter, E. and B. Kragelj (2007). Digital Divide Reconsidered: A Country- and Individual-Level Typology of Digital Inequality in 26 European Countries. Presented at the QMSS Conference, Prague: Czech Republic (June). Available from http://www.s3ri.soton.ac.uk/qmss/conf07/schedule.php.

Sciadas, G. (2005). Infostates Across Countries and Over Time: Conceptualization, Modeling, and Measurements of the Digital Divide. Information Technology for Development 11, 3: pp. 299-304.

Segev, E. and N. Ahituv (2010). Popular Searches in Google and Yahoo!: A 'Digital Divide' in Information Uses? The Information Society 26: pp. 17-37.

Segger, M.C. and A. Khalfan (2004). Sustainable development in policy and in law. Sustainable Development Law: Principles, Practices, and Prospects, pp. 45-50.

Selhofer, H. and H. Mayringer (2001). Benchmarking the Information Society Development in European countries. Communications and Strategies, 43(3): pp. 17–56.

Sethi, Neerja and Vijay Sethi. E-Government Implementation: A Case Study of Dubai E-Government. E-Government in Practice.

Seychelles. National ICT Policy. Available from http://www.ict.gov.sc/resources/policy.pdf.

Shah, Bimal (2010). Increasing E-Government Adoption through Social Media: A case of Nepal. University of Norway.

Singapore (2011). Go Mobile with Government. Available from http://www.ecitizen.gov.sg/mobile/index.html. Accessed January 2012.

Smith, Aaron (2010). Government Online: The internet gives citizens new paths to government services and information. Pew Internet and American Life Project. (27 April 2010).

Social media strategy (2010). Social media isn't a prerequisite for open government. (19 February 2010).

Society of IT Management (2008). Green ICT? Current research into the environmental impact of ICT. Report for the Department for Communities and Local government.

Stoiciu, A. (2011). The Role of E-governance in Bridging the Digital Divide. *UN Chronicle*, 18 November 2011. Available at http://wwwupdate.un.org/wcm/content/site/chronicle/cache/bypass/home/archive/thedigitaldividend/theroleofegovernanceinbridgingthedigitaldivide.

Susanto, T. D. and R. Goodwin (2010). Factors Influencing Citizen Adoption of SMS-Based E-Government Services. Electronic Journal of E-Government. vol.8, Issue 1, pp. 55 - 71. Available from http://www.ejeg.com/.

Teisesforumas (2012). Valdžios elektroniniai vartai (e-government portal). Available from http://www.teisesforumas.lt/index.php/it-teise/224-valdzios-elektroniniai-vartai.html. Accessed January 2012.

Tolbert, C. and K. Mossberg (2006). New Inequality Frontier: Broadband Internet Access. EPI Working Paper 275. Economic Policy Institute. Available from http://www.epi.org/page/-/old/workingpapers/wp275.pdf.

Torsen, M. (2005). The domination of the English language in the global village: efforts to further develop the internet by populating it with non-Latin-based languages. *Richmond Journal of Law and Technology* 12, 1. Available from http://law.richmond.edu/jolt/v12i1/article2.pdf.

United Nations Development Programme (2008). Gender Responsive E-governance: Exploring the Transformative Potential.

___ (2011). Country Profiles and International Human Development Indicators. Available from http://hdr.undp.org/en/countries/.

United Nations Environment Programme (2005). Register of International Treaties and Other Agreements in the Field of the Environment. (UNEP/Env.Law/2005/3).

___ (2010). Auditing the Implementation of Multilateral Environmental Agreements: A Primer for Auditors. Data on treaty participation has been compiled from the United Nations treaty database and websites of the various convention secretariats.

United Kingdom (2011). Delivering Open Public Services – and Open Data.

United Kingdom, Cabinet Office (2011). Open Public Services White Paper.

United Nations (2008). United Nations E-Government Survey 2008. United Nations, New York, p.4.

___ (2010). Objective and themes of the United Nations Conference on Sustainable Development. Report of the Secretary-General. (22 December 2010) A/CONF.216/PC/7.

___ Rio+20 Secretariat (2011a). Discussion paper prepared for the high-level dialogue on institutional framework for sustainable development held at Solo, Indonesia. (19-21 July 2011).

___ Statistics Division (2011b). Social Indicators. New York. Available from http://unstats.un.org/unsd/demographic/products/socind/inc-eco.htm.

___ Statistics Division (2011c). Grouping (4 October). Available from http://unstats.un.org/unsd/methods/m49/m49regin.htm#least.

United States, Internal Revenue Service. Available from http://www.irs.gov/efile/article/0,,id=118986,00.html.

van Veenstra, A. and M. Janssen (2010). Migration Strategies for Multichannel Service Provisioning in Public Agencies. Electronic Journal of E-Government, vol.8, Issue 2, pp. 215-226. Available from http://www.ejeg.com/.

Vencatachellum, I. and S. Pudaruth (2010). Investigating E-Government Services Uptake in Mauritius: A User's Perspective. International Research Symposium in Service Management, Mauritius (24-27 August 2010).

Vicente, M. R. and A.J. Lopez (2010). A Multidimensional Analysis of the Disability Digital Divide: Some Evidence for Internet Use. The Information Society 26: pp. 48-64.

Voigt, Kevin (2011). Mobile phone: weapon against global poverty. CNNTech, 9 October 2011. Available from http://articles.cnn.com/2011-10-09/tech/tech_mobile_mobile-phone-poverty_1_mobile-phone-cell-phone-rural-villages. Accessed January 2012.

Von Haldenwang (2002). Allocative efficiency measures how well service of infrastructure bundles match consumer preferences.

Wang, Yih-Jeou (2009). OECD Rethinking E-Government Services: User-centred Approaches.

Wimmer, Maria A. (2002). Integrated Service Modelling for Online One-stop Government. Electronic Markets, Volume 12 (3): pp. 149-156. Available from http://www.electronicmarkets.org/.

Wimmer, Maria and Roland Traunmüller (2002). Integration – The Next Challenge in E- Government. EurAsia-ICT, Shiraz-Iran, (29-31 October).

Wolff, L. and C. Castro (2003). Education and Training: the Task Ahead. After the Washington Consensus: Restarting Growth and Reform in Latin America. P. Kuczynski and J.Williamson, Eds., Washington, D.C.: Institute for International Economics.

World Bank (2009). Information and Communication for Development: Extending Reach and Increasing Impact. Washington, D.C.

___ (2011a). Mobile Phones Help Liberia Map Rural Water Points and Informs Poverty Reduction Strategy. (16 June 2011). Available from http://go.worldbank.org/Q97TZ-VXGI0. Accessed January 2012.

___ (2011b). Paying taxes.

World Bank Instituted (2010). Available from http://wbi.worldbank.org/wbi/devoutreach/article/375/mobile-technology-one-core-lesson-many-possible-solutions.

World Economic Forum (2011). Global Agenda Council on the Future of Government: The Future of Government Lessons Learned from around the World. Cologne and Geneva.

___ (2008). Mobile Web Best Practices 1.0. (July 2008) Available from http://www.w3.org/TR/mobile-bp/. Accessed January 2012.

___ (2009). Improving Access to Government through Better Use of the Web: W3Interest Group Note. (May 2009). Available from http://www.w3.org/TR/egov-improving/#multichannel. Accessed January 2012.

Yeo, Vivian (2011). Asia speeds up E-Government efforts. *ZDNet Asia*, 14 June 2011.

Yih-Jeou Wang (2009). Rethinking E-Government Services, Presentation at the OECD-India meeting, New Delhi, India. (4 December 2009)

Yonazi, Jim, Henk Sol and Albert Boonstra (2010a). Exploring Issues Underlying Citizen Adoption of eGovernment Initiatives in Developing Countries: The Case of Tanzania. *Electronic Journal of E-Government*, vol. 8, Issue 2 (2010): pp. 176-188.

___ (2010). The Role of Intermediaries in facilitating E-Government Diffusion in Saudi Arabia.

Yong, James S.L. (2004). Promoting Citizen-Centered Approaches to E-Government Programmes – Strategies and Perspectives from Asian Economies. Paper presented at the Second APEC High-Level Symposium on E-Government, Acapulco, Mexico. (6-8 October 2004).

Yung, J., and others. (2010). Low Income Minority Seniors' Enrolment in Cybercafé: Psychological Barriers to Crossing the Digital Divide. *Educational Gerontology* 36: p. 194.